MALCOLM BALEN is the author of a biography of Kenneth Clarke and *A Very English Deceit*, a history of the South Sea Bubble. He is senior editorial adviser to BBC News, where he was previously executive editor. He was educated at Peterhouse, Cambridge, where he took a First in History.

Visit www.AuthorTracker.co.uk for exclusive information on your favourite HarperCollins authors.

D0766018

By the same author

Kenneth Clarke: A Biography

*A Very English Deceit: The Secret History of the
South Sea Bubble and the First Great Financial Scandal*

Portrait of Captain William Siborne

MALCOLM BALEN

A Model Victory

Waterloo and the Battle for History

HARPER PERENNIAL
London, Toronto, New York and Sydney

Harper Perennial
An imprint of HarperCollins*Publishers*
77-85 Fulham Palace Road
Hammersmith
London W6 8JB

www.harperperennial.co.uk

This edition published by Harper Perennial 2006

1

First published in Great Britain in 2005 by Fourth Estate

A catalogue record for this book is
available from the British Library

ISBN-13 978-0-00-716030-3
ISBN-10 0-00-716030-5

Typeset in Minion by
Rowland Phototypesetting Ltd, Bury St Edmunds, Suffolk

Printed in Great Britain by Clays Ltd, St Ives plc

Henry Balen

The duty of the Historian of a battle . . . is to prefer that which has been officially recorded and published by public responsible authorities; next, to attend to that which proceeds from Official Authority . . . and to pay least attention to the statements of Private Individuals.

The Duke of Wellington, 24 September 1842

The communication by the media of information . . . on matters of public interest and importance is a vital part of life in a democratic society. However the right to communicate such information is subject to the qualification . . . that false accusations of fact impugning the integrity of others, including politicians, should not be made.

Lord Hutton, 28 January 2004

Contents

List of Maps and Illustrations

Key				
XXXX	Army	◇	Skirmishers	
XXX	Corps	▭	Infantry	Anglo-Allied
XX	Division	▱	Cavalry	
X	Brigade			
III	Regiment	▬	Infantry	Prussian
II	Battalion	▱	Cavalry	
I	Company			
⚑	Artillery	◆	Skirmishers	
✂	Battle site	▬	Infantry	French
		▱	Cavalry	

PICTURES

A MODEL VICTORY

I

Truth is history, and history without truth does not deserve the name; and I am anxious for the sake of the gallant men I commanded, that one day at least the truth may be known.

Sir Richard Hussey Vivian, letter to William Siborne, 18 January 1830

The advice is always to walk a battlefield, and so this is what the officer did. In itself, then, his action was not remarkable, but what was surprising to those who did not know him was the level of his commitment, a devotion to duty which was reflected in the time he spent crossing and re-crossing a few miles of rolling countryside out-side Brussels. A day, perhaps, would have been deemed too short a time for most visitors, as if they were in an almost indecent haste to see the killing-fields, but a week at most would have sufficed. To go for eight months, therefore, was the sign of an interest bordering on obsession.

But then the lieutenant, prim and proper, was no ordinary tourist, and if he was there for pleasure (and it gave him plenty, although he might have cavilled at using such a word in so bloody a context) then this was an incidental benefit of the curious military exercise that he had campaigned so hard to carry out. His task was both arduous and precise but it was made the more so by his unrelenting search for perfection, for he was not a man to tolerate a hair out of place. Perhaps we should say, given the military training which lay behind his approach, he could not abide a tunic button which did not shine as brightly as the Duke of Wellington's star still shone in the firmament of British society. It was the Duke, indeed, who was unwittingly responsible for the officer's task though it was not one which came to meet with the approval of the great commander. This was one of many curiosities which came to attach themselves to the lieutenant's project as the years went by.

That Wellington should become at best indifferent and at worst hostile to the officer's work was in itself an oddity because, in truth, the lieutenant was doing little more than paying homage to him, an act of obeisance that was charted by the pen and paper which accompanied him as he trudged across the land. For he had set out to map the ground of the Duke's most famous victory, the glory of his life, the triumph which exceeded all others in a military career which had glittered as none other: the defeat of Napoleon on the fields of Waterloo, fifteen years before.

It was entirely in character that the lieutenant intended his map to be the most accurate the army had ever seen. It may have been his military training which infused him with a taste for exactitude, so that, as he grew older, he even changed the spelling of his name as if to render it more accurate: he was called William Siborn, and why he became Siborne at thirty-seven years of age, we do not know. He was born near the century's turn, on 18 October 1797, at Greenwich in south London: a meridian child who became fascinated by maps. His father was called Benjamin, and his mother Charlotte, and he was an only son. Perhaps his upbringing gave him a taste for isolation, for self-containment, for favouring a world which was neat and tidy and above all precise.

It was an upbringing which revolved around the army. A year after his birth his father became an ensign in the West Kent militia, and a year later moved into the 9th (East Norfolk) Regiment, where he stayed for two decades. Unlike his son, Siborn senior saw active service. We find him first in the 2nd Battalion under General Sir John Moore in 1808/9; then at Walcheren in 1809, under Lord Chatham; we glimpse him in the Peninsula with Wellington from 1810; and then at the Battle of Nivelles, where, on 10 November 1813, he was gravely wounded, never fully to recover. At the end of the war he sailed with his regiment to Canada, returning too late to take part in the Battle of Waterloo. The trail ends on 14 July 1819 at St Vincent in the West Indies, where Siborn was serving on peacetime duties, and where finally he succumbed to his wartime wounds.

William Siborne, brought up in a country perpetually at war and proud of his father's exploits in Spain, devoted himself to a military career, too: while still fourteen, he became a gentleman cadet at the Royal Military College, first at Great Marlow and then at Sandhurst. He was one of the first professionally trained staff officers, and he was educated in mathematics, languages and military drawing. He was commissioned as an ensign in the same regiment as his father, the 9th Foot, in 1813, but he was too young for the great Napoleonic battles of his era, serving, somewhat less glamorously, at Chatham and Sheerness. The nearest he came to fighting was in the year after he had passed out from Sandhurst with distinction: in 1815 he joined his father as a member of the army of occupation in Paris, once the Battle of Waterloo had been fought and won. If the son ever felt the need to win the approval of higher authority (and, at the end, he came to resent it) his father's distinguished battlefield career may have played its part. Perhaps it made the son feel that while his father had seen action, his role was merely to record it, a task which made him feel part of the glorious whole which was the victorious British army, but left him curiously unsatisfied as a man.

We know what William Siborne looked like from a single surviving portrait. For this we must thank a man of many parts – Samuel Lover, sometime novelist, musician, and painter. Granted, the pose is a touch mannered, too ornamental even, as if, through the surrounding objects, the artist is trying to invest him with a status which he does not yet possess. In his blue military undress coat, William Siborne leans on a prop, a tiny cannon, and his left hand holds a plumed hat. He has a high forehead framed by brown curls; a pair of steady eyes; a long, large nose, and a round jaw, which in combination with the domed forehead, make his face seem curiously egg-shaped. A precise, exact, soft face, of which the most certain feature is the mouth: a small, pursed mouth, resolute and hard-set. It says he is a determined man; an exact man; a man who likes order; a man who likes things just so.

Fittingly, for such an exact man, the killing-fields of Waterloo were divided into areas of geometrical precision.

A large triangle with Brussels at its northern apex is formed by two long roads, one running south to Nivelles, the other, which lies further east, heads to Charleroi. The triangle's base is a shorter road which runs between the two. Heading south from Brussels, the Charleroi road cuts through the Forest of Soignes, emerging from dense wood at Waterloo, then heads for the village of Mont St Jean. Leaving Mont St Jean, a traveller can journey along a smaller triangle of roads, by stopping at the crossroads of Quatre Bras, turning west to Nivelles, and then returning north to where he started.

The base of another shape, an imperfect rectangle, is formed by the road which runs east from Nivelles to Namur, with Ligny just outside it; the Brussels to Charleroi road forms its western side, while its eastern side runs from Louvain, twenty miles east of Brussels, to Namur. In the centre of the rectangle lies Wavre. Quatre Bras, Ligny, Wavre and Mont St Jean: four places linked by the battles which determined the fate of Europe in four days of June, though all were overshadowed by the name which was given, imprecisely, to the last, the most famous conflict of them all: the Battle of Waterloo.

Waterloo has earned its lasting fame by virtue of being one of the bloodiest and most decisive one-day battles in European history. Never before had armies deployed a mixture of old and new forms of warfare with such destructive consequences. Men rode to war on horseback, their swords flashing, or formed themselves into protective squares of infantry to resist attack, but guns and shellfire were deployed too, to devastating effect. Rarely had there been slaughter on such a scale.

Though the glory of the victory soon came to overshadow any notion of its gore, nearly fifty thousand died or were wounded in the single bloody day which it took to conclude the business. A few weeks afterwards, one visitor, Charlotte Waldie, recalled how she had seen a long line of burial pits: 'the effluvia which arose from them . . . was horrible; and the pure west wind of summer, as it passed us, seemed pestiferous, so deadly was the smell that in many places pervaded the field. The fresh-turned clay which covered those pits betrayed how recent had been their formation. From one of them the scanty clods of earth which had covered it had in one place fallen, and the skeleton of a human face was visible. I turned from the place in indescribable horror.'

It was fitting, then, for such a bloody confrontation, that victory brought with it such a conclusive prize, an outcome which defined the course of the nineteenth century. Waterloo was one of the most conclusive armed confrontations of the century, the crucible in which modern Europe was fashioned. It saw Britain and Prussia emerge triumphant, the two countries eclipsing the shattered might of France. It also marked the military and political end to the career of the greatest soldier of modern times, the soldier who dared to become an emperor.

Over the years, the horror of the battle had diminished, eroded by the passage of time and the growth of legend, which dwelt more on the triumph than on the cost in flesh and blood. It is here, in this cleansed landscape, that Siborne tried to make order of the ground which had played host to the carnage, mapping the land as exactly as he knew how, an academic exercise imposed on human slaughter. First, he prepared his drawing-board as if he was following a recipe in the kitchen, to guard against the expansion and contraction of the paper in the atmosphere. 'Lay upon that side of the sheet of paper which is to be fixed to the board the white of an egg well beat up,' he told students of his methods. 'Press the paper gently and gradually down upon the board from one side to the opposite one, and paste the edges which hang over to the under part of the board.' Not even a downpour would put him off. 'With drawing-boards thus prepared,' he declared solemnly, 'I have stood with an umbrella over the instrument during heavy showers of rain, without the slightest alteration taking place in the smoothness or firmness of the paper.'

If Siborne had followed the exact sequence of the battles as he mapped the countryside, and it would have been in character, he would have started at the River Sambre, with Napoleon's unexpected crossing into Belgium, so sudden and brilliant a manoeuvre that, by noon on the first day, the town of Charleroi had fallen. The topographer in Siborne would have noted how rapidly the terrain changes, falling away into the valley of the River Orme, between Genappe and

Gembloux. Within five miles, the land is broken up into hills and valleys around the River Dyle, and as the river meanders north to Louvain, the country becomes close and wooded.

Then comes the landscape of the final battle. Near the hamlet of Frischermont, there is a crossroads where a lane becomes a track, and about four hundred yards later it dips into a slope which leads, through a long hollow, to the village of Plancenoit, near the Lasne stream. Both the French and Allied positions can be seen from here, perhaps the finest general view of Waterloo that Siborne could have obtained, indeed a clearer view than the participants gained for themselves, surrounded as they were by battle-smoke and the head-high crops. At the church at Plancenoit, a few battalions of the French Old Guard held off thousands of young, inexperienced Prussians, until the Prussians finally won the day. Further north still, and the road from Braine l'Alleud to Ohain follows the crest of the Mont St Jean plateau, which formed a natural obstacle along the entire front of Wellington's army. A lone elm tree on the ridge, on the west side of the crossroads, marked Wellington's position during much of the battle. But it is the Duke's advanced defences which stand out for inspection – the farm of La Haye Sainte, and the château of Hougoumont. La Haye Sainte was the centre of the Allied line, from where Major George Baring's small band of men threw tiles at the attackers, and where, the night before the battle, they tore down the great barn doors for firewood, unaware that they would have to defend the building the next day. The enemy dead, piled up on the threshold, proved to be a barricade which was almost as effective.

Hougoumont was the key to the Allied position, a fortification whose defences never fell, despite the terrible punishment its occupiers endured, and whose resistance served as a metaphor for Wellington's tactics during that long day. By the close of battle, hundreds of its defenders had died, but Hougoumont's survivors claimed divine protection when a fire stopped, miraculously and marvellously at the feet of the figure of Our Saviour in the chapel, and barely singed His toes. Charlotte Waldie, on holiday in Brussels, visited the château a few weeks after the battle and found herself in a different world.

'The carnage here had been dreadful. Amongst the long grass lay remains of broken arms, shreds of golden lace, torn epaulets, and pieces of cartridge-boxes; and upon the tangled branches of brambles fluttered many a tattered remnant of a soldier's coat. At the outskirts of the wood, and around the ruined walls of the Château, huge piles of human ashes were heaped up, some of which were still smoking. The countrymen told us that so great were the numbers of the slain, that it was impossible entirely to consume them. Pits had been dug, into which they had been thrown, but they were obliged to be raised far above the surface of the ground. These dreadful heaps were covered with piles of wood, which were set on fire, so that underneath the ashes lay numbers of human bodies unconsumed.

'At the garden gate I found the holster of a British officer, entire, but deluged with blood. In the inside was the maker's name – Beazley and Hetse, No. 4, Parliament Street. All around were strewed torn epaulets, broken scabbards, and sabre tashes stained and stiffened with blood.'

When it was over, the French had lost half their men, while the two opponents who had united against them, the Anglo-Allied army led by the Duke of Wellington and the Prussian army led by General Blücher, had lost a third: out of 190,000 men who took part in the battle, the French casualties totalled more than 30,000, the British and Dutch, under Wellington, about 15,000, and the Prussians lost about 7000 men. At one point, 45,000 men lay dead or wounded within an area of three square miles. Half the 840 British infantry officers were dead, and their cavalry had lost a third of its number. The 12th Light Dragoons alone lost three officers, two sergeant-majors, five sergeants, three corporals and thirty-eight dragoons.

Despite the death toll, the soldiers themselves remembered it as a glorious victory. But in the stories they told of the battle they did not forget its horror, even if none of them appeared to dwell unduly on the cost. Among the survivors was Private Tom Morris of the 73rd Foot, who described how he had roamed the battlefield in search of water after the fighting had ended: 'By the light of the moon I picked my way among the bodies of my sleeping as well as of my dead comrades . . . I thought I heard the man call to me, and the hope that I could render him some assistance overcame my terror. I went towards him, and placing my left hand on his shoulder, attempted to lift him up with my right; my hand, however, passed through his body, and then I saw that both he and his horse had been killed by a cannonball.' Another soldier from Staffordshire, Frederick Mainwaring, found a loaf of bread in a French officer's knapsack, covered in the brains of a British guardsman. Mainwaring was so hungry he scraped off the brains and ate the loaf. Captain Cavalié Mercer of the Royal Horse Artillery remembered that 'from time to time a figure would raise itself from the ground, and then, with a despairing groan, fall back again. Others, slowly and painfully rising, stronger, or having less deadly hurt, would stagger away with uncertain steps across the field in search of succour. Many of these I followed with my gaze until lost in the obscurity of distance; but many, alas! after staggering a few paces, would sink again on the ground, probably to rise no more. Horses, too, there were to claim our pity – mild, patient, enduring.'

Only at first light did the men begin to comprehend the enormity of their sacrifice. Captain Mercer buried one of his drivers, James Crammond, simply because his injuries were so horrifying. 'I had not been up many minutes when one of my sergeants came to ask if they might bury Driver Crammond. "And why particularly Driver Crammond?" "Because he looks frightful, sir; many of us have not had a wink of sleep for him." Curious! I walked to the spot where he lay, and certainly a more hideous sight cannot be imagined. A cannon-shot had carried away the whole head except barely the visage, which still remained attached to the torn and bloody neck. The men said they had been prevented sleeping by seeing his eyes fixed on them all night; and thus this one dreadful object had superseded all the other horrors by which they were surrounded.'

An ensign, seventeen-year-old Edward Macready, calculated that of the 460 men in the 30th Foot, 279 were casualties. Sixty-nine of Captain Mercer's horses were dead, and more than 1500 in all. 'Some lay on the ground with their entrails hanging out, and yet they lived,' wrote Captain Mercer. 'These would occasionally attempt to rise, but, like their human bedfellows, quickly falling back again, would lift their poor heads, and, turning a wistful gaze at their side, lie quickly down again.'

Hougoumont, still smouldering, smelled of burnt flesh and death. It looked, thought John Kincaid of the 95th Rifles, as if the world had nearly come to an end. 'The field of battle next morning presented a frightful scene of carnage; it seemed as if the world had tumbled to pieces and three-fourths of everything destroyed in the wreck. The ground running parallel to the front where we had stood was so thickly strewed with fallen men and horses, that it was difficult to step clear of their bodies; many of the former were still alive, and imploring assistance, which it was not in our power to bestow. The usual salutation on meeting an acquaintance of another regiment after an action was to ask who had been hit? But on this occasion it was "Who's alive?"'

The villages around Waterloo were filled with the injured, their churches acting as hospitals. In Brussels, the mayor launched an appeal for its citizens to take as much bedding as they could to the Hôtel de Ville, especially mattresses, bolsters, bedsheets and blankets, and to give linen or lint to their local priests. But it would take several days until all the injured had been recovered, taken by wagon to nearby farm buildings or cottages. Accidents caused the death toll to rise still further: 'Two of our men, on the morning of the 19th, lost their lives by a very melancholy accident,' Kincaid recalled. 'They were cutting up a captured ammunition waggon for firewood, when one of their swords, striking against a nail, sent a spark among the powder. When I looked in the direction of the explosion, I saw the two poor fellows about twenty or thirty feet up in the air. On falling to the ground, though lying on their backs and bellies, some extraordinary effort of nature, caused by the agony of the moment, made them spring from that position five or six times, to the height of eight or ten feet, just as a fish does when thrown on the ground after being newly caught. It was so unlike a scene in real life that it was impossible to witness it without forgetting, for a moment, the horror of their situation.'

A professor of military surgery, John Thomson, saw one patient whose neck had been cut by a sabre, revealing part of the brain which was seen pulsating for eight weeks. There were many victims with sabre wounds to the face and neck, where the eyelids, nose, ears, cheeks and lips had been divided, wounds which were held together by adhesive straps, and by bandages. In many cases, bullets had passed directly through one or both eyeballs. There were many chest wounds, too, some inflicted by the lance and bayonet; but most by musketballs. There were patients whose bladders had been penetrated by musketballs, and, in several cases, men had lost large portions of the buttocks and thighs to cannonballs.

More than five hundred amputations were carried out by the surgeons in an age without anaesthetics, their most famous patient Lord Uxbridge, whose knee had been shattered. He talked calmly to his surgeons as they cut through his flesh and bone, in a house a few miles from the battlefield, and he was heard only once to complain, when he remarked that the knife did not seem very sharp. 'Take a look at that leg,' he commanded his visitor, Sir Hussey Vivian, pointing to the severed limb which was still in the room. He regretted its loss deeply. 'Some time hence, I may be inclined to imagine it might have been saved.'

Wellington was far from immune to the human cost of victory, to the lives wrecked and to the men racked with pain in Brussels hospitals. Many of his friends and fellow-officers were dead, a mournful list which included a dozen of his senior staff. 'Do not congratulate me. I have lost all my friends,' he insisted, on his return to Brussels. Many men died from exposure as they lay on the battlefield for two, sometimes three days, waiting to be rescued, while scavengers moved among them, stripping valuables from the dead and injured before the stretcher parties arrived. 'I hope to God,' said Wellington later, 'that I have fought my last battle. I always say that, next to a battle lost, the greatest misery is a battle gained.'

So intense had been the fighting that the landscape was altered by the conflict, with the trees reduced to stumps. It was killing on the scale of the First World War, a century ahead of time.

It was fifteen years after the battle that William Siborne began his great project. He was invited by the commander-in-chief of the army, Lord Rowland Hill, a Waterloo veteran, to map the ground where the Battle of Waterloo had been fought, and from this to create a scale model, with the work paid for by public funds. Over the years which followed the Model grew in size and detail and ambition so that when it was finally finished few exhibition rooms in the land were large enough to hold it. Tens of thousands of toy soldiers, carefully crafted so that their different parts should move, came to take up their positions in the gently rolling landscape of its perfectly contoured terrain.

One of the reasons that Siborne was commissioned to map the land which came to grip his imagination was the threat that a housing development would scar the battlefield, altering irreversibly the scene of one of Britain's most famous military victories. For eight months he stayed at La Haye Sainte farmhouse, the scene of some of the bloodiest fighting fifteen years before. Though he became obsessed by the need to map the terrain as accurately as possible, Siborne also determined to gather together the recollections of many of the surviving officers who had fought at Waterloo. His cartographic skills were unquestionable. But, to create his Model, Siborne had resolved to become a historian, too. To gather the information he needed, and arrive at what he hoped would be 'a most faithful and authentic record of the battle despite the passage of time' Siborne decided to send out a circular letter to British officers at the battle. From it, we get a clear sense of a precise, particular, man in search of historical accuracy:

Sir,

Having for some time been occupied in constructing a Model of the Field and Battle of Waterloo, upon a scale sufficiently large to admit of the most faithful representation of that memorable Action, I have accordingly the honour to request you will have the goodness to reply to the following queries, as far as your recollection and circumstances of your position at the time will admit.

What was the particular formation at the moment when the French Imperial Guards, advancing to attack the right of the British Forces, reached the crest of our position? What was the formation of the Enemy's Forces?

Would you have the goodness to trace these formations, according to the best of your recollection, upon the accompanying Plan?

If Officers will, however, but favour me with their remarks and opinions, freely and without reserve, I trust that, by fairly weighing and comparing the data thus afforded me, I shall be enabled to deduce a most faithful and authentic record of the Battle, the surest means of imparting to the Model that extreme accuracy which in a work of this nature, not dependent like a pictorial representation on effect for excellence, must always constitute its real value.

I have the honour to be, Sir,

Your most obedient, humble Servant,

W. SIBORNE

Lieut.-Assist. Mil.Sec.

Siborne collected and kept his replies, the eyewitness accounts of the survivors of the battle, so that today we can read the handwritten evidence of the men who fought at Waterloo. Hundreds of letters with diagrams and maps, and thoughts and views, were gathered together in six volumes, the matter-of-fact commentaries of the men who survived the killing-fields.

The replies came in angular writing, usually in black ink but occasionally in blue, on paper large and small. Some were neatly written, and were well thought out. Others were written down without forethought, and with many crossings-out. Siborne also sent out maps which he had drawn and printed, to establish the exact location of the troops, and often these came back cut into smaller pieces to focus on a relevant sector, coloured-in or marked in pencil. There were letters from as far away as Corfu, from Ketley in Southampton, from Maltings in Suffolk, from Leamington, from Derby, from Mansfield, from Belper, Knutsford, Brighton, Edinburgh, and Kelso; in London, from Carlton Terrace, Bryanston Square, Portman Square and Woolwich. He had letters, too, from the Prussian general staff and some French marshals. One envelope addressed to The Captain Siborne, Royal Military Asylum, Chelsea was forwarded to a new address in Yorkshire with the sender's name, the King of Prussia, casually written on the back. Today the large red seal of Le Roi De Prusse, bearing his crown, looks incongruous against the blue Post Office stamp which declares: Harrogate August 8 1848. A second envelope was simply sent to 'Captain Siborne at Dublin, Officer of the Commander of the Forces' and a third addressed 'À Monsieur le Capitaine Siborne à Londres.' As Siborne's fame spread, both found their destination.

In addition to creating his extraordinary Model, Siborne came to write a history of the battle, based on these replies. In outlook, he was no different to the general run of historians of his time. He, too, was patriotic to a fault, and his history reflected his nationalism, but he was prepared to ask questions of the veterans, to list and document all their accounts. Nearly two hundred years on, these accounts read as if the battle had been fought yesterday. Siborne was prepared to go beyond a ritualistic celebration of national pride. He researched what actually happened, and then inch by inch, piece by piece, he tried to reconstruct events with the exactitude which might be expected from such a meticulous map-maker. But Siborne was to struggle with the obstacles history places in the path of its pursuers, trying to peel away the layers laid down by time, before he could begin to make sense of the material he had so patiently gathered together. For all his information-gathering, he was to find that history has a way of revealing itself, not always willingly, but obstinately, like a reluctant relative yielding up the hidden secrets of a family's past.

For if history is a search for truth, and it was in exactly this spirit that Siborne embarked on the enterprise which would ruin him, then there are always forces which oppose it. And, unfortunately for the good officer, the truth can be maddeningly imprecise, if not lost for ever, then at least shrouded in the fog of time and war. It certainly does not always admit of the exactness which is needed when a terrain has to be mapped. Honestly held views and accounts have to be recorded, reconciled, crosschecked against a hundred others, sifted for evasions, exaggerations and misunderstandings. 'You speak of the difficulties you have in reconciling different accounts of eyewitnesses,' replied Major Evans of the 5th West India Regiment, to one of Siborne's enquiries. 'This is only what invariably occurs. There is scarcely an instance, I think, of two persons, even though only fifty yards distant from each other, who give of such events a concurring account.'

Truth and facts in history, as Siborne would learn to his cost, admit of many interpretations, often honestly held. To map a battlefield is one thing: to record the twists and turns of the battle quite another, to impose upon it order and stratagem, to reduce it, tidily, to a clear series of linear events which join together and connect to reach their natural conclusion, is another still. In short, the witnesses Siborne had sought, whose accounts he uniquely captured, did not always tell the same story. More importantly, they did not tell the story that the high command, both political and military, always wished to hear.

More than fifty history books were written in the year of the battle alone, some of them reprinted several times, such was the public appetite to celebrate the victory. Of the many accounts written by veterans of the battle, some were vainglorious, some misleading, some ostentatiously romantic. Such accounts were, however, uncontroversial. Glorying in victory, they were personal, anecdotal, narrow, exciting books, which would cause the Duke of Wellington no harm. As Captain Mercer noted in his diary: 'Depend upon it, he who pretends to give a general account of a great battle from his own observations deceives you – believe him not. He can see no farther (that is, if he be personally engaged in it) than the length of his nose; and how is he to tell what is passing two or three miles off, with hills and trees and buildings intervening, and all enveloped in smoke? I write . . . only pure simply gossip for my own amusement – just what happened to me and mine, and what I did see happen to others about me.'

Siborne's history, however, in its complexity and reach, was different, ranging far and wide in its gathering of witnesses. In this way, eventually, he made a name for himself as a historian, and in so doing surpassed his previous career as a soldier and topographer. Siborne sought to describe a whole battle by sorting historical truth from the chaff of confusion, and although he relied upon, indeed courted, army testimony which was overwhelmingly officer-based, his was a unique exercise in the search for truth. But it was, in its scope and reach, far too democratic for the times.

Using hundreds of eyewitness statements, the Model he created tried to capture the exact moment of victory, the Crisis of the Battle as it was called, with the precision only he could bring to such an enterprise. But models, of course, cannot show the great sweep of history; they cannot demonstrate the irresistible tide of events which flows inexorably in one direction, towards a single inevitable conclusion. They cannot make allowances for nuances of analysis. They cannot hedge or dissemble, or allow extraneous factors or influences to intrude upon the carefully crafted conclusion they have created. They are fixed in their certainty, frozen in time, their central characters immobile, as if paralysed by the mighty forces which they have unleashed. Such a fate awaited Siborne's Model, because he dared to pose the central question: who won the Battle of Waterloo? Was it Wellington's forces, or Blücher's Prussians, or a combination of the two? Siborne was forced to provide an answer, and the question nearly destroyed him. The next decade, for Siborne, would come to be dominated by the need for money for his Model, and the military establishment's growing opposition to the exercise in historical democracy it had unwittingly unleashed. These two forces would collide, undermining Siborne's search for truth, eroding his atavistic belief in the army and his own view of the historical facts he had spent half his lifetime assembling.

'What are you to do with the Prussians?' asked the Waterloo veteran, Sir Richard Hussey Vivian, presciently, about the army of model soldiers the junior officer was assembling. His question would find an echo in the army, and among the political leadership of the country. It would reverberate among the high command and in the corridors of power. It would even tap uncomfortably at the door of the great commander himself. Sometimes tacitly, and sometimes overtly, Siborne's obstinate search for the facts would be seen as the barrier to the further, official, funding of his Model. What was he to do with the Prussians? The question pursued Siborne to the grave.

II

When varying circumstances, witnessed at the time under great interruption, are sought historically after the lapse of many years, suggestion occurs as remembrance, surmise as fact; the difficulty then, with
whatever veracious intention, is to tell the truth, the whole truth and
nothing but the truth.

Lt.-Col. Henry Murray, letter to William Siborne, 27 December 1834

It would be the biggest, most detailed model the world had ever seen,
but it was almost impossible to make. First, there was its size.
Siborne's creation would be so large, it would have to be made in
more than thirty sections, which would have to dovetail perfectly, or
it could never be moved. Then, too, there was the question of Siborne's
own experience. The project was far more ambitious than anything he
had ever attempted. He was used to making relief maps, indeed he was
quite brilliant at creating them, but never before had he attempted to
fashion so many model soldiers or tiny buildings, all of which would
be needed for a proper battlefield model of Waterloo. But when his
superior officer asked him if he was up to the task, he had to accept
the challenge. Apart from anything else, he must have thought it would
be the making of his career.

Siborne needed the high profile the work would bring him, for the
military had been slow to recognise his skills, and he had a wife, Helen,
the daughter of a Fifeshire banker, and children to support. By 1830,
when he mapped the battlefield, he had already been assistant military

secretary to the commander of the forces in Ireland for four years. It was not the most prestigious post he could hope for, and he would have to remain in it for another thirteen years. It seemed the army was overlooking Siborne's talents. One officer, quoted in W.M. Fitzpatrick's *The Life of Charles Lever*, suggested that 'he was a perfect gentleman and a most able officer. A man of fine intellect and judgement, truly unpretending in his manner and very well informed. Pity that the British Army was so constituted as to condemn a man like Siborne to an utterly subordinate and inadequate sphere of duty.'

Part of Siborne's career problem was that mapping was a relatively new development, so his skills were not fully recognised by the army. The first large-scale survey of any part of the British Isles had been the military survey of Scotland, carried out in response to the Jacobite Rebellion of 1745/6, under the leadership of a civilian recruited from the Post Office, William Roy. But it had taken another half-century for the army to realise the importance of accurate maps in planning its military campaigns. At the start of the Napoleonic Wars, the only formal training in surveying was to be found at the Royal Military Academy at Woolwich, where cadets from the Royal Engineers were taught, and at the Board of Ordnance Drawing Room at the Tower of London.

Siborne could see the need to improve the craft. His aim was to create a style of topographical drawing which 'impresses at once upon the mind of the person viewing it as a correct image of nature' so that even 'the most fastidious will not require a greater approximation of perfection.' He wrote two technical books on the subject, one of which he dedicated to his superior, the commander in Ireland, Sir George Murray. Siborne considered that Ordnance Survey work in England, then in its infancy, had been woefully executed, because the resulting maps, first of Kent and then of Essex, had been so badly drawn that they had failed to match the great skill with which the surveyors had carried out their task. He agreed with evidence heard by a parliamentary committee which was considering how to make a complete survey of Ireland. The engineer William Bald, who won later renown for designing the Antrim coast road to replace the dangerous Old Irish

Highway, had told the enquiry that the mapping should be carried out so accurately that, from it, an exact model of the land it represented could easily be made.

Siborne quoted approvingly Bald's dictum that a model 'is the nearest approximation of art in representing the features of a country, and, for military purposes, superior to any map representation.' And he put his mind to inventing a new system of topographical drawing, from which accurate models could be made. Models were ideal, he opined, for studying the tactics of past battles, according to the differing terrains on which they had been fought. Through a system of laying down lines and points, Siborne found a way to make maps which were easier to read and more accurate in their topographical detail so that the army could judge the suitability of the land for its different types of troops. He laid down complicated and detailed instructions to surveyors – on how to find the depth of an object; on how to find the angle of inclination of ground; on how to carry on work from one survey-sheet to another ('always allow an inch margin upon your board, upon which you can determine any conspicuous objects which properly belong to the adjoining sheets'). There were even instructions on how to shade a map in diluted Indian ink to represent changes in the slope of the ground.

Much of this might have escaped the army's attention. But in 1830, the twin skills of surveying and model-making were suddenly high on its agenda, for reasons of vanity and prestige. Fifteen years after their triumph at Waterloo, the country's military leaders were still trying to find an appropriate way to commemorate the battle and to preserve its legend. They thought there should be a museum in London dedicated to the army and the navy, which should contain a suitable exhibit to celebrate Waterloo. Lord Hill, who as a lieutenant-general at Waterloo had gained Wellington's complete trust, was deputed to find a modeller who could create a miniature version of the battlefield. The French had displayed them for years at Les Invalides, so why not the British?

Siborne had already made a model of the Battle of Borodino, in 1812, and his former colleague in Ireland, Sir George Murray, was now a cabinet minister under Wellington. Murray considered Siborne to be the ideal candidate to make a model of the Battle of Waterloo: he was held to be loyal, diligent, meticulous – and eager to get on. For the first time in Siborne's career, preferment beckoned. He could not have seen that the twin forces of politics and money would conspire to bring him down.

When Siborne had been chosen to build the Model, Lord Hill contacted the Secretary at War, Sir Henry Hardinge, to arrange the necessary financial backing. The Tory government readily paid his first bill of more than sixty pounds, for the survey of the battlefield. Ministers considered it to be money well spent, an appropriate cele-bration of the Duke's great triumph. Then, for Siborne, came disaster. Three years after the election of a Whig prime minister, Earl Grey in 1830, and three years into his project, the government decided it no longer wished to fund such a costly enterprise. Over the next twenty years, the Whigs would cut spending on the army by nearly a fifth, and the Model was seen as an unnecessary cost. Added to which, the new men in the War Office, led by Edward Ellice as Secretary at War, had had a number of run-ins with the Duke. It was clear that Ellice would refuse to sanction spending public money on the project and in this he would find ready acceptance from the Whigs, who thought that the Model would glorify the Tory Welling-ton. It was an irony which was to rule Siborne's life for the next decade that the public purse was closed to him by the political opponents of the Duke, who were not overly anxious to celebrate his achievements, while the great man's supporters came separately to the view that work on his Model should be stopped because it did not celebrate him enough.

Ellice was on safe ground, because he could find no record of the financial agreement Siborne considered he had struck. Siborne was convinced that Sir Henry Hardinge, the previous Secretary at War, had agreed to pay for the whole, completed project, but, curiously for such a meticulous man, Siborne does not seem to have confirmed the deal in writing. The War Office and the Treasury debated the matter between themselves, concluding that Lord Hill had not anticipated the full cost of building the Model, and that Hardinge had only agreed to pay Siborne for the cost of his initial survey. The result was that the government decided to postpone any decision on funding the whole project, leaving Siborne with a deep-felt sense of injustice which would stay with him until his death.

The great expense of creating the Model was outlined in a memorandum written by Siborne in August 1833. In fourteen months, he said he had spent £217 12s 6d, and 'the principal expenses, namely the moulding and casting of the figures representing the troops, remain to be incurred.' Yet, he complained, for four months he had heard nothing from the commander-in-chief's office, or from the Secretary at War, about his mounting bills. So he had himself taken the decision to continue with the Model 'upon the supposition that the government would not wish me to abandon the undertaking and thus sacrifice the £400 already laid out upon it.' Siborne calculated that the cost of creating his toy soldiers would amount to between £600 and £700, and the engraving and painting of them to about £100. There would be, he estimated, other expenses of between £200 and £300 before the Model was completed. In short, he needed to find at least £1000.

Siborne's supporter, Sir Hussey Vivian, wrote to the Secretary at War on 10 November 1833 to make a new plea for funding, but also to suggest, if this failed, that there should be a subscription amongst Siborne's military friends: 'I speak from having been three times over the Field since the Battle, and to the expression of my own opinion, I can add that of the Marquess of Anglesey, who inspected the Model with me and who in the strongest terms expressed his approbation. As a National Work I consider the Model will be highly valuable.'

Siborne was not immediately convinced that a public subscription was the right way forward, and feared losing ownership of his project. But the withdrawal of public funding had placed him in an impossible position. Within months, in January 1834, he was so deeply in debt that he acquiesced and formally proposed a subscription. In the draft handbill for the appeal, he revealed the full details of the Model he was trying to build. 'It may be right to mention,' he stated, 'that it will afford an accurate representation of the Battle and its Field, at a particular moment, the Crisis; that the whole of the Troops engaged will be faithfully represented, every corps in its correct position and formation, and that the superficial extent of the Model will occupy a space of about 420 square feet.'

This final paragraph of the subscription was the key to the saga which was about to unfold. Not the staggering size of the great Model, which was extraordinary in itself, nor the cost at which the government had balked. The problem was Siborne's intention to display the Crisis of the Battle, the point at which the day was won. For as Siborne recorded the views of the participants in the engagement and allotted due weight to their roles in the day's proceedings, so he increasingly came into conflict with the Duke of Wellington's account of the battle.

Siborne's revolutionary idea was to allow the participants in the battle to have their say, not in the personal, romantic way in which some of them wrote their own accounts, but by mediating their stories, crosschecking the facts they provided, and weighing up their evidence. In doing so, he flew in the face of the official version of events, and opposed the Duke of Wellington's desire to control the narrative of the day. Wellington had refused to endorse any of the books which had been written about the battle, even saying they disgusted him. For history, as Wellington put it, was simply what lay in official reports, and he referred authors to his own brief description of the battle, his Waterloo Despatch.

'The people of England may be entitled to a detailed and accurate account of the Battle of Waterloo, and I have no objection to their having it,' Wellington once declared, disingenuously. 'But I do object to their being misinformed and misled by those novels called "Relations", "Impartial Accounts", etcetera, etcetera, of that transaction, containing the stories which curious travellers have picked up from peasants, private soldiers, individual officers ... and have published to the world as truth ... there is not one which contains a true representation, or even an idea, of the transaction; and this is because the writers have referred as above quoted, instead of to the official sources and reports.'

Siborne had failed to predict that he would be in conflict with the official version of events, laid down in the Duke's own account. In its sweep and compass, and in its devotion to firsthand accounts of the men who actually fought the battle, Siborne's historical evidence-gathering was far too revolutionary. His project stood to threaten not just the official view of the battle, but the official view of history – that it was a subject which was best left to those in political and military charge of the country: in short, to Wellington himself.

The Duke of Wellington, by virtue of his deeds in the Peninsular War and then his astounding triumph at Waterloo, had found fame and wealth and a status which, even while he was alive, had made him a hero of the century and a bulwark against political instability. Industri-alisation and the growth of the big cities had triggered political unrest which the country's leaders struggled to contain. England felt like a country which, at any point, might lose its balance, and in these circumstances it looked for certainty, and the Duke of Wellington's glorious victory at Waterloo had provided an anchor. Wellington reflected the country's standing in the world, both real and imagined. It was an image he was keen to foster once he had fought his last battle, almost as if he was observing detachedly the man he had become: 'I am the Duke of Wellington,' he would say, 'and must do as the Duke of Wellington doth.' To this extent, he controlled his image as carefully as any modern politician, sitting for many portraits, attending public functions, and keeping a wary eye on the publication of his military despatches. For many years, the Duke held political power too: as prime minister for two years, until 1830, as foreign secretary under Sir Robert Peel (1834–5), and then as a cabinet minister for five years, again under Peel, from 1841. Despite the hostility he attracted because of his opposition to the electoral Reform Bill, he was still, for many, the embodiment of the age, patriotic, modest, honourable, a gentleman hero, and he was understandably anxious to ensure that the image did not prove to be at variance with reality.

To this end, the Duke had a firm rule when it came to the historical accounts of the battles he had fought: he never read any. Aware that he might be irritated or angered by false comment, he preferred to rise above the storm entirely, to embrace the peace of ignorance and avoid debate or controversy. This, however, was not quite the full story. He was quite prepared to visit the many popular Waterloo entertainments which had become an industry in themselves, and which included vast paintings, theatricals, and even planting trees in public parks in the pattern of troop deployments.

If these events had anything in common, it was that they were only loosely based on fact. But Wellington had also been persuaded, somewhat against his better judgement, to sanction an authorised account of his career, a twelve-volume set of his despatches, edited by Colonel John Gurwood, who became Wellington's private secretary. Gurwood effectively became Siborne's rival, approved by the establishment. Like Siborne, he too had a military background. He had been badly wounded in the Peninsular War and was injured in the knee at Waterloo. At the precise point that Siborne was walking the battlefield of Waterloo, he too had set about the task of recording the period of history he had lived through. In 1830, he had been stationed at Portsmouth as a major. 'Soon after my appointment,' he recalled, 'I set to work on the project I had designed 12 years previous, of condensing all the Duke of Wellington's orders, and obtaining His Grace's sanction for their publication.'

Gurwood, like Siborne, sought to adhere strictly to the facts. But to do this, he was intent on portraying the Duke in his own words, even at the price of editorial freedom. 'I will trouble Your Grace to mark any part which may be thought foreign to the purposes for which the Despatches are printed,' he told him at one point. Wellington was, nonetheless, initially resistant to the idea of publication and rebuffed the approach – 'Whoever heard of a true history?' he insisted. But eventually, flattered by Gurwood's approach and reassured by his own control of the project, he gave his assent. The first volume, his *General Orders*, was published two years later, in September 1832, and Wellington became an instant convert. The Duke could clearly see that he had managed to control the content as skilfully as he had commanded any army throughout his long military career. The Conservative MP Charles Arbuthnot, whose wife Harriet was a close friend of Wellington, wrote to Gurwood that the Duke 'has taken the greatest interest in your book. He was so delighted with reading his old orders that he did nothing else all yesterday but read them aloud.'

Within a year, Gurwood had completed the task of putting all Wellington's public despatches in order so that they might be published. Wellington still had editorial control ('Your Grace may draw your pen through what may be deemed unnecessary to print'), but by 1835, as another volume was readied for publication, the Duke was again assailed by doubts about the original wisdom of his decision. To complete the publishing task he had set himself Gurwood was forced to fight his corner, as diplomatically as possible, telling Wellington: 'without the publication of these despatches, the truth will never be known; and posterity will be led into error by the imagination of historians whose narratives will otherwise become hallowed by time as uncontradicted authorities.' Cautiously, Wellington kept the original proofs for himself so that the changes he made could not be discovered.

Gurwood kept to his task and acquitted himself so well in his balancing act that he was awarded, at Wellington's instigation, a pension of £200 a year from 1839, and was given the post of Deputy Lieutenant of the Tower of London. 'You have brought before the publick,' a grateful Wellington told him, 'a work which must be essential to statesmen and soldiers as containing the true details of important and military operations of many years duration.' The *Waterloo* volume, the twelfth in the series, came out in the late summer of 1838. It was a work which stood as if in contradistinction to the unmediated, democratic access Siborne had gained to the soldiers of Waterloo.

For Siborne, history could not be as straightforward as Gurwood made it. His was neither the official version, nor those of individuals, but the product of intensive evidence-gathering from a wide range of witnesses. This approach was to cause him no end of difficulties. Meticulous both as a modeller and as an historian, Siborne had to reconcile the firsthand accounts of the battle he was obtaining with the official version laid down by the great Duke himself. For a relatively humble member of the army, who wished to present an accurate celebration of a famous victory, but also to further his own career, the pressure must have been enormous. At a personal level, he wished to be true to himself and model exactly what he had found. But on a professional level, he was pressurised by the very military leaders he admired. He could only offer the reassurance that his intentions were noble, and that he would, in keeping with his uncontroversial ambitions, submit the plan of his Model to the Duke of Wellington for approval, not least because, as he had protested, he aimed to do nothing which contradicted one syllable of the Duke of Wellington's Despatch. But the years ahead would be marked by a growing row over the money he still felt the government should pay him, and by the gathering storm over the nature of his project.

As if to make this clear, the imposing figure of Wellington's ally, Lord James Henry Fitzroy Somerset, stood in the way of Siborne making further progress with his Model. Somerset, later Lord Raglan of Crimean fame, was a Waterloo veteran whose friendship with Wellington had been a long one. He had served on his staff in the expedition to Copenhagen, and was alongside him during the whole of the Peninsular War first as aide-de-camp and then, from 1811, as his military secretary. In the same role at Waterloo, as military secretary in the general headquarters, he had dealt with all Wellington's correspondence during the campaign, reading all incoming reports, keeping a register of all documents and liaising with the non-British formations. He was no mere bureaucrat: he had himself been injured in the battle, and his right arm had been amputated. Afterwards, he had taught himself to write with his left hand, and in between two spells as an MP for Truro, he was appointed secretary to the Duke of Wellington when the Duke became master-general of the ordnance in 1819. From 1827 he was again his military secretary, when the Duke became commander-in-chief of the army and he stayed in this role for another twenty-five years, for the rest of the Duke's life.

But Somerset's connection with Wellington went deeper than his many decades of service. In 1814 he had married Emily Harriet Wellesley-Pole, the Duke of Wellington's niece. In army and family matters, Somerset was tied to Wellington, and in the years after Waterloo, he acted as his gatekeeper. Early on, Somerset became unhappy with Siborne's desire to interview the participants in the battle and to portray its Crisis. In the icily polite but dismissive language of the bureaucrat, a language with which the model-maker was to become familiar in the years ahead, Siborne was sent the first sign that he had become an irritant, and that the military was beginning to wish it had not sanctioned his project. He received this letter from Maj.-Gen. Sir James Charles Dalbiac, the Inspector-General of Cavalry and a

Peninsula veteran himself. It was the beginning of years of cuttingly formal exchanges with the country's bureaucrats.

> 34, Cavendish Square
> 5 March 1834

My dear Siborne,

   Since the receipt of your letter, I have had several conferences with Lord Fitzroy Somerset.

   We think that it would greatly increase your difficulties rather than lead to elucidation to write a circular for information to different general officers who commanded brigades and who from a variety of circumstances must give such very different versions of what passed before their eyes . . .

   Yours faithfully,

   J. Chas Dalbiac

Siborne, convinced of the accuracy of his methodology in matters both topographical and historical, would not take the hint. At one point he asked Lieutenant Samuel Waymouth, of the 2nd Life Guards, who was wounded at Waterloo and had been one of the very few officers to be captured by the French, to approach Fitzroy Somerset on Siborne's behalf. Waymouth reported back: 'he cannot conceive the possibility of your being able to attain to accuracy, considering how conflicting are the statements one continually hears from persons, all whose testimonies one considers undeniable. If you succeed in giving a tolerably correct representation, it is all you can expect.'

But Siborne was as determined to follow his own course as his portrait by Samuel Lover suggests. His mouth was hard-set against change. His dogged determination blinkered him to ways which might smooth his path ahead to achieve his overall objective, so that he was not in the slightest bit sensitive to recognising any of the political niceties which Somerset raised. Nor was he moved by the idea, put forward by Lord Fitzroy Somerset, that he should give the finished Model to the Duke of Wellington, refusing to realise that such a gesture might win him the necessary political support for its creation.

The result was that Fitzroy Somerset did not receive the most diplomatic of responses. From this point on, conflict was inevitable and Wellington was forced, as on the battlefield, to try to keep events under his absolute control. Siborne had started his project with a naïve belief that he was doing nothing other than bringing credit on the army he so admired, and the generalship of Wellington of which he stood in awe. But as the Model progressed, and he found himself at war with the authorities, his weapons were his doggedness, his obsession with the demands of historical accuracy, his determination to make his precious Model so exact, so meticulously accurate, that the soldiers he so admired would marvel at his powers. Both attributes, his naïveté and his determination, blinded him to the gradual process of obstruction and denigration which came to undermine his finances and his health. Unwittingly, he was challenging the Duke's Despatches, and taking on the state, by adhering to the simple, if democratic, dictum that history should consist of the properly weighed claims of eyewitnesses, whatever their station in life.

Dublin

8 March 1834

My dear General,

Surely it will be conceded that officers may be able to give a very good version of what passed before their own eyes, *as far as relates to themselves and their own corps.*

Fortunately, there still exists a considerable number of eyewitnesses of the Battle of Waterloo and it appears to me that the principal utility and advantage of constructing a Model ... is to secure, before the favourable opportunity is gone for ever, a well-authenticated representation and record of the positions and movements of the troops engaged ...

The only mode of arriving at accurate conclusions essential for such a purpose, is to weigh and compare the statements of those eyewitnesses ...

I cannot proceed upon any other principle – it would be useless to trust to the very imperfect unsatisfactory accounts that have hitherto been published, which though they might serve the purpose of the general historian, or of the designer of a battle-piece, become of little or no value to the modeller, who, from the nature of his work, especially when that is constructed upon an unusually large scale, can make no progress without correct data – *accuracy, not effect,* being the sole object of *his* labours.

    I remain,

        My dear General

            Your very faithful servant

              WS

By the year's end, a weary Lord Fitzroy Somerset had made his one and only concession, replying tersely, through the chief clerk in the commander-in-chief's office: 'Then let him issue his circular and the Lord give him a safe deliverance.' It was a concession he would bitterly regret, as Siborne's evidence-gathering reached epic proportions, with dangerously democratic results. With the building of William Siborne's Great Model of the Field of Waterloo, a new conflict had broken out – the Battle of Waterloo's history.

Why this should be so is a mystery that lies in the eyewitness accounts which Siborne gathered, and in the separate version the commanders wished to tell. It lies deep in the course of the fighting itself, in the twists and turns of battle, and most importantly of all, in the fragile and sometimes fractious alliance of armies which came together to face the greatest soldier of the age. It is the story of how William Siborne decided how much credit should be awarded to the Prussians, rather than the Duke of Wellington, for the victory which defined the age.

III

To the Secretary at War, Edward Ellice
From Sir Hussey Vivian, Commander-in-Chief in Ireland

Dublin, 20 August 1833

My dear Ellice,

I send you a memorandum on the subject of a great national work undertaken under the authority of the general Commander in Chief – a model of the Battle of Waterloo.

Mr Siborne is a very intelligent and clever person. He has taken great pains with this work and has been at a great expense – he was many months on the spot surveying the ground. It is impossible for any thing to be more correct than it is.

Under these circumstances I hope he will not be allowed any longer to remain under pecuniary difficulties, but that the means he proposes may be taken to supply him with the sum requisite to finish the Model.

Ever my dear Ellice,

Very faithfully yours,

Hussey Vivian

War had come to threaten Europe so quickly, it was hard to believe it was less than four months since the emperor had returned from his island exile. It was harder still to remember that, when Napoleon had landed at the end of February, his invasion force had consisted of eleven hundred soldiers and a fleet, if such it could

33

be called, of three ships. Not that the size of his army had mattered when he set foot on French soil. Many thousands of French soldiers, ranged against him at Grenoble, had simply laid down their arms and cheered their emperor's return. Soon the miniature army, swelled by deserters, was built upon an altogether grander scale and a country which contained an emperor and a king could not hold both within its boundaries. Within a month, Louis XVIII had fled the country and the French monarchy had collapsed. But that was not the end of Napoleon's ambitions, and his enemies knew it. Europe's political masters, whose representatives had gathered at the Congress of Vienna, realised it was only a matter of time before war broke out. Now it had actually happened, but still Napoleon had managed to take everyone by surprise.

Through the brilliance of his manoeuvres, Napoleon was able to dictate the course of events, and to scatter the two armies, of Britain and Prussia, which had hoped to unite against him. In doing so, he not only gave himself a chance of victory which would have been denied him if they had joined forces, but he placed their alliance under a strain which nearly broke it. In this way, he so undermined the little trust that the two armies placed in each other that the British military authorities would give little or no credit to the Prussians for the victory they came to win. The seeds of this discord lay in the speed of Napoleon's attack which kept Wellington's army and the Prussian forces apart until the very end of the Battle of Waterloo. As William Siborne discovered, the eventual result of their separation was to infect the battle's history beyond his cure.

When the first dozen regiments of French cavalry thundered through the countryside, it was not yet dawn, and Wellington had no idea that his enemy was on the move. The horsemen, brass-helmeted, spurred on their charges, and barely noticed the land as it fell away behind them. Their road led north, and soon it brought them to a small river which marked the frontier of France and Belgium. A hundred hooves, followed by many hundreds more, came crashing through the river at its shallow fording-place, so that spray was sent high into the air, to hang for a moment in the half-light. The horses climbed up and over the riverbank and took their thunder with them. The River

Sambre resumed its gentle course, and the birds returned to their resting place in the trees. But the world was no longer at peace. The enemy had crossed the border and there were thousands more waiting to follow the bridgehead they had made. It was 15 June 1815 and the invasion had begun.

If Napoleon was to narrow the odds against him, he had to catch the enemy off-guard. To take on the Duke of Wellington, who was undefeated in battle, was one matter, even though the Emperor did not rate his tactical abilities: too slow, too cautious, and no flair, he thought. But to take the Anglo-Allied army on at the same time as the Prussian army of old Blücher was military madness. The Emperor must keep the two sides apart or else be hopelessly outnumbered. That was why speed was all. His spies had told him that it would take many hours to bring together Wellington's scattered army, and many hours more for the two armies to become one force. If he could take on each army separately, then they might never unite. And that was entirely their own fault.

Wellington and Blücher had first met only six weeks earlier to discuss their joint campaign. They met again in Brussels at the end of May, where Blücher had been granted the rare honour of inspecting some of the Duke's cavalry. Their discussions had led to them to agree that their armies would cooperate in battle, but their pact was incomplete. United by a common enemy, the two armies were not brought together on the ground. There was no joint command, and their forces operated in different parts of the country, which made coordination difficult. Wellington's base lay in Brussels, and his supply lines ran from Ostend and Antwerp. Blücher's headquarters were being transferred from Liège to Namur, and his supply lines ran in the opposite direction to those of Wellington. If the two armies were forced to retreat, they would be pulled even further apart. But the two leaders had, at least, agreed on tactics. They planned to advance into France on 27 June to attack Napoleon, and to try to defeat him through the use of overwhelming force. If the plan failed, then the Allied army and the Prussians would try to protect each other. Now, although they did not know it, the plan *was* failing, and their pact would be tested to destruction.

The alliance with the Prussians was, in any case, an unlikely one, because in battle as in life, Wellington and Blücher were polar opposites. Blücher was born to be obstinate, and he had lived his life according to his own drumbeat in a military career which was as rich as it was varied. A member of a military family, he had joined the Swedish army as a cavalryman in 1742 and had taken part in three campaigns against Prussia's Frederick the Great. When he was captured by his enemy in 1760, he changed sides and became a loyal, but uncontrollable soldier. He then served with distinction against France's revolutionary armies, but the disastrous 1806 campaign had led to his enforced retirement. When Prussia again took up arms against the French in 1813, Blücher returned to fight with typical ferocity until the emperor was defeated at Laon, forcing his abdication. Now the two rivals were to face each other again, with Blücher, at seventy-two, the oldest man on the battlefield, and the only man to have beaten Napoleon more than once in battle.

In contrast, Wellington was cautious and conservative, a methodical commander who considered defence was the best form of attack, who wanted to lure his enemy into making mistakes, and who instinctively eschewed unnecessary risks. He had never met Napoleon directly in battle though the two had circled each other warily. The Duke had forced the Emperor into exile on Elba the year before, and there was a certain inevitability in their meeting now, the scion of the establishment ranged against the avowed outsider, the imperial usurper of monarchy and tradition. The son of an Irish aristocrat, albeit an impoverished one, Arthur Wellesley had been educated at Eton, and had then taken a commission in the 73rd Infantry. India was the making of him. The war with France had effectively moved there, with the French encouraging native princes to resist the East India Company's control. As brigade commander under General George Harris in 1799, Wellington impressed his superiors throughout the Seringapatam expedition against the rebellious Tippoo Sahib of Mysore, who had been stirred into action by his French allies, and he was made administrator of the conquered territory.

It was the Peninsular War against the French in Spain, however, which had cemented Wellington's growing reputation and which taught him a mastery of defensive warfare. Between November 1809 and September 1810 he had supervised the construction of protective lines of trenches and redoubts, north of Lisbon, stretching from the Atlantic to the Tagus. The 'Lines of Torres Vedras' were crafted out of two successive ridges of hills. Buildings, sunken lanes, olive groves and vineyards were all erased from the landscape, denying any cover to an attacking force. It was a brilliantly successful tactic, and after driving the French from the Peninsula, Wellington pushed on into France itself in 1814 until Napoleon, pressed by Wellington in the south and by a triple alliance of Prussia, Russia and Austria in the north and east, had been forced to abdicate.

But a year later, with every mile of Belgian countryside covered by his light dragoons, his hope of revenge was growing. After securing the crossing at the River Sambre, his Armée du Nord had moved fast to form a wedge between its two enemies. Marshal Ney led the left wing towards Frasnes and Quatre Bras, while Marshal Grouchy took the right wing towards Fleurus and Sombreffe. A mobile reserve was kept at Charleroi to reinforce either of the commanders. By seizing Quatre Bras, the French would control the main highway, and the chances of the two armies joining up against them would be as likely as this year's harvest failing, and already the crop was as high as the tallest cavalryman. Instead, Wellington and Blücher would be forced to fall back across country, slowed down by the rutted landscape and the sun-baked soil. The Emperor had sprung his trap before his enemies knew anything about it. Soon, he would be the conqueror of Brussels.

That evening, in a large room on the ground floor of the Duchess of Richmond's residence, the young ladies of Brussels were dancing with the British officers, resplendent in their scarlet, gold and white uniforms. The ball, it should be said, was the scene of the first of many myths which came to cloak the history of the Battle of Waterloo. As William Siborne was to find, the imprecision of legend began even before the combatants reached the battlefield.

The building in which the ball was held has long since disappeared, enabling novelists, painters and poets to let loose their imaginations, so that the ball has entered the classical literature of England without regard to fact. Over the years, it became a grand affair, in a magnificent ballroom, with sparkling chandeliers, great sweeping curtains and sumptuous furniture. But it was a memory based on fiction, created partly by Thackeray, by Turner, who painted a ornate ballroom modelled on an entirely different building, and especially by Byron, who ensured that romanticism prevailed, rather than historical accuracy. It was left to the son of a Waterloo veteran, Sir William Fraser, to prove, though not conclusively, the mundane truth: that the ball had in fact taken place, not in a high hall, but in a long, low-ceilinged room supported by square wooden posts.

The guest list for the ball is, however, well documented. More than two hundred people had been invited: His Royal Highness the Prince of Orange was there, and the Duke of Brunswick and the Prince of Nassau and the Duc d'Aramberg and a clutch of counts and countesses. There were more than eighty British officers, too, on the guest list, many of whom would play a prominent part in the battles which lay ahead, including the Earl of Uxbridge, Wellington's deputy; Maj.-Gen. Lord Edward Somerset; Lord Hill; Lt.-Gen. Sir Henry Clinton, and his wife, Lady Susan; Lt.-Col. Lord Saltoun; Sir John Byng; Sir William Ponsonby; Maj.-Gen. Sir Hussey Vivian and Maj.-Gen. Sir James Kempt. They did not know that the room they occupied had more humble origins as the storeroom of a coachbuilder who still owned the rented property, for its rose and trellis wallpaper camouflaged its previous existence from the party-goers, as if their evening's pleasure was a veneer which could be stripped away.

During the morning of 15 June, there had been rumours in the city that the Emperor had invaded the country. But although there is a dispute about when reports reached Wellington, it seems there was no definite information on which he could rely. A messenger on a good horse would take only three hours to gallop the distance which separated the city from the border. And yet there had been no definite sighting, not even a suggestion of a cloud of dust created by an army on the move. Besides which, the Duke of Wellington needed to keep up appearances: there were too many supporters of Napoleon in the city who resented the yoke of the Dutch rule. It would not do to raise their hopes or give them encouragement, which was why he intended to go to the Duchess of Richmond's ball.

By mid-afternoon, Wellington knew that there had been an attack, but he could not discern if it was merely sabre-rattling by the Emperor or if a full invasion had been launched. A clash of Prussian and French skirmishers did not tell him anything, for he knew enough of Bonaparte's brilliance not to be lured into a false move: the attack might simply be a feint, to mask his true intentions. Was Napoleon really heading directly through Charleroi? Or would he attack more centrally, with a strike at Mons? Perhaps further east still, darting between Condé and Tournai? It was impossible to judge. If the Duke was tricked into sending his men to Charleroi, then the road from Mons would lie open. In the end, he thought his army was most vulnerable to an attack on its supply links to the Channel, and so he issued orders for his divisions to gather at their assembly points in readiness for battle, a decision which pulled men away from Brussels, in the opposite direction to where they were needed.

At nightfall, more reports arrived. Wellington learned that the Prussians were mobilising at Sombreffe, against a French push east; he learned too, from the young Prince of Orange, that there had been the sound of gunfire near the border. But still he was unable to calculate the position of the main French force. So he did not commit his men to Quatre Bras, as he should have done, and its strategically vital crossroads remained unguarded.

In the end, given the confusion the day had brought, it was appropriate that the threat of war should finally come to wrap itself, incongruously, around Brussels society as it paraded on the dance floor. For as the guests danced and talked and ate, Lieutenant Henry Webster, of the 9th Light Dragoons, an aide-de-camp to the Prince of Orange, was pounding the road between Braine-le-Comte and Brussels, bearing news of the French advance from Maj.-Gen. Jean-Victor Constant-Rebecque, the incisive chief of staff of the Prince of Orange. 'I was in my saddle without a second's delay; and, thanks to a fine moon and two capital horses, had covered the ten miles I had to go within the hour! Such was the crowd of carriages, that I could not well make way through them on horseback; so I abandoned my steed to the first man

I could get hold of, and made my way on foot to the porter's lodge.' Even so, Webster was forced to wait because the Duchess of Richmond had just given orders for the band to go upstairs, and he was told that if he burst in suddenly it might disturb the ladies. Peering in between the doors he saw two couples on their way to the ballroom, the Duchess of Richmond with the Prince of Orange, and Lady Charlotte Greville on the Duke of Wellington's arm. Webster slipped quietly into the house to deliver his vital message.

After reading Rebecque's despatch, Wellington remained at the ball for twenty minutes, then quietly asked his host if there was a good map in the house. The Duke of Richmond took him upstairs into his own dressing-room, and as the two men pored over the chart, the full impact of Napoleon's lightning strike became clear. It was only now that Wellington realised how disastrously he had miscalculated. Famously, he was said to have declared, 'Napoleon has humbugged me, by God! He has gained twenty-four hours' march on me,' and he ordered men to move to Quatre Bras. 'But we shall not stop him there,' Wellington reflected, 'so, I must fight him here.' And he put his thumbnail on the map, on the village of Mont St Jean, just south of Waterloo.

Wellington was to say afterwards that this was the first he had heard of Napoleon's attack on the Prussian outposts. But the Prussians were convinced that Wellington had received news of the attack which they had sent in the afternoon, and that he had broken his promise to support them. Tonight, there would be no help for the Prussians from the Duke of Wellington's army, and they would come to connect his apparent failure to help them with the terrible defeat they were to suffer the next day. With every minute that went by, and with every mile his men pushed on into Belgium, Napoleon was on his way to victory.

Both armies paid the price for Wellington's mistake. At the crossroads of Quatre Bras on 16 June the gunfire started at first light. Eight thousand men in the Dutch-Belgian army had spread out in a wide circle, south of the crossroads, facing twenty-eight thousand of the enemy. There were not enough of them to hold the French but there were enough to delay them if Wellington's men arrived, and their skirmishers were already at work, sniping at enemy forces. But they would have to wait several hours for reinforcements, for Wellington's orders of the night before were only just beginning to get through to some units, so that new orders which referred to previous orders confused the men who had not received the first set of paperwork. Captain Alexander Cavalié Mercer of the Royal Horse Artillery was told to head for Braine-le Comte: 'that we were to move forward, then, was certain . . . but the suddenness of it, and the importance of arriving quickly at the appointed place, rather alarmed me . . . First, all my officers were absent; secondly, all my country waggons were absent; thirdly, a whole division (one-third of my troop) was absent at Yser-ingen.' Ensign Edward Macready, who was the brother of a famous actor, William Charles Macready, had lost contact with his regiment, the 30th (Cambridgeshire), which had been billeted in the little town of Soignes, the headquarters of the 3rd British Division. Macready was only seventeen, and had joined the 2nd Battalion of the 30th Foot the previous year as a volunteer, serving in Holland. He kept a private journal of his experiences. That morning he had ridden over to the regiment 'and pulling up in the market-place, was thunder-struck. Not a soul was stirring. The silence of the tomb reigned where I should have met 10,000 men. I ran into a house and asked, "where are the troops?" "They marched at two this morning," was the chilling reply.' If it was a shock for such a young soldier, then soon he was acting like a veteran: by the end of the Battle of Waterloo, such was the casualty rate, he was commanding his own light company.

When Wellington arrived to take charge at Quatre Bras, he was facing a crisis of his own making. Not only were the defending forces in disarray, but he had to fight the battle in a place which was not of his own choosing. The landscape was flat and featureless, its only features a brook which ran parallel to the Nivelles road and the Bossu Wood towards which it meandered, where the Dutch troops had taken shelter. There could be no question of the Duke developing a con-sidered strategy or dictating the pace of events. His army was not yet fully assembled and it would grow incoherently and unpredictably as the hours went by, so that each fresh unit would be flung straight into the fray as soon as it arrived.

Wellington improvised brilliantly to disguise the weakness of his forces and his lack of cavalry. He pushed forward two brigades, to slow down the French advance and to stop the enemy from moving beyond the lake. But his army took heavy casualties. Sergeant James Anton, shrewd and tough, was a Scottish soldier who had joined the 42nd Regiment ten years earlier. Coming from a poor background, and brought up by his mother after his father died when he was still a child, he was so small that he had only been accepted by the Aberdeen militia at his second attempt, by standing on tip-toe. He made up for his lack of inches by being steady under fire: 'We instantly formed a rallying square; no time for particularity; every man's piece was loaded, and our enemies approached at full charge; the feet of their horses seemed to tear up the ground. Our skirmishers . . . fell beneath their lances, and few escaped death or wounds; our brave colonel (Sir Robert Macara) fell at this time, pierced through the chin until the point of the lance reached the brain . . . Colonel Dick assumed the command . . . and was severely wounded; Brevet-Major Davidson succeeded, and was mortally wounded; to him succeeded Brevet-Major Campbell. Thus, in a few minutes, we had been placed under four different commanding officers.'

Lt. Frederick Pattison of the 33rd Regiment, who published a short account of his experiences fifty years after the battle, remembered the impact of the French artillery: 'The destruction was fearful. At this time, Captain Haigh, having moved from the head of his company to encourage the face of the square, fronting the enemy, was cut in two by a cannonball, and poor Arthur Gore's brains were scattered upon my shako and face.'

Reinforcements again came to Wellington's rescue, two more Brunswick battalions and the 1st British (Guards) Division led by Maj.-Gen. George Cooke, which moved into the Bossu Wood. For the first time in the battle, Wellington had more men than the French, though he was still short of cavalry, and for the first time, too, he could dictate the pace of events. When his left wing captured the village of Piraumont, to the east, he gambled on a central push against the enemy. The 92nd was sent forward to tackle the French infantry which had occupied a house just east of the Charleroi road, braving the fire which rained down on them from the windows and from behind the hedge which ran from the back of the house. They took severe casualties. At the end of the battle, Lieutenant Robert Winchester of the 92nd – who was wounded at both Quatre Bras and Waterloo – recalled that 'Sir Thomas Picton, to whose division we belonged, saw the remains of the regiment, and when he enquired what this was, he was told it was the 92nd, on which he asked, "Where is the rest of the regiment?"' But the 92nd's bravery was a crucial turning-point, allowing Wellington's army to push south along both sides of the road. In the space of half an hour, the battle swung decisively towards the Duke, and the Anglo-Allied army recaptured all the ground lost by the Dutch-Belgians in the morning.

But Wellington's success had been costly. More than two thousand British troops lay dead or wounded. Ensign Robert Batty of the 1st Foot Guards remembered that 'as we approached the field of action we met constantly waggons full of men, of all the various nations under the Duke's command, wounded in the most dreadful manner. The sides of the road had a heap of dying and dead, very many of whom were British ... too much cannot be said in praise of the division of Guards, the very largest part of whom were young soldiers and volunteers from the militia, who had never been exposed to the fire of an enemy, or witnessed its effects.' The 32nd had two hundred casualties in its ranks, and the 79th, three hundred; half the 42nd and half the 92nd were dead or wounded, more than five hundred men in all.

It was less than twenty-four hours since the Duchess of Richmond's ball, and some of the victims were still dressed for the dance. But with their lives, the Duke had bought time, the very commodity which Napoleon had stolen from him by the speed of his invasion. And through fighting a brilliant, instinctive battle he had stopped the two wings of the French army from making a pincer movement on the Prussian army. Now he could now try to retreat to Mont St Jean, the place where he had left the mark of his thumbnail on the map, to make a stand in ground of his own choosing.

But, caught up in his own desperate struggle to survive, Wellington had not sent any troops to help his Prussian allies, deepening their suspicion of his leadership. More than fifteen years later, when he came to make his Model, William Siborne would discover the depth of the distrust in which the two allies held each other. On the Prussian side such feelings were, perhaps, understandable. From the east, there could be heard a faint rumble of thunder, the sound of guns at Ligny. A few miles beyond the horizon, they were dying in their thousands.

On the night of the Duchess of Richmond's ball, as Wellington's men hurriedly took to the roads towards Quatre Bras, the Prussian army had marched urgently to support its forces which had been chased east by Marshal Grouchy and the right wing of the French army. The next day, as the two sides readied themselves for battle, it became clear that the French had seized the best position: they were on the high ground overlooking Fleurus, while the Prussians had spread out through the villages in the bottom of a valley, from Ligny in the west to Wagnelée in the east, placing them within range of the French artillery.

For seven long hours, in the scorching sun, the two sides waited for battle, the yellow cornfields dazzling their eyes in the harsh summer light. The two armies were evenly matched, some 84,000 Prussians, with 226 guns, against a French army with 78,000 men and 242 guns. Then the French advanced. Their infantry marched in columns towards St Amand, while their artillery launched a fearsome cannonade on Ligny. Their skirmishers spread out quickly in the ground between the villages, fighting for possession of the Ligny stream. Prussian musket-fire rattled out from the loopholes cut into the walls of every house on the front line, from hedges and orchards and from behind stone walls, but still the French pressed forward, and soon the village of St Amand fell. When Pirch, the leader of the Prussian 2nd Corps, sent his men out from Bry to counterattack, they were slaughtered by French artillery, or destroyed by musket-fire. Each time the Prussians, bravely, wrested the shattered buildings on the front-line from the French, superior enemy firepower rained down on them and forced them back. The fiercest fighting was at Ligny, where the bodies were piled up in doorways and alleys, and where the cobbled road ran with blood.

As they fought, the Prussians hoped that Wellington might come to their rescue, but he was too hard pressed at the crossroads of Quatre

Bras. The French, too, were hoping for support from General d'Erlon, commanding I Corps, but because of a communication breakdown, he had spent fruitless hours galloping between the battlefields of Quatre Bras and Ligny in utter confusion as to whether he should be fighting the Anglo-Allied army or the Prussians. By crossing the River Sambre so swiftly, Napoleon had achieved his aim of dividing the two armies so that he might tackle each in turn. The irony was that a tactic intended to give him a greater chance of success, had also, in effect, divided his own army, reducing his chances of a quick victory.

But even without d'Erlon, the French were winning the battle. By nightfall, the Prussian defences could hold out no longer. They were short of ammunition while Napoleon had ten thousand men in reserve, and now they swarmed forward towards Ligny, forcing the Prussians to retreat. For Blücher, staring at defeat, there was only one response he could make: he would attack, heroically, and go down fighting with his men. He ordered his cavalry to form into line and led the charge himself, on the fine stallion which had been a present from the Prince Regent of England. A shot rang out, tearing into the horse's flank, and suddenly Blücher was falling, pitching forward onto the ground, the horse on top of him. Then darkness: he remembered nothing more. It was left to Blücher's deputy, his chief of staff, Lt.-Gen. August von Gneisenau, to signal the retreat.

It was a long, dark night of confusion for the shattered Prussian forces, their only solace the fact that the French were too exhausted from their efforts to pursue them through the dark. Men were scattered across the countryside in no formation, and the Prussian commanders had to try to round them up, to create order out of chaos. The plan was to make for Tilly but this was changed after the intervention of Lt.-Col. Ludwig von Reiche, the chief of staff of I Corps, who noted that, although it was almost dark, he could see that the place was not marked on his map. He realised that, if other officers had the same map, there would be confusion, so he proposed that another town further back, but on the same line of march, should be named as the assembly point. 'I found that Wavre was just such a place.'

The Prussians had failed to hold their own against Napoleon, and, separated by miles of countryside, they could not easily link up with the

Anglo-Allied army. But the distance between the allies was not just a physical separation, for it reflected too the gap between the two armies' thinking, and the ambiguous relationship they had forged. Gneisenau was a leading critic of the Duke, and had previously accused him of being a 'master in the art of duplicity' because of his ability to 'outwit the Nabobs' during his time in India. Now he thought Wellington had reneged upon a commitment to send help to the Prussians at Ligny, and he blamed the Duke for the defeat. He recorded bitterly that 'on the 16th of June in the morning the Duke of Wellington promised to be at Quatre Bras at 10 o'clock with 20,000 men . . . on the strength of these arrangements and promises we decided to fight the battle.' Gneisenau, so long as he remained in charge, would not offer any further help.

Fifteen years later, William Siborne came to realise that the distrust still ran deep, and that it was mutual. Wellington claimed that the Prussians had been defeated because they had chosen the wrong position. 'I told the Prussian officers that according to my judgement, the exposure of the advanced columns and, indeed, the whole army to cannonade was not prudent. The marshy banks of the stream made it out of their power to cross and attack the French, while the latter had it in their power to cannonade them, and shatter them to pieces, after which they might fall upon them by the bridges at the villages. However, they seemed to think they knew best, so I came away very shortly. It all fell out exactly as I had feared . . .' There was no reflection that he, himself, might have precipitated their problems through the late deployment of his troops.

That night, the two armies were fighting a common enemy whose aim was to divide them. And they were falling into the trap.

While the French were masters of the battlefield, there was still hope for the Anglo-Allied forces. Napoleon was fearful that the Prussians were regrouping and so he decided he could not throw the weight of his full army against Wellington's forces, lest the two enemies encircle him. And in doing so he let his enemies off the hook.

It was not until midday the next day, 17 June, that Grouchy received orders to follow the Prussians north. He then sent out cavalry to try to find out where the Prussians had gone and whether they had managed to reassemble as one force. By then it was nearly too late. Grouchy was unsure, he told his Emperor by messenger, of the location of the Prussians, though he thought, correctly, that they must have taken the road to Wavre. But he also thought, wrongly, that some of their army had moved even further east, so he divided his forces for the chase. By now, however, the weather had turned against the attacking army, clouding over and raining hard, making reconnaissance impossible.

And, by a miracle, Blücher was not dead. He had been carried from the field of battle to survive an ordeal which would have killed a lesser man. Gneisenau found him propped up on a camp bed in some farm buildings at the village of Mellery, north of Ligny. His right shoulder was very sore, and he smelled strongly of the medicaments which had been rubbed into his bruises, including brandy, gin, rhubarb and garlic. A British liaison officer, Sir Henry Hardinge, later to be Secretary at War, witnessed a fierce debate between the two men, as Blücher resisted pressure to resign because of his injuries. With firsthand experience of fighting Napoleon, he saw his old adversary as the enemy, and not the Anglo-Allied army. He told Hardinge 'he should be quite satisfied if in conjunction with the Duke of Wellington he was able now to defeat his old enemy.' Gneisenau, having successfully led the retreat of the exhausted troops, had to cede command to his Field-Marshal and his British ally. At Quatre Bras, Wellington finally learned what had happened to the Prussians, an event witnessed by Captain George Bowles of the Coldstream Guards: 'The Duke of Wellington came to me and said he was surprised to have heard nothing of Blücher. At length a staff-officer arrived, his horse covered with foam, and whispered to the Duke, who without the least change of countenance gave him some orders and dismissed him. He then turned round to me and said, "Old Blücher has had a damned good licking and gone back to Wavre, eighteen miles. As he has gone back we must go back too. I suppose in England they will say we have been licked. I can't help it; as they are gone back, we must go too."' The need to withdraw to safer ground was urgent. There would be no repeat of the tactical mess and barren terrain he had inherited at the crossroads.

In retreat, Wellington showed his strategic brilliance, ensuring that all four main routes into Brussels would be blocked by his army. It was a manoeuvre that was witnessed by Lieutenant Basil Jackson. Jackson was one of the longest-surviving Waterloo veterans, dying in 1889 at the age of ninety-four. The son of a major, he had entered military college in 1808, from where he was transferred to the Royal Staff Corps, where he was taught engineering, and the duties of the Quartermaster-General's department. With this background, he could appreciate the organisational skill of Wellington's retreat: he remembered that 'the first intimation that the army was about to retire was the getting in of the wounded; troopers were sent to the front, who placed such disabled men as could manage to sit, on their horses, they themselves rendering support on foot. At times a poor fellow might be seen toppling from side to side, requiring two men to keep him on his seat; the horses moving gently, as if conscious that their motions were torturing the suffering riders. Some again required to be carried in a blanket, so that every man with life in him was in one way or another brought in and sent to the rear. It was about mid-day ere this important duty was completed, and the troops then began to move off by brigades . . .' The men who had fought for Quatre Bras were to pull back along the main Charleroi highway, with their retreat covered by cavalry and horse artillery, and about two battalions of light troops, led by Lt.-Gen. Henry William Paget, the Earl of Uxbridge. Behind their shield, some 46,000 men would attempt to slip away by the road north, to fight another day. Invaluably, for three hours, their protection was not needed, and Wellington's men were eight miles up the road before the French attacked the crossroads they had left. It was just as well, for the retreat was a logistical nightmare. The entire centre column of artillery and two brigades of heavy cavalry, with the 7th Hussars and 23rd Light Dragoons, the smallest light dragoon regiment, in the rearguard, had to cross a small river by the narrow bridge at Genappe.

Only when the truth dawned on Napoleon that Wellington's army had escaped, did he give the order to advance. Manning a gun battery at the crossroads, Captain Mercer was in effective charge of the gunners, drivers and horses of 'G' troop of the Royal Horse Artillery. He saw the enemy silhouetted against the horizon as the sky darkened threateningly overhead. Mercer was thirty-two, and he had been brought up in a military family. His father had been a general in the

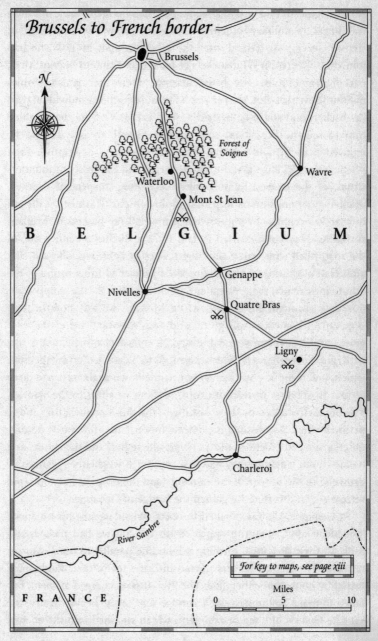

Brussels to French border

N

Brussels

Forest of
Soignes

Wavre

Waterloo

Mont St Jean

B E L G I U M

Genappe

Nivelles

Quatre Bras

Ligny

Charleroi

River Sambre

For key to maps, see page xiii

Miles

0   5   10

F R A N C E

Royal Engineers, and he had already spent half his life in the army: after training at the military academy in Woolwich, he was commissioned at sixteen, serving in Ireland after the rebellion and, in 1808, he had joined Lt.-Gen. John Whitelocke's ill-fated expedition to Buenos Aires, part of an ambitious, even absurd, attempt to seize the Spanish colonies of South America. But Mercer was a far more rounded individual than his background suggests: he had a quizzical view of life that enabled him to see the occasional eccentricities of military service and he enjoyed painting and writing, which he did in a descriptive, even poetic, vein. On this night, he wrote, 'large isolated masses of thunder-cloud, of the deepest, almost inky black hung suspended over us, involving our position in deep and gloomy obscurity; whilst the distant hill lately occupied by the French army still lay bathed in brilliant sunshine.' Heavy rain started to fall, and the ditches on either side of the road filled with water. Blinding flashes of lightning followed clap after clap of thunder. Uxbridge ordered Mercer to fire a round at the advancing French, then retreat as quickly as possible. 'We galloped for our lives through the storm,' wrote Mercer. 'Retreat now became imperative. The order was given, and away we went, helter-skelter – guns, gun-detachments, and hussars, all mixed pele-mele, going like mad, and covering each other with mud, to be washed off by the rain, which, before sufficiently heavy, now came down again as it had done at first in splashes instead of drops, soaking us anew to the skin . . . The obscurity caused by the splashing of the rain was such, that at one period I could not distinguish objects more than a few yards distant. Of course we lost sight of our pursuers altogether, and the shouts and halloos, even laughter, they had first sent forth were either silenced or drowned in the uproar of the elements and the noise of our too rapid retreat . . . In this state we gained the bridge of Genappe.'

At Genappe, Uxbridge halted to make a stand against his pursuers. 'Squadron after squadron appeared on the hill we had passed, and took up their positions, forming a long line parallel to ours,' Mercer recalled. The French lancers moved into the town, their flanks protected by houses on either side. The 7th Hussars charged at them, but failed to make any impact, so Uxbridge sent in the heavy cavalry, the 1st Life Guards, the senior regiment, which smashed into the enemy, trapping it in the narrow streets. The rocket division sent missiles flying towards the French army, causing them to desert their gun batteries in alarm as the rockets spluttered and sparked and burst overhead. But the missiles, though spectacular, were notoriously inaccurate and Mercer noted that none of them ever followed the same course 'whilst some actually turned back upon ourselves – and one of these, following me like a squib until its shell exploded, actually put me in more danger than the fire of the enemy throughout the day.' Uxbridge thought that his cavalry had deployed 'beautifully' but the ground was so heavy from the downpour that the horses were quickly exhausted and he ordered their retreat. And still it rained.

The Mont St Jean ridge, chosen by Wellington as the ground on which he would make his stand after the retreat from Quatre Bras, was a defensive line in the exact image of Torres Vedras of the Peninsula, a natural fortification, a barrier against which, he hoped, the enemy forces would throw themselves and be wrecked in the process. The difference, however, was that the Portugal campaign had been long and drawn-out, a trial of patience and delay. This next battle would be warfare at its rawest and most concentrated, conflict distilled into a single day, as if Wellington and Napoleon had conspired to boil down the military art into its ultimate, bloody essence.

'I had never yet heard of a battle in which everybody was killed,' thought Lt. John Kincaid of the 95th Rifles. 'But this seemed likely to be an exception.'

But there was still hope. An hour before midnight, on the night before the battle, the terms of the deal between the two armies which faced Napoleon were finally sealed. Blücher, at Wavre, received full details of the Anglo-Allied army's position, and heard Wellington's request for the assistance of one corps. 'Gneisenau has given in,' Blücher told the British officer waiting for a reply. 'We are going to join the Duke.' He promised to lead the troops himself against the enemy's right flank as soon as Napoleon made any move against the Duke. The two armies would cooperate after all.

But the day ahead would stretch their fragile trust to breaking-point. William Siborne would find that it had still not been repaired when he came to make his Model.

IV

To Lord Fitzroy Somerset, Military Secretary to the Duke of Wellington
From Sir James Willoughby Gordon, Quartermaster-General
PRIVATE

1 November, 1834

My dear Lord Fitzroy,

It appears to me that the clearest point of view under which both armies could be represented on a Model upon a large scale would be that of their position at the *commencement* of the action, when each successive movement could best be followed up by an attentive study of the Duke's Despatch – whereas if the action is to be represented as it stood at the close, and the information to be obtained from each commanding officer or perhaps from others even less informed, this must in great measure tend to weaken the high authority of the Duke's Despatch and to substitute in its stead divers minor accounts and those too not detailed at the time but after a lapse of 20 years.

This is the way in which the matter strikes me, and I merely throw it out for the better judgement of those who have thought more about it.

Yours faithfully,

J.W. Gordon

The military authorities who came to oppose William Siborne's Model had a simple reason for doing so. It was not that they objected in principle to his plans, but that they could not abide the practice. Partly this was because of their view of history: Siborne was gathering information about the Battle of Waterloo in greater detail than anyone before him, so that he was becoming a repository of knowledge and expertise which far outstripped that held by the military commanders. Yet history was held to be the preserve of those who led the soldiers into battle, rather than the rank and file themselves. When Captain Michael Childers, of the 11th Light Dragoons, forwarded a letter to Siborne from his commander, Lt.-Col. James Sleigh, he took the liberty of commenting that it 'only shows how hopeless it is to expect (after such a lapse of time) an account from those who were actors in what then took place, in which we should all agree.' Wellington could not have put it better. History was like an army: it had to be led, controlled and organised by those in charge.

But armies have to adapt to events, and despite the unwelcome democracy of its evidence-gathering, Siborne's project would have been supported by the military leaders who had sanctioned it, if they had not objected to his specific choice of which battle-scene to represent. He was determined to model the end of the battle, at which Prussian troops were present, and in doing so he unwittingly brought himself into conflict with the military authorities whose view of history was very different from his. That the defiance of Napoleon had lasted all day, without Prussian support, and that many glorious individual deeds were performed by British soldiers, only sharpened the desire for a model to celebrate the role of the British. In particular, the authorities wished William Siborne to model the 'commencement of the action'.

That the morning of 18 June 1815 provided a glorious spectacle, there is no doubt. On the easternmost side of the Anglo-Allied line, the officers of the 18th Hussars wore blue-grey overalls with scarlet stripes, as if they were trying to draw attention to themselves; gold or silver or crimson lace adorned the uniforms of the 11th and 12th Light Dragoons, and they had yellow and black stripes on their breeches; three cavalry regiments had dark blue facings and gold lace on their uniforms; four branches of the Royal Horse Artillery had blue and gold braided jackets and a white sash. Officers in the 23rd Light Dragoons sported turquoise jackets; for the rest, including the Foot Guards and the Corps of Royal Engineers, there was a theme of red and white.

Then there were the hats – a vast, swirling, colourful array of military headgear. The Life Guards had a black and red woollen crest and a white plume curling over their helmets, like a squirrel's tail; the Scots Greys wore bearskin caps with a red cloth patch bearing the white horse of Hanover. There were red shakos, bell-topped shakos, Belgic shakos covered with oilskin, stovepipe shakos and dark-blue shakos, bonnets and busbies. There were white pompoms and yellow pompoms, green pompoms and light-blue pompoms, white plumes, black plumes, green plumes and red plumes, red and white plumes and yellow and white plumes, and for officers in the Brunswick Lancer Squadron a vast, absurd plume of blue and yellow.

Napoleon's army was no less colourful than Wellington's. Among the elite Imperial Guard, there were bright blue uniforms for the heavy cavalry, the Grenadiers à Cheval, and green for the Guard's Dragoons, both edged with orange lace. The 1st and 2nd Carabiniers were dressed in white, with sky-blue collars and cuffs of red and white or sky-blue and white, while the helmets of their officers and troopers sprouted a vast red quiff. Then there were the red pompoms of the tirailleurs, and the green pompoms of the voltigeurs; the great black plumes of both the cuirassiers and of the dragoons; the black or red wool crests on the brass helmets and fur turbans of the Chevaux-Légers-Lanciers. Among the hussars, colours varied widely from regiment to regiment as if each was trying to outdo the others, sky-blue and red, red and yellow, green and red, sky-blue and white and yellow. This was not the age of camouflage. Men faced death in colour.

But if there was one thing the men agreed upon when they wrote their own histories, and when they gave William Siborne their eyewitness accounts, it was the depths of misery they had suffered on the night before the battle. No model could have reflected that. The three armies had spent hours sitting on their knapsacks, sleepless in the pouring rain, ankle-deep in mud. The soldiers knew the enormity of the battle ahead, and they knew too that many of them would die. But their bodies had more pressing concerns. They were cold, and damp and hungry, and their limbs ached from the many miles they had marched, and from the battles already fought. There was little shelter in the midst of such an overwhelming storm, except for a few trees and some brushwood. Captain Mercer remembered how their horses were better provided for than the men. One soldier had found a sack of corn in the road near Genappe, and he had carefully transported it all the way on an ammunition waggon, so the horses had plenty to eat. 'For ourselves we had nothing! – absolutely nothing!' said Mercer.

Both sides sent out search parties to forage for food and wood; every house in the area, and every farm, was looted. Animals spilled their blood as liberally as the men would the next day, with the soldiers using their bayonets and bullets to slaughter any cattle they came across. Hogs and hens, chickens and cows died to feed the soldiers, while shutters and doors, tables and chairs were sacrificed to warm their bodies. For miles around, hundreds of small fires twinkled in the gloom, some extinguished by the rain before they could catch hold, others burning fiercely as the furniture caught light. John Gordon Smith, an assistant surgeon, recalled bivouacking with his regiment, the 12th Light Dragoons, in open clover fields, behind the farm of Mont St Jean. For Smith and the men with him, the nearby village furnished fuel in abundance. Doors and window-shutters, furniture of every description, carts, ploughs, harrows, wheelbarrows, clock-cases, casks and tables were carried to the bivouac, and set alight in the rain. Chairs were bought by the officers for two francs each, the price of a seat for the night. Others were less comfortable. Private Edward Cotton of the 7th Hussars found some beanstalks at the farm Mont St Jean and sat on those all night. Twenty years after the battle, after he had risen to become a sergeant-major, he would come to live in the village, marrying a local woman and writing a book about his experiences, called *A Voice from Waterloo*. He died a wealthy man from many years of acting as a battlefield guide, and from collecting relics, which he displayed in his own museum.

Other soldiers tried to put up small tents, or fill trenches with straw.

But both soon filled with water. William Gibney, an assistant surgeon of the 15th Hussars, felt thoroughly miserable: 'There was no choice; we had to settle down in the mud and filth as best we could . . . we got some straw and boughs of trees, and with these tried to lessen the mud and make a rough shelter against the torrents of rain which fell all night; wrapping around us our cloaks, and huddling close together . . . it was almost ludicrous to observe the various counten-ances of us officers, smoking cigars and occasionally shivering, we stood round the watch-fire giving out more smoke than heat.' Twenty-year-old Private Matthew Clay of the 3rd Foot Guards tried to rig up a blanket for shelter: 'we fixed our muskets perpendicular at each end of the blankets and then slipping the loop of the cord around the muzzle of both muskets . . . All four of us crept under the cover, taking the remainder of our equipment with us. The storm still con-tinued with equal force and our covering became very quickly soaked . . .'

The only comfort for the Anglo-Allied army was that it was the same for the enemy. Lieutenant J.L. Henckens was a member of Napo-leon's light cavalry, the 6th Châsseurs. Neither he nor his horse could sleep, nor could they lie down on the soaked ground, so he spent the night leaning against his horse as it slept. No one could stay dry for long, and some simply gave up the attempt, choosing to walk all night, waiting for dawn and for the weather to let up. Of that, there was little sign. Rumbles of thunder continued to echo through the night, a dull angry sign of disquiet with the men below whose guns had so impu-dently sounded at the battles of Quatre Bras and Ligny. If it had been light, the British would have noticed that the rain had caused the dye in their red coats to run, staining their white belts, so that it appeared as if they were bleeding.

Throughout the night, men from each army had continued to arrive, clogging the roads with their supplies and baggage carts. The French marched along the roads and meadows to their front line in the pitch-dark, their path lit only by the occasional flashes of lightning which forked through the sky. The rain drove straight into their faces, and the water soaked into their greatcoats, weighing them down still further. They were wet and tired and hungry. They were also thirsty, despite the rain which poured down upon them. Some men could take no more, and fell over into the mud. Others crawled into hedges, or under trees, to try to escape the driving rain. They may have been fortified by the knowledge that they were advancing while their enemies were retreating, but the chase had been long and arduous, and they were in no shape for battle.

As the morning broke, the rainclouds gradually lifted, but they never quite disappeared; they hung over the battleground, protecting the world's gaze from the horrors which would enfold. The sun's rays eventually broke through the cloud cover, but only as if puncturing it, so that misty shafts of light travelled to the ground. Dawn was the signal for the armies to repair the damage of the night before. Lt.-Col. William Tomkinson, of the 16th Light Dragoons, looked at the battle-field with a dispassionate, professional eye: 'The whole field was covered with the finest wheat, the soil was strong and luxuriant; conse-quently, from the rain that had fallen, was deep, heavy for the transport and moving of artillery, and difficult for the quick operation of cavalry. The heavy ground was in favour of our cavalry from the superiority of horse, and likewise, in any charge down the face of the position, we had the advantage of moving downhill, and yet we felt the incon-venience in returning uphill with distressed horses after a charge.' Tomkinson, quiet and unassuming, but nonetheless decisive, was the fourth son of a Cheshire squire, who had joined the 'Scarlet Lancers' eight years earlier at the age of seventeen. An excellent rider, as his upbringing might suggest, he had been promoted to captain in 1811 on Wellington's recommendation, and he later wrote a diary of his experience as a cavalry officer.

Muskets were dried and cleaned, and then fired to check that they were still in working order, that the damp had not penetrated the powder. The rapid, if irregular, sound of gunfire echoed round the countryside as if battle had already commenced. The noise of drums, bugles and trumpets could be heard from both sides, raising the spirits before the final call to arms. Staff officers galloped off in different directions, checking on the position of the men who had bivouacked overnight, issuing orders for them to regroup so that each unit of each army was in the position determined by its commander. Lt. John

Kincaid had spent the night on the Namur road behind the farm of La Haye Sainte. His leader had been lucky enough to find a mud cottage for his quarters: 'We made a fire against the wall of Sir Andrew Barnard's cottage, and boiled a huge camp-kettle full of tea, mixed with a suitable quantity of milk and sugar, for breakfast; and, as it stood on the edge of the high road, where all the bigwigs of the army had occasion to pass, in the early hour of the morning, I believe almost every one of them . . . claimed a cupful.'

The French had the larger force, so long as the Prussians failed to arrive. Napoleon had nearly 72,000 men under his command, and 246 guns. The Anglo-Allied army amounted to 67,661 men, and it had only 157 guns, and only 15,000 of its infantry were British, less than half of which had been on a battlefield before. The lower ranks came mainly from the lower reaches of society, deemed by Wellington to be 'the scum of the earth', and they were attracted to the army simply because they found it was hard to earn a living as a manual worker or a tradesman. Half of the 23rd Foot, for example, were labourers, and many had been textile workers; the rest were from the trades, among them watchmakers, bookbinders and gunsmiths. In the 73rd Foot, too, most of the regiment were labourers; among the rest, men whose occupation reflected the level of the country's industrial progress: there were several bakers, butchers, brass founders, carpet weavers, cord-wainers, cotton spinners, cutlers, framework knitters, gunmakers, hosiers, tailors, locksmiths, miners, ribbon weavers and shoemakers. There were two clerks, potters, musicians, stonemasons and woolcom-bers, and there was a single blacksmith, bleacher, bricklayer, bronze maker, chairmaker, coach harness maker, cabinet maker, collier, cooper, currier, farmer's boy, farrier, gardener, gun-stocker, hatter, iron founder, leather grinder, needle maker, miller, painter, plater, ropemaker, sword-blade maker, tinsmith and watchmaker. There were soldiers as young as sixteen and veterans of more than sixty, though the average soldier was in his twenties.

Some of the troops were very raw. Ensign George Keppel, the future 6th Earl of Albemarle, had been commissioned into the 3/14th Foot when he was fifteen, and was sixteen only five days before the battle. In his memoirs, he said that his battalion 'was one which in ordinary times would not have been considered fit to be sent on foreign service at all, much less against an enemy in the field. Fourteen of the officers and 300 of the men were under twenty years of age. These last, consisting principally of Buckinghamshire lads straight from the plough, were called at home "the Bucks", but their unbuckish appearance procured for them the appellation of "the Peasants."' Few of the infantry regiments, which were notionally based on county names in order to encourage recruitment, had as much connection with their locality as their titles suggested, and many were filled out with volunteers from the militias, coerced by persuasion and bribery, with a payment on enlisting.

Ensign William Leeke, the most junior subaltern in the 1/52nd, was only seventeen, and his father, a Hampshire squire, had wanted him to enter the church. Leeke had refused to become a cleric, and thought briefly of becoming a lawyer. Fourteen years after the battle, he did indeed become a curate, at West Ham, but as a young man his imagination had been captured by an officer who had told him of the delights of serving under Wellington. Leeke persuaded his family to buy him a commission, and he was about to go to India when Napoleon escaped from Elba. Leeke realised that the Napoleonic wars were not over after all, and ditched his plans to go abroad. Instead he wrote to a cousin in the 52nd, caught up with the regiment in Belgium, and joined up just five weeks before the battle. He did not suffer on the way: he bought the best of everything in London shops before departing, including unbreakable wine glasses, a soup tureen and several pints of brandy.

Private Tom Morris was not yet twenty, a Cockney gunmaker, who had joined the Loyal Volunteers of St George's, Middlesex in 1812, when he was only sixteen, and a year later he had enlisted with his brother's regiment, the 2nd Battalion of the 73rd, after accidentally meeting a friend of his brother. That same night he wrote a note for his parents, asking for their forgiveness. 'I made up my mind to take life as it should come,' he decided, aware of the privations which would face him. A kindly sergeant suggested he should pretend to be eighteen, so that he could qualify for extra pay and a pension.

Most of the officers came from the rural gentry, or from leading military families, or from backgrounds in commerce, or the professions. The gentry, naturally, knew how to handle a gun and ride a horse, and a battle required both those abilities, as well as a chivalric disregard for danger. The bloody course of the Napoleonic wars could be traced in the careers of many of the officers. John Kincaid, the officer who thought everyone might be killed at Waterloo, was a gentleman and a Scot, who had held a lieutenant's commission in the North York Militia. In 1809, he had volunteered to join the 2nd Battalion of the famous Rifles, taking part in the Walcheren expedition where he had caught the swamp-based fever which had destroyed the campaign. Nonetheless, he said he had joined up because it was the glamorous thing to do, and in 1811 he was to be found fighting in the Peninsula, defending the lines of Torres Vedras, and taking part in all the great battles from Fuentes to Vittoria. At the age of twenty-eight, he was already a battle-hardened veteran.

Few of the officers were from the aristocracy, but most had risen through the recommendation of a person of importance either in society or in the army, or through buying their promotion, and both methods of progression required a degree of social standing. One ensign, Rees Gronow, was an old Etonian, whose family came from the landed gentry of Glamorganshire, and it was natural that he should see the army as a career, either in itself, or as a springboard for success in life. He was a dandy who had persuaded Sir Thomas Picton to let him go to battle, even though his own battalion had been left at home. So that he might fight in style, he borrowed two hundred pounds, tripled his money through gambling, and with the profits bought a new uniform and two horses. Appearances could be deceptive: Gronow, with his neat moustache and perfectly coiffed hair, may have been fastidious about his appearance, but he was held to be the best pistol shot in the army. Later, he published his account of the battle in a book called *Reminiscences of Captain Gronow* and became MP for Stafford.

Among the Allied troops were 3300 King's German Legion infantry, nearly 15,000 cavalry and infantry of Hanover; 6000 Brunswickers; 2880 independent Nassauers; and more than 17,000 infantry, cavalry and artillerymen from the United Netherlands. This army, commanded by the Prince of Orange, was a volatile mixture of Dutch, Belgian and Nassau soldiers, their mutual uneasiness stemming from their forced marriage. The Dutch were Protestant, the Belgians Catholic, and the latter had been hoping for independence from the geopolitical settlement which had decided Holland's future a year before Waterloo. France had taken control of the country until Napoleon's defeat at the Battle of Leipzig in 1813, and the subsequent Treaty of London had created the new Kingdom of the Netherlands, to the Belgians' disgust. Extraordinarily, two out of the three Netherlands divisional commanders had fought for France, and their men even wore blue uniforms which looked similar to those of the French. Many of them were inexperienced, and some of them would have preferred to fight for France. It did not provide a basis of trust within the Anglo-Allied army, before, during or after the battle.

Wellington had more faith in the crack troops of the King's German Legion. Although it had been formed by refugees from Hanover, which Napoleon had overrun in 1803, it was less foreign than its name suggested. Indeed, it had been based at Bexhill-on-Sea for the last eleven years, and its increasingly distinguished service record had reached an apogee in the Peninsular War. It was more or less integrated within the British army, adopting its military structures and tactics on the battlefield and wearing the same uniform. But the Duke had less confidence in the men from Nassau and Hanover, and little or none in the Dutch and Belgian battalions which, generally, he placed well away from the front-line. 'We were, take us all in all, a very bad army,' thought a jaundiced John Kincaid of the 95th Rifles as he eyed the men. With few exceptions, he rated the foreign auxiliaries as little better than a raw militia. They were, he thought, 'a body without a soul, or like an inflated pillow, that gives to the touch and resumes its shape again when the pressure ceases – not to mention the many who went clear out of the field, and were only seen while plundering our baggage in their retreat...' Kincaid looked back enviously at past campaigns. 'If Lord Wellington had been at the head of his old Peninsula army, I am confident that he would have swept his opponents off the face of the earth immediately after their first attack.'

In contrast, the French army was battle-hardened and united.

Corporal John Dickson, of the 2nd (Royal North British) Dragoons, the Scots Greys, could see the enemy drawn up just a mile away. 'The grandest sight was a regiment of cuirassiers dashing at full gallop over the brow of the hill opposite me, with the sun shining on their steel breastplates.' Dickson had risen through the ranks from a humble Paisley background and, at the age of twenty-six, had eight years service under his belt. 'It was a splendid show. Every now and then the sun lit up the whole country. No one who saw it could ever forget it.' Then there was a sudden roll of drums along the whole of the enemy's line. 'A burst of music from the bands of a hundred battalions came to me on the wind. I seemed to recognize the Marseillaise, but the sounds got mixed and lost in the sudden uproar that arose. Then every regiment began to move. They were taking up position for battle.' Dickson noted the great columns of infantry, and squadron after squadron of cuirassiers, red dragoons, brown hussars and green lancers, with little swallow-tail flags at the end of their lances.

At nine in the morning the rain finally ceased, though the ground was still boggy underfoot. In the hours ahead, the mud would save lives, becoming the captor of roundshot, a soft cushion for bursting shell. 'We stood in the right square, not on rye, or wheat trampled down, but, I think, on clover or seeds which had been recently mown,' William Leeke remembered. 'I furnished information to Captain Siborne with regard to this crop . . . when he was forming his beautiful model of the Field of Waterloo, and was very anxious to procure accurate information on the subject. It was generally supposed that there would have been a much greater loss in killed and wounded at Waterloo, if the heavy rain on the nights of the 16th and 17th had not well saturated the ground.' But the soldiers were not initially disposed to see the wet ground as their ally. It was another inconvenience, one of many, as they waited for their commanders to order them into battle. Napoleon inspected his lines, and the Emperor's headquarters, under Marshal Soult, dispatched orders to the divisional commanders to be ready for battle. Otherwise, both sides held still as if waiting for the other to show its hand. For Wellington's part, this was because he approached the battle like a game of chess, and he wanted to see what pieces Napoleon would move first before committing himself.

Napoleon himself wanted the earth to dry out so that his troops could cover the ground which separated his forces from the Anglo-Allied army more freely and more quickly.

A quiet descended: the lull after the night's storm. As the two sides prepared for action, they were observed by Edmund Wheatley, who, at twenty-one, was an ensign in the 5th Line Battalion of the King's German Legion. Little is known of Wheatley's career, though he lived in Hammersmith, and his diary suggests he was brave, if a little moody. He was certainly headstrong: he had already fought a duel with a rival from his schooldays, and he had joined the King's German Legion at its depot in Bexhill in 1812, although the corps was considered vaguely unsuitable for an English gentleman. For much of the time Wheatley's thoughts were with his girlfriend, Eliza Brookes, although her family had clearly forbidden her to see him: his diary begins with a secret assignation at Hyde Park Turnpike. Now the battle was upon him, and it was unclear if he would ever see her again. 'About ten o'clock, the order came to clean out the muskets and fresh load them. Half an allowance of rum was then issued, and we descended into the plain, and took our position in solid Squares. When this was arranged as per order, we were ordered to remain in our position but, if we like, to lay down, which the battalion did.'

There was a feeling of excitement, almost of being on parade. As Wheatley looked around, 'shoals of cavalry and artillery' arrived behind him 'as if by a magic wand. The whole of the horse guards stood behind us. For my part I thought they were at Knightsbridge barracks or prancing on St James's Street.'

Wellington blended his troops carefully into the demands of the land. More than thirteen thousand men in the second line of the Anglo-Allied army, which was made up entirely of British and German cavalry, were concealed behind the reverse slope of the ridge, and in the hollows of the ground. Rather than following conventional military practice by protecting his flanks, he placed most of his cavalry behind the infantry on the centre and right of the ridge, where he thought that the battle would be concentrated.

The artillery was spread out along the front line, generally half a dozen guns at a time, in a wholly defensive role. The heaviest place-ments were on the army's right, behind the two main roads – here, there was a gun or howitzer every twenty metres. To bolster the central defences of Wellington's army, the horse artillery batteries were taken from the cavalry and made static, by placing them among the foot artillery. Their orders were to conserve ammunition, rather than try to destroy enemy guns. Early on, Captain Mercer disobeyed orders, irritated by the French batteries on the Nivelles road. His fire was returned with interest from guns 'whose presence I had not even suspected, and whose superiority we immediately recognised by their rushing noise and long reach, for they flew far beyond us. I instantly saw my folly, and ceased firing ... But this was not all. The first man of my troop touched was by one of these confounded long shot. I shall never forget the scream the poor lad gave when struck. It was one of the last they fired, and shattered his left arm to pieces as he stood between the waggons. The scream went to my very soul ...'

The Duke himself took up a position next to the elm tree which grew in the corner formed by the intersection of the main road and a lane. It was a good, though far from perfect, vantage-point from which to watch the battle unfold – he had a clear view to his left, down the valley, and to his right the farm of La Haye Sainte. His battle orders were perfunctory, his tactics straightforward. There were no stirring speeches, no summoning up of the Shakespearean spirit of Agincourt. The Earl of Uxbridge reported that, going into battle, Wellington gave him full command of all the cavalry, including that of the Prince of Orange, who had relinquished his control: 'I felt that he had given me *carte blanche*, and I never bothered him with a single question respecting the movements it might be necessary to make.'

The main work had been done in choosing the position; all that remained was for the men to use the protection of the terrain to blunt the French advance. Left implicit in Wellington's choice of position was the fact that the main Anglo-Allied position, while defensively sound, was also one from which a quick retreat could be sought, along the two great thoroughfares, while the right wing of the army could withdraw through the network of villages and smaller roads which linked them. The Forest of Soignes, too, gave deep, dark shelter to an

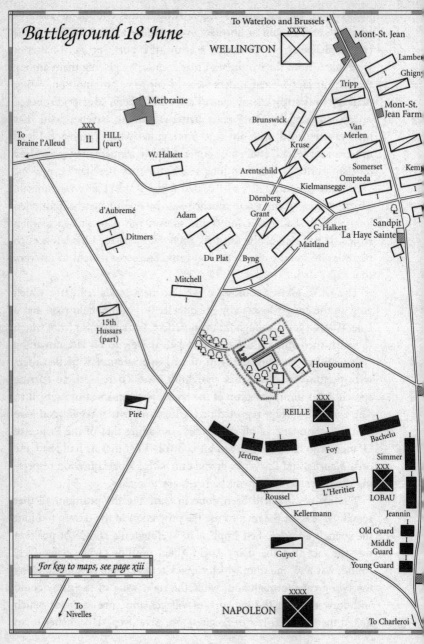

Battleground 18 June

To Waterloo and Brussels

WELLINGTON

Mont-St. Jean

Lambe

Ghign

Tripp

Mont-St.
Jean Farm

Merbraine

Brunswick

Van
Merlen

To
Braine l'Alleud

II   HILL
(part)

Kruse

Somerset

Kem

W. Halkett

Arentschild

Ompteda

Kielmansegge

Dörnberg

Grant

d'Aubremé

Adam

C. Halkett

Sandpit

La Haye Sainte

Ditmers

Du Plat

Maitland

Byng

Mitchell

15th
Hussars
(part)

Hougoumont

Piré

REILLE

Bachelu

Jérôme

Foy

Simmer

L'Heritier

LOBAU

Roussel

Kellermann

Jeannin

Old Guard

Middle
Guard

Guyot

Young Guard

For key to maps, see page xiii

To
Nivelles

NAPOLEON

To Charleroi

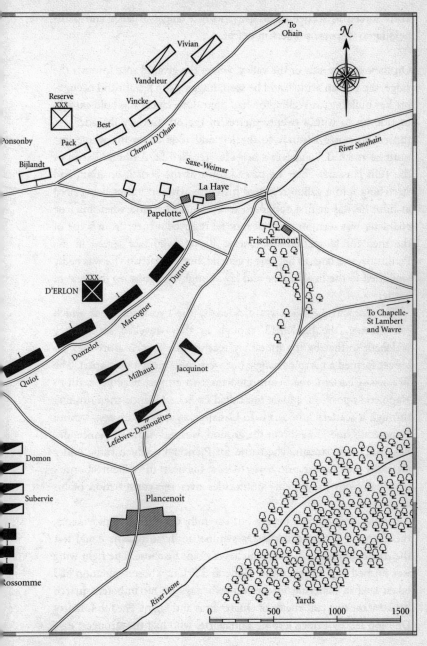

army forced to scatter in disarray, with a tangle of lanes and paths helping to disperse soldiers in defeat.

On the opposite side of the valley, where the ground rose towards the ridge, the French army could be seen, hugging the terrain and occupying key buildings as Wellington had done. One lancer was bold enough to ride up to within twenty metres of the 6th Cavalry Brigade. 'He turned his horse leisurely to the left and rode down the whole line until he reached Vandeleur's brigade,' recalled Lt. Anthony Bacon of the 10th Hussars. Then 'he turned towards the French position, and stretching into a gallop regained his corps without a shot being fired at him; he was at first supposed to be a deserter, and when his true character was seen, in place of shot he received a cheer from some of the men for his extreme boldness.' Bacon, who had served in the Peninsula, was later to become a general, but at Waterloo he was badly wounded in the final charge and lay all night in agony on the field of battle.

The French line, too, was divided by the two great roads which ran through the battlefield, though as they travelled south, they widened, so that by the time they reached the French army they no longer formed a narrow triangle but were more than a mile apart. The Brussels–Charleroi road connected the two armies, heading south to Napoleon's position, and an inn called La Belle Alliance, then running through a scattering of farms to Genappe. A mile to its east, behind Napoleon's lines, in a dip in the ground, was the village of Plancenoit, near the Lasne stream. The battle for Plancenoit, which came under attack by the Prussian army, was to lie at the heart of William Siborne's problems with the military authorities over the construction of his Model.

Unlike Wellington's untidy but carefully considered deployments, the Emperor arranged his forces symmetrically so that he could test the Anglo-Allied position at whichever point he chose. The right wing was formed by 1 Corps, under General d'Erlon, whose reputation had taken such a battering in the last two days by his impotent march between the two battlefields of Quatre Bras and Ligny. The 6th Infantry Division led by Prince Jerome Bonaparte, who had the strongest division in the army with nearly 8000 men, was placed along the ridge which formed the western boundary of Hougoumont. Jerome was Napoleon's youngest brother, though he had little or none of his military skill. At Quatre Bras he had lost a thousand of his men, and his recklessness on the battlefield was matched by the wastefulness of his lifestyle in his own kingdom of Westphalia.

Napoleon placed the centre of his second line to the west of the Charleroi road, but his third line was key. Although this was his reserve, it consisted of his crack troops, the Imperial Guard, cavalry and infantry, under General Drouot. The Imperial Guard was Napoleon's creature, an elite force which had never before been beaten in battle, whose bond of loyalty to the Emperor was unbreakable. They were the Emperor's men. He had created them, and then courted them, securing their affections by using them as his personal guard and by rewarding them handsomely. They had privileges which caused resentment in the wider army: they had better uniforms, higher rates of pay, better food, the best barracks, and even their own dedicated hospital in Paris. Its services were not needed as much as they might have been for an ordinary unit: because of their special place in Napoleon's affections, he would only commit the Guard on the battlefield as a last resort.

The Guard constituted a small army in itself, and was divided into regiments known as the Old Guard, the Middle Guard and the Young Guard. There were more than 12,000 of them at Waterloo – infantry, heavy cavalry, light cavalry, foot artillery, horse artillery and engineers, who were posted in front of the farm of Rossomme, with their centre divided by the Charleroi road. Two batteries of guns were placed with the infantry, with a reserve of twenty-four guns in the rear. The right wing of the third line consisted of light cavalry, the chasseurs and lancers of the Guard, the left wing their heavy cavalry. The Old Guard, more than 4800 strong, was placed at the rear of the reserve; in effect they were the reserve of the reserve, the Emperor's insurance policy. If they should be destroyed, his ambitions would be lost. But it had never happened, and no one in the French army ever thought it would.

Before the battle started, the Earl of Uxbridge, second-in-command of the Anglo-Allied army, asked his leader if he might be told the details of the battle-plan. Wellington dismissed the question abruptly: 'Well, Bonaparte has not given me any idea of his projects: and as my plans will depend upon his, how can you expect me to tell you what mine are?' His tactics would be entirely reactive. The Duke would try to hold on to his strategic position, until the Prussians came from Wavre to shore up his left wing. Napoleon, on the other hand, had no intention of playing for time. He would try to force his way through the Mont St Jean crossroads and then strike rapidly for Brussels. The Prussians, he considered, could not possibly recover from their defeat at Ligny to be of any use to the Anglo-Allied army. The military genius would take on the master of defence.

The forthcoming battle would be the first between the two greatest commanders of their day and no one dared to predict the outcome. 'The approaching contest was contemplated with anxious solicitude by the whole military world,' wrote William Siborne. 'Need this create surprise when we reflect that the struggle was one for mastery between the far-famed conqueror of Italy, and the victorious liberator of the Peninsula; between the triumphant vanquisher of Eastern Europe, and the bold and successful invader of the South of France! Never was the issue of a single battle looked forward to as involving consequences of such vast importance – of such universal influence.'

If Siborne had left it there, by acceding to the military's demand to depict the start, rather than the end, of the battle on his Model, he would have been able to show only two armies on the field of Waterloo. In this way, the clash would have been seen simply as a great and glorious contest between Wellington's essentially British army and Napoleon's France. But, in the interests of accuracy, Siborne wanted to show Prussian soldiers arriving in their thousands at the close of the battle, to illustrate their contribution to a joint victory. For at Wavre, a third commander was still determined to join the action. Field-Marshal Prince Gebhard Leberecht von Blücher, as he had promised, ordered IV Corps under General Bulow to lead an attack on the French flank, with II Corps in support, though his men had ten gruelling miles to march before they reached the enemy. The fate of Europe hinged upon their journey.

Afterwards, no one could agree on what time the fighting started, although Edmund Wheatley was convinced he knew. 'A ball whizzed in the air. Up we started simultaneously. I looked at my watch. It was just eleven o'clock, Sunday morning. In five minutes a stunning noise took place and a shocking havoc took place.' Nor could anyone agree on exactly how long the fighting lasted. To some it felt like minutes, to others an eternity. So intense was the battle, many agreed, it was as if time itself stood still.

V

To Lord Fitzroy Somerset, Military Secretary to the Duke of Wellington
From Sir James Willoughby Gordon, Quartermaster-General
at the Horse Guards

PRIVATE

1 November, 1834

My dear Lord Fitzroy,

If Mr Siborne persists in his intention of representing upon his Model 'the Crisis of the Battle' I do not see any prospect of his being enabled to obtain any information that can be depended upon.

The Commanding Officer of each regiment could certainly say where his regiment was posted at any period of the day, but to require such information for the purpose of the plan or Model would in my opinion lead to anything but an accurate exposition of the Battle.

Two, three, or more Regiments might be, and probably were, posted exactly on the same spot, within a few minutes each after the other, & this could not be clearly represented either on a plan or Model, but on the contrary would lead to a scene of indistinctness and confusion in the mind of any spectator, whether civil or military.

Yours faithfully,

J.W. Gordon

William Siborne could have chosen many glorious scenes of British derring-do for his Model, rather than showing the battle's end. Indeed, when he finally completed the magnificent tableau that would provoke such controversy, he started to make a series of further models, showing key moments from the action. Of these, for most observers, it was the battle for Hougoumont that encapsulated the strength of the Duke of Wellington's leadership and the valour of his army against overwhelming odds throughout the nine hours of fighting.

William Siborne paid close attention to Hougoumont, taking care to draw a detailed plan of the building during his survey of the battlefield. In 1830, he found it in very nearly the same ruined state to which the fighting had reduced it. 'The château itself,' he wrote, 'and the buildings surrounding the old farmyard, present to the eye nothing more than crumbling walls, scattered stones, bricks and rubbish ... The identical loopholes with the innumerable marks of shot indented around them, are still permitted to remain as they were left by the brave defenders of the place.' Inevitably, however, the many tales that were told of its valiant defence overshadowed the story of the Prussian army's battle to join up with Wellington, away from the main theatre of war. It was one of several scenes that lived on in the nation's imagination, sharpening the difficulties Siborne would face in choosing to model the end of the battle with the Prussian army present.

Hougoumont was the sum of many different parts, variously a château, chapel, farm and home, but the two sides could see a fortified position in a collection of buildings which looked as if they had been gathered together by accident. Hougoumont was strategically important, not so much for itself but because it overlooked a thin strip of valley which ran across the high road from Nivelles from a point close to La Belle Alliance. Unless the Anglo-Allied forces held Hougoumont, or at least controlled the land around it, the French could move around their flank by using the valley floor as a line of advance, and yet still be protected against artillery fire from the ridge above. Although it was not essential to capture Hougoumont, unless he did so Napoleon could only attack the Anglo-Allied army by moving through a narrow thousand-metre gap between its eastern orchard and the farm of La

Hougoumont – The Great Model

Haye Sainte. His initial aim was to draw in Wellington's reserves, before he launched the main assault against the Anglo-Allied army. Wellington, on the other hand, declared that the buildings must be defended to the last extremity. That nearly a quarter of the French infantry, in the course of the next few hours, was thrown into the fight for Hougoumont was a sign that the French priorities had shifted out of all proportion to their leader's stated purpose.

Hougoumont was said to have taken its name from the resin or *gomme* which was extracted from the lofty pine trees which grew on the high ground, or Gomme Mont, nearby. The modest château was unoccupied and unfurnished, as if waiting to be filled by the troops who had taken up station there, and the farm had been let out by its elderly owner. But the buildings had been built so close together that they formed an impressive wall against the world, a defensive barrier which was weakened only by the huge doors cut into its brickwork which gave access to its inner reaches.

The buildings were grouped around two courtyards, divided by an archway. In the southern half there was a private chapel, built of red brick, which was so small that it was barely the length of three men.

The chapel, which contained a fifteenth-century wooden figure of Christ on the cross, came to invest the forthcoming fight, retrospectively, with religious fervour, as if Napoleon was the infidel seeking to seize a hallowed corner of Christendom. To the chapel's side, like a much larger elder brother, stood the cream-coloured château itself, its pitched roof proud above the accompanying buildings, with a solitary corner tower, topped by a weathervane, rising higher still. But Hougoumont was also a working farm. There was a well in the north courtyard, and next to its west gate there was a barn, known as the Great Barn, running two thirds of the length of the side. Beyond it lay a small kitchen garden. There was the usual scattering of small buildings which would be found on any farm, a cowhouse and stabling to the side of the north gate, with the stables continuing at right-angles down the east side of the farm where they met the farmer's house. A gardener's house, offices and store sheds lay on either side of the arched south gate. Beyond the east gate, near the farmer's house, there was a formal garden, which was meticulously laid out with shrubs and flowers and divided precisely into a square and a rectangle, each of which was cut by angular paths into symmetrical parterres, a horticultural exactness which sat oddly with the chaos of war soon to envelop Hougoumont, sweeping away four centuries of patient effort to place order upon its world.

The formal garden was bordered on its south side by a brick wall more than a man's height, which was strong enough to resist musket-fire, though not artillery fire. Beyond it lay a strip of open land, and a small wood which was defended by a few hundred Hanoverians and Nassauers. The brick wall dog-legged north to run up the eastern side of Hougoumont, and outside it there was an apple orchard, called the Great Orchard, which was defended by more men from the Nassau Regiment. Further north, there was a narrow strip of orchard, which was divided from the garden by a hedge. This Small Orchard, as it was known, ran west to a pond, and led to the so-called Hollow Way, a sunken road on marshy ground which was lined on each side with hedges, and which ran along the northern perimeter of the orchard. From there, it was only a short distance to the Anglo-Allied position on the ridge, across rolling, open fields. Overall, the farm was 'well-calculated' for defence according to Colonel Alexander Woodford, a

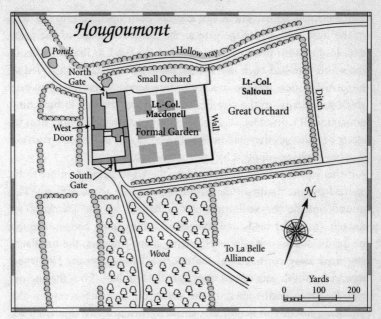

Peninsula veteran with sixteen years' service in the 2nd (Coldstream) Foot Guards, which came to play a key role in trying to prevent the château falling. But if Hougoumont was a fortification which could be defended against an all-out assault, its layout was too random and dispersed for it to be held without casualties.

To begin with, there were barely a thousand men inside the château and its grounds but they were determined to defy the odds and repel the enemy, despite the overwhelming numbers ranged against them, resisting a siege as if in medieval times, their only ally the strength of the structure they were occupying. Throughout the night the men had created firing platforms and had cut loopholes in the walls, to enable them to fire their guns from behind the protection of the brickwork into the wood which lay beyond. The gates of Hougoumont were the weakest part of its defences, though they were strongly built. Colonel Woodford noted that, while the barns and granaries formed a near-square, a door led to the small yard to the south; from that yard there was a door into the garden and a double-gate into the wood, under or near the small house. There was another door opening into the lane on the west, and a carriage gate at the northwest angle of the great yard, leading into the barn, which led to the road to Braine l'Alleud. The south gate had been barricaded, while the east gate, which led to the formal garden, was too small to be threatened. It was the north gate which gave access to the Nivelles road that was the key to breaching Hougoumont's defences. Its two wooden panels could be held firm by a long bar, though they had been left open so that the defenders could be more easily re-supplied by their fellow-soldiers.

If this was a strategic mistake, then there was some comfort to be gained from the nature of the terrain which made access difficult. The ground outside the walls presented a hazard for the attackers, an obstacle course of fields and ditches and thick, high hedges, though the height of the corn concealed enemy sharp-shooters, the tirailleurs who fired away constantly at the doors to Hougoumont. The wood beyond the south gate served to protect the buildings from the enemy, with the trees both screening the defenders from observers in the advancing forces and acting as a shield against artillery fire. Even so, the fight would be a close one, lasting the length of the entire battle, and much would depend on the determination and bravery of the defenders.

Two light companies from the 1st Guards, under their thirty-year-old commander, Lt.-Col. Alexander George Fraser, were originally stationed in the Great Orchard, though they were withdrawn when the Nassauers arrived. Fraser was the 16th Baron Saltoun and his father had bought him a commission in the 1st Foot Guards at great expense in 1804, when he was nineteen. It turned out to be money well spent, for a decade later at Waterloo, the son's bravery would become a legend: he had four horses shot from under him, and two thirds of his men became casualties. After Waterloo, Wellington was said to have called him 'a pattern to the army both as a man and a soldier.'

The bravery of another man, lower down the social scale, would also be remembered: that of Lt.-Col. James Macdonell. Macdonell came from Glengarry, joining the 19th Foot in 1796, then the Coldstream Guards as a captain in 1811, serving in the Peninsular War. He was a huge man, a massive, reassuring presence for the light companies of the Scots Guards and Coldstream Guards which were under his command. They were positioned in the kitchen garden, to the west of the château, towards the narrow valley which the château overlooked. A light company from the 23rd (Royal Welch Fuzileers) manned part of the avenue leading out of Hougoumont's northwestern corner, which connected with the Nivelles road. To reinforce this key route, an artificial barrier, known as an abatis, made from felled trees and sharpened branches, was placed across the road, and a company of the 51st Regiment was stationed by it. At around eleven o'clock, when Wellington visited them, he fell into conversation with the Prussian liaison officer, Maj.-Gen. Baron von Muffling. Muffling insisted that Hougoumont could not properly be defended, that it was inevitable that the place would fall as it was closer to the French lines than the Anglo-Allied position. 'Ah, but you do not know Macdonell,' replied Wellington, pointing to the imposing presence of the Scottish colonel.

If he was wise to invest his hopes in the giant Scotsman's abilities, then Wellington was also expecting reinforcements from the Prussian army before the day was old. Hougoumont, in a sense, then, reflected his wider ambitions. It was a symbol of his wish to turn the day into a long, slow encounter, in which his forces took no risks, allowing the French to become spent in their attempts to overcome not just the Anglo-Allied army but the defensive advantage its position had afforded it. Wellington's strategy was to soak up the enemy attacks, and to look towards the east, from where the Prussians would emerge to join him. But the wait would be far longer, and even more of an ordeal, than Wellington had calculated.

The first shots which rang out across the valley were fired by the French, when Napoleon finally signalled his intent after the delay caused by the appalling weather. He had waited to launch the battle to let the muddy ground dry out, but it had failed to do so completely when, before midday, he began his long-awaited attack. Under the cover of fire from two horse artillery batteries, Prince Jerome Bonaparte, who was leading the left-hand division of Reille's II Corps, launched the first assault against Hougoumont's wood and Great Orchard.

With every gun that was fired, the gunsmoke thickened and swirled

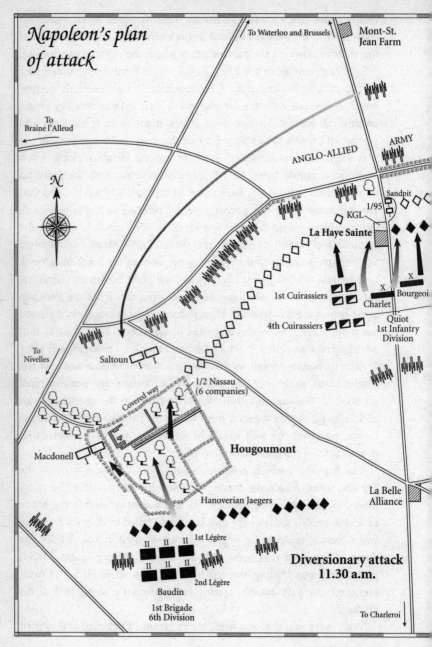

Napoleon's plan of attack

To Waterloo and Brussels

Mont-St. Jean Farm

To Braine l'Alleud

ANGLO-ALLIED

ARMY

N

Sandpit

1/95

KGL

La Haye Sainte

1st Cuirassiers

X Charlet

X Bourgeoi

Quiot

1st Infantry Division

4th Cuirassiers

To Nivelles

Saltoun

1/2 Nassau (6 companies)

Covered way

Hougoumont

Macdonell

La Belle Alliance

Hanoverian Jaegers

1st Légère

Diversionary attack 11.30 a.m.

II II II

II II II

2nd Légère

Baudin

1st Brigade 6th Division

To Charleroi

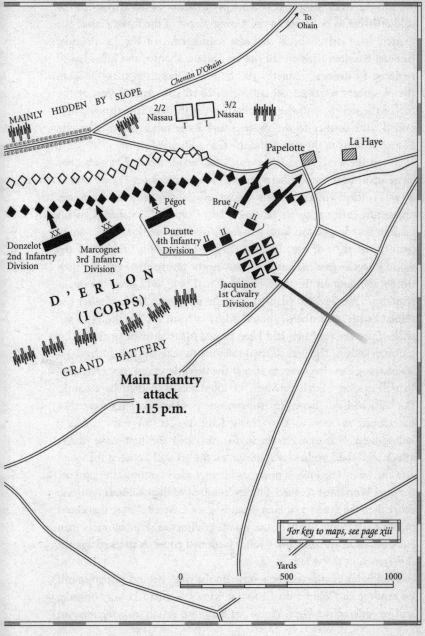

around the trees, so that it became even harder to discern where the soldiers were to be found in the hiding-places of the forest. Twice the French were driven back, and the commander of the 1st Brigade, General Bauduin, was picked out by a sharp-shooter and killed, to be replaced by Colonel Cubières. As the French began to make ground, the Nassauers retreated behind a row of closely-planted trees at the top of the woods, but when the French cut through it with axes, they pulled back further to the château and its grounds. By midday the French had taken the wood and the Great Orchard.

But as the attackers emerged from the wood, scenting victory, they came up against the southern wall of Hougoumont only thirty metres away. 'I heard voices and the drummers beating the *pas de charge*, apparently belonging to Jerome's left Column,' recalled Captain George Standen of the Scots Fusiliers, who was stationed in a small field to the right of the château. There was constant firing from the wood into the garden, but there was heavy return fire from the men inside, standing on the platforms they had built, and from the upper windows. The French were trapped in no man's land. Musket-fire rained down upon their exposed position from the loopholes in the walls. Even the roof tiles had been ripped off to provide openings for gunmen within. The French tried valiantly to scale the two-metre-high walls, using their bayonets to stab at the defenders, and they even tried to pull musket barrels through the loopholes with their bare hands. But they had no answer to Hougoumont's defences. They were shot or stabbed as soon as they reached the top of the wall. It was a killing-field. Not one French soldier survived the first wave of the attack, and their bodies lay in heaps on the ground between the wood and the wall. 'The French never, as far I recollect, got into the garden,' Colonel Woodford recalled. Fifteen hundred of their soldiers lay dead, more than the number of men defending the château. Those that could pulled back to the safety of the wood. Wellington sent Saltoun's men back to retake the orchard, while Macdonell counter-attacked against the French in the wood.

Wellington reinforced the reserve on the ridge behind Hougoumont by sending in Colonel du Plat's 1st King's German Legion Brigade, and he ordered the Royal Horse Artillery into action, moving forward a battery of short-barrelled howitzers. Lt.-Col. Augustus Frazer was commanding the Royal Horse Artillery: 'By this time the enemy had forced a battalion out of the orchard to the left of the wood, and there was a hot fire on a battalion of the Guards, stationed in the buildings, and behind the walled garden. The Howitzer troop came up, handsomely; their very appearance encouraged the remainder of the division of the Guards, then lying down to be sheltered from the fire. The Duke said, "Colonel Frazer, you are going to do a delicate thing; can you depend upon the force of your howitzers? Part of the wood is held by our troops, part by the enemy." The battery, which came under the command of Captain Bull, started firing from a position just behind Hougoumont, over the heads of the soldiers within its walls. 'We moved to the heights on the right of our first line,' said Bull, 'and immediately came into action with spherical case-shot with the intention of dislodging the enemy's infantry from the left of the small wood . . .' Jerome's battalions continued to take heavy casualties.

Under Colonel Cubières, the French again pressed forward, along the western wall and towards the north gate. Private Matthew Clay of the 3rd Foot Guards, the young man who had spent such a damp night under his blanket, found himself left behind by the rest of his company as it retreated towards the great gate. Clay, who had enlisted from the Nottinghamshire militia, climbed the higher part of the sloping ground on which the outside wall of the farm was built. 'I thought that I would be able to single out the enemy's skirmishers more correctly, but I very quickly found that I had become a target for them because my red coat was more distinctly visible than theirs. Remaining in this position I continued to exchange shots with the enemy across the kitchen garden, but they, having the advantage of the fence as a covering, their shots freely struck the wall in my rear . . . We were now left to ourselves and could see no one near us. The enemy remained under cover and continued firing at us, and we fired back and retired down the road we had advanced . . .'

The leading detachment of Soye's 2nd Brigade was led by a huge *sous-lieutenant* called Legros, whose nickname was L'Enfonceur. Carrying a great axe he led the way towards the north gate of the château. With the French attacking the weakest spot in the defences, the situation for the defenders of Hougoumont was now critical. The soldiers tried desperately to close the gates, and nearly succeeded, but the weight of the French troops pressing against them was too great, and the gates took repeated blows from L'Enfonceur's axe. The gates trembled, then gave, and L'Enfonceur and his men forced their way into the courtyard. Some thirty or more French soldiers had, for the first time, penetrated the outer walls of Hougoumont. For all the ranks of cavalry and infantry and the batteries of guns lined up against each other, the battle for Waterloo had turned into desperate, bitter, hand-to-hand fighting between a few dozen men. Now that they were inside the complex some of the French soldiers tried to make their way towards its most obvious landmark, the château itself. But they found themselves in the middle of a firestorm. Gunfire rained down on them not just from the château but from buildings on all sides. Private Clay: 'On turning my eyes to the gates, I saw they were open . . . and we hurried towards them. On entering the courtyard I saw the doors, or rather the gates, were riddled with shot holes, and it was also very wet and dirty. In its entrance lay many dead bodies of the enemy. One which I particularly noticed appeared to be a French officer, but they were scarcely distinguishable, being to all appearance as though they had been very much trodden upon and covered with mud.'

The fate of Hougoumont hung in the balance. More French soldiers were trying to follow their colleagues through the gate in a renewed push. Lt.-Col. Macdonell saw the danger and, realising that the gates must be closed at all costs, shouted for help from three Coldstream Guards officers, Captain Henry Wyndham, Ensign James Hervey and Ensign Henry Gooch. Another six soldiers grouped near the well in the courtyard joined them as they rushed towards the gate – Sergeants Fraser, Macgregor and Aston, and Private Lester, and two Irish brothers from the Coldstream Guards, Corporals James and Joseph. These ten men then took part in what would be seen as one of the most heroic episodes of the battle. Some of them fought with bayonets and swords to keep the enemy at bay, while the others tried to close the gates. It was just as well that men like Macdonell were built so solidly. They put their shoulders to the gate, and using all their weight pushed it back against the French soldiers who were trying to force their way in. Inch by painful inch the panels of the gate were slowly pushed back, and reinforced by whatever objects the defenders could lay their hands on, bits of timber, pieces of stone, ladders, posts and barrows, until the two parts of the gate were sufficiently close together for the large crossbar to be dropped into position across them. Hougoumont had been sealed against the outside world.

But still the French tried bravely, if in foolhardy fashion, to break through. Realising that the gates could not be forced, one of their number, a grenadier, volunteered to climb over to try to open them from the inside. It was a suicidal mission, which summed up the French desperation at a morning of fruitless effort and wasted lives. The defenders had so much time to deal with the intruder that Captain Wyndham was able to call out to Corporal James Graham to drop the wood he was carrying, pick up his gun and shoot the attacker. The bullet went through his brain. So few French had managed to make it through the north gate that, even allowing for the shortage of defenders, those who were inside were easily outnumbered, and gradually a combination of their numerical disadvantage, and the exposed position they found themselves in, began to tell. One by one, including L'Enfonceur, they were killed, apart from a young drummer-boy whose life was spared.

By three o'clock, more than 12,500 French infantry were trying to prise Hougoumont away from a reinforced garrison of just 2500 men. But Hougoumont, its orchard and garden, were still in Allied hands, and that this was so was in no small measure down to the handful of men who had won the struggle to close the north gate. But, unwittingly, they had helped to close the gate, too, on history's perception of the battle as an alliance with the Prussians. How could William Siborne think of sharing the credit for victory on his Model when Wellington's army had fought on its own at Hougoumont to such brilliant, brave effect?

VI

Memo from Colonel Sir Charles Grene Ellicombe, Ordnance Office

29 October 1834

84 Pall Mall

I fear this office cannot assist Lieut. Siborn in any of the points referred to except it be from two printed sketches and a general plan by W.B. Craan in French which appears to be very detailed shewing the position of all the Corps engaged – but as for the 'Crisis' I don't know how the information is to be got at and I fear the answer to the proposed Circular would only bring a mass of information that never could be got together with any degree of accuracy.

C.G. Ellicombe

If William Siborne had chosen to make the fight for Hougoumont the centrepiece of his Model, rather than simply including it on his vast tableau of the battle, he would have run into no difficulties with the military authorities. Courage, determination and sheer bloody-mindedness had ensured that Hougoumont had not fallen. There was nothing in the history of the fighting that could tarnish the Duke of Wellington's image. More than that: on any model of the fighting in and around the château, not a single Prussian soldier would be seen. But Siborne wanted to portray, in both his Model and his written history, a comprehensive picture of the battle, so while he was still prepared to glorify individual deeds of bravery and praise the Duke of

Wellington's leadership, he took care to understand the importance of the Prussian manoeuvres away from the main theatre of war.

That the Prussians had not yet arrived lent the battle a curious effect, as if their absence weighed more heavily on the minds of the commanders than the reality of the troops and weaponry under Blücher's command. The missing Prussians affected the tactics of both sides, forcing both to be wary of what was happening to the east, and both kept a constant lookout. Wellington waited for the Prussians' arrival, almost to the point of immobility, and gave the Prussian liaison officer, General Muffling, *de facto* command of his left flank, so that he might try to keep in touch with the forces heading towards the battlefield. For his part, Napoleon posted a cavalry lookout on his right wing, and decided against an attack on the Anglo-Allied right partly because he feared that if the battle took hold here, the Duke would still be able to fall back towards the advancing Prussian army. Speed was all. Should Napoleon seize control of the battlefield by winning a quick victory, then Blücher's support for Wellington would be rendered redundant. The battle would hinge on his ability to keep the two forces separate.

In the end, the Prussian threat forced Napoleon to weaken his battlefield army. When he looked to the east of the battlefield with a telescope from his position on a knoll by the road at Rossomme, he thought he spotted a column of troops moving towards Chapelle St-Lambert, a small village which lay east of the Lasne river, two miles from Ohain, and nearly five from Plancenoit. The view was far from clear, and even when his officers followed his lead and trained their telescopes in the same direction, they could not be sure what they were looking at. Were they merely trees? Or was it the Prussian enemy? Or was it, as Napoleon fervently hoped, Marshal Grouchy's men riding to join up with their Emperor? Napoleon sent out a party of men to find out the truth. Soon after they left, however, a prisoner of war brought Napoleon the information he was so anxious to discover. The prisoner, a Prussian, had been caught carrying a letter from General Bulow, informing Wellington that he had arrived at Chapelle St-Lambert. The troops that Napoleon could see were not French but were, instead, members of the advanced guard of Bulow's army. The prisoner also told Napoleon that there were three other corps of Prussian troops stationed close to Wavre, and that he had seen no sign of the French troops on which the Emperor had pinned his hopes. A message from the scouts seemed to confirm the prisoner's story. But Bulow's advanced guard had been mistaken for the main body of his men, so that Napoleon, as well as Wellington, believed that the Prussians would shortly be among them.

At around half-past-one, therefore, Napoleon reduced the size of his army facing Wellington by detaching 7000 infantry, more than 3000 cavalry and twenty-eight guns, the whole of Lobau's VI Corps, to stop the Prussian advance. Lobau stationed his men on a high point of ground southwest of the Bois de Paris, to block the road south to the small village of Plancenoit and the tracks which led north to the hamlets of Frischermont and Smohain. The battle was beginning to tilt against the Emperor. 'This morning we had ninety odds in our favour,' Napoleon reflected. 'We still have sixty against forty.' The Prussians had already altered the balance of the battle, despite the slow progress they were making towards it.

The Prussian IV Corps, under Bulow, had already been on the move for four hours. But although their military burden had been lightened by the failure of Marshal Grouchy's men to stop them, it by no means removed their difficulties. There were still miles of virtually impassable countryside to cross, heavy, slow, painful going with death on the battlefield the likely reward for such back-breaking endeavour. 'I have given my word to Wellington and you will surely not make me break it,' exhorted the redoubtable Blücher. 'Only exert yourselves a little longer and certain victory is ours.'

The reasons for the Prussians' delay were, at best, confusing. Of all their forces, it was odd that Bulow's men in IV Corps had been chosen to come to Wellington's aid, when they were the most easterly of the Prussian troops, although they may have been chosen because they had missed the fighting at Ligny. But they were some three to four miles away from Wavre, where the rest of the Prussian army had bivouacked. More curiously, perhaps, the men of II Corps, led by Maj.-Gen. Pirch, had been ordered to wait for Bulow, so that they might follow him. Similarly, Lt.-Gen. Ziethen's I Corps were ordered to follow a roundabout route which took them further to the north, and they were not allowed to march until Bulow and Pirch had passed by. Was it conspiracy, or simply the result of an inefficient system of command and control? Was it possible that the malcontent Gneisenau had deliberately slowed down the Prussian advance, so that he could be seen to be carrying out the orders of which he so strongly disapproved, while doing as much damage as he could to Wellington's cause? Whatever the reason, the outcome would be the same. None of it would bring rapid aid to Wellington's army, nor improve his army's relations with the Prussians.

If that was Gneisenau's aim, then his treachery gained the approval of the elements. Fire and water delayed IV Corps still further. The roads which had taken such a drenching in the storm had turned to mud, slowing the movement of men, animals and guns, clogging their wheels and forcing them deeper into the tracks carved out by their weight. The progress of Bulow's men was slow. They had to negotiate sunken lanes which cut through deep ravines; an almost impenetrable forest grew on each side, so that the troops had to keep to the road, and in many places men and horses could only pass through one at a time. The column was frequently split up, and every now and then, wherever the ground allowed it, the head of each column had to halt to give time for the detachments to catch up.

Then, as if out of nowhere, the fire had started, spreading so quickly that it rose high above Wavre, blocking the route of Bulow's men, and cutting in two the columns of his army, creating an hour's gap between the soldiers who had marched beyond the flames and those who were in the rearguard when the fire broke out. In the circumstances, the lead party of Bulow's corps did well to make Chapelle St-Lambert by noon, just as the battle for Hougoumont was underway, and where his commander, Blücher, caught up with him. From here, however, the journey posed further difficulties. To leave Chapelle St-Lambert, Bulow's men would have to go down a hill, cross a stream by a small bridge and climb up the other side, on a road which was so waterlogged that the Prussian artillery would have great trouble in forcing its way through. But, symbolically, it was an even tougher journey for Gneisenau to sanction. Once his troops had travelled through Chapelle

St-Lambert, he was beyond the point of no return, heading for the French right wing and committed against his better judgement on the orders of his commander to come to the aid of the man he so detested. So while the Battle of Waterloo began, the Prussians delayed at Chapelle St-Lambert for two hours, their soldiers the unwitting pawns in the game of chess played out in the high command by Blücher and Gneisenau. It was not until about two o'clock in the afternoon, with his 14th Brigade still an hour behind, that Bulow's IV Corps started to climb the steep hill which took the men out of Chapelle St-Lambert and towards the Bois de Paris.

If the Anglo-Allied army, and particularly the British, came to claim the spoils unfairly when victory was won, then the divisions within the Prussian army did little to help its own cause, and its late arrival was not forgotten, for all Blücher's steadfastness and the incalculable influence his men eventually exerted on the outcome. If he had been a wiser man, when he came to choose his battle-scene, William Siborne should have taken note.

While the Prussians were still far away from the action, the Anglo-Allied army was facing more than seventy guns, which were pointing at its left wing from no more than 600 metres, so the accounts of the men, understandably, reflected the forthcoming ordeal they endured, rather than any wider sense of their ally's military manoeuvres. Their battle, increasingly, was one of defiance in the face of adversity, for the forthcoming onslaught of Napoleon's artillery signalled an all-out offensive. He aimed to seize the farm of La Haye Sainte and, further north, of Mont St Jean, both of which lay alongside the Brussels to Charleroi road, and then cut Wellington's main line of communication. If he could take the road, he would prevent the Prussians from fulfilling Blücher's promise to join up with Wellington. If he failed, and if the Prussians linked up with the Anglo-Allied troops, Napoleon's forces would be hopelessly outnumbered.

The course of the battle now depended on the defensive capability of Wellington's army as Napoleon's 'Grand Battery' began to roar across the valley, the guns simultaneously spitting their fire from the spur of land below La Belle Alliance. If William Siborne had chosen to model this moment he would have been on as safe ground as the Duke's army itself, hidden behind its defensive ridge. Forty-two six-pounders, including eighteen guns from the Guard artillery, eighteen twelve-pounders, which were known as the 'beautiful daughters', and twenty howitzers were lined up to take part in the barrage. They were stationed on the open ridge which ran for more than a thousand metres from east of the Brussels highway all the way to the valley which led to Papelotte. From here the guns could fire over the battlefield into the Anglo-Allied ridge which ran parallel to theirs, but which was slightly higher. To the rear of the French artillery, in a valley, were hundreds of soldiers and more than a thousand horses pulling limbers and caissons of ammunition, two or three for every gun, and wagons carrying equipment for repairs. Behind this obstacle course, waiting for the signal, were more than sixteen thousand infantry, the advance divisions led by d'Erlon.

It was, quite simply, the heaviest bombardment the men in Wellington's army had ever experienced, even the veterans of the Peninsular War. The shelling at Hougoumont had been the equivalent of a light shower; now the skies turned heavy with thundering great iron balls which came hurtling down upon the Allied side. 'One could almost feel the undulation of the air from the multitude of cannon shot,' remembered Edmund Wheatley, the ensign from Hammersmith who had left behind his girlfriend. 'The first man who fell was five files on my left. With the utmost distortion of feature he lay on his side and shrivelling up every muscle of body he twirled his elbow round and round in acute agony, then dropped lifeless.'

Firing the guns was hard, labour-intensive work for a team of artillerymen, whose practised, coordinated actions made sure that cannonball after cannonball could be fired as quickly as possible. The drill was virtually the same for both sides in the battle. As soon as the gun had been fired, a 'spongeman' swabbed out the barrel. Once it was clean, a loader on the other side of the gun placed a new projectile in the muzzle, ready for the spongeman to force it home with a rammer. Behind the loader was the gunner. The gunner pierced a cartridge bag by pushing a pin down into the gun's vent, then placed a priming tube inside it, and gave the order to fire. To the side, the 'ventsman' turned the elevating screw to correct the gun's range, following the orders of a corporal. Opposite the gunner, the firer lit the priming tube and the gun boomed out. For all the hard work, however, it could take a full minute to fire the next shot from a twelve-pounder, not least because the gun might jump, and would have to be manhandled back into position. It was dangerous work: Gunner Butterworth was one of the first casualties in Captain Mercer's troop. 'He had just finished ramming down the shot,' Mercer explained, 'and was stepping back outside the wheel, when his foot stuck in the miry soil, pulling him forward the moment the gun was fired. As a man naturally does when falling, he threw out both his arms before him, and they were blown off at the elbows. He raised himself a little on his two stumps, and looked up most piteously in my face. To assist him was impossible . . .' Gunner Butterworth managed to find his way back through the lines but bled to death, near the farm of Mont St Jean.

As if out of nowhere, a vast column of men fanned out along the valley accompanied by the thud of drums, sixteen Eagles raised high towards the sky. Marshal Ney, the commander of the left wing of the Armée du Nord, rode at the front with the commander of I Corps, General d'Erlon, at his side. Ney was a tall, redheaded man with a foul temper and a coarse tongue, and his wing of the army consisted of I Corps, II Corps under Reille and the Imperial Guard light cavalry, a total of 47,000 men and a hundred guns. They thought him to be an erratic leader, despite the brilliant rearguard action he had led in the winter retreat from Russia. The empty valley and the deserted main road were filled with vast columns of his infantry, thousands upon thousands of men, all of them shouldering arms and marching in step to a steady drumbeat to create an impression of invincibility, of inexorable might and confidence, a ritualistic advance to a relentless rhythm designed to shred the nerves of any opponent not self-possessed enough to look beyond the spectacle. 'With drums beating, colours flying, and eagles soaring above their huge headdresses, the enemy advanced in solid column to attack,' recalled Lt. James Hope of the 92nd in his memoirs. It was war as theatre, but Hope had seen it all before: he was a veteran, like Kincaid, of the Walcheren expedition, and had been severely wounded in the Peninsula campaign, in which he had won the General Service Medal and three bars.

Theatre soon became reality, for the French soldiers were gradually becoming caked in mud which pulled at their ankles, tugging at their feet and clinging to their gaiters, causing them to slip and slide and even lose their boots. Then Wellington's army opened fire. 'Their progress was considerably retarded by the fire of our artillery, and volleys of musketry from the Belgian infantry,' Hope noted. But the foreign infantry in Wellington's army was to prove less than courageous: 'The enemy having almost gained the summit of the ridge, our allies partially retired from the hedge.' The 1st Netherlands Brigade led by Maj.-Gen. Bijlandt had scattered suddenly, abandoning its position to break away through Picton's division, a concerted movement which gave rise to the suspicion that their officers had issued formal orders to run. 'The enemy continued to advance in columns under cover of a tremendous cannonade, which was answered by our artillery with great spirit,' Ensign Thomas Mountsteven of the 28th Regiment told Siborne. 'A body of Belgian infantry which had been posted some distance in front fled on the enemy's approach and were honoured with hisses and cries of shame in passing our troops.' The brigade may not have been placed on the forward slope in an exposed position, as some veterans suggested. But even if they had been withdrawn to the comparative safety of the ridge, they nonetheless wilted under the relentless fire as General Donzelot's men pressed forward. One by one, their leading officers fell, including Bijlandt, who was wounded. Further back the men of Sir Thomas Picton's 5th British Infantry Division, a polyglot mixture of hardened Scottish, English and German soldiers, could only watch in alarm. Even some of the more experienced troops were forced to retreat. 'The post abandoned . . . was instantly re-occupied by the 3rd Battalion the Royals, and the 2nd Battalion 44th Regiment,' remembered Lt. James Hope of the 92nd. 'Those two weak battalions poured on the assailants a heavy fire of musketry, but the latter continued to advance with unflinching courage, till they succeeded in compelling our friends also to retire from the hedge.'

Despite the ordeal endured by the Dutch-Belgian brigade, their colleagues who occupied more sheltered ground were dismissive of their behaviour. Major Evans of the 5th West India Regiment commented that 'the Dutch Belgian Infantry yielded with slight or no resistance to the advancing columns, and got quickly to the rear; and not in the stubborn, reluctant, deliberate way of our infantry.' In this way, the retreat of the Dutch-Belgian brigade did nothing to help the cause of foreigners in the Anglo-Allied army, while promoting that of the British, and it also helped dent, as if by association, the importance of the Prussians' contribution to the battle. 'They commenced a hurried retreat,' wrote William Siborne of the Dutch-Belgian brigade, 'not partially and promiscuously, but collectively and simultaneously ... As they rushed past the British columns, hissings, hootings, and execrations, were indignantly heaped upon them.' In contrast to the Dutch-Belgian brigade, Lt.-Gen. Picton was held to be 'calmly watching' the French movements and those of his wavering colleagues with a 'quick and practised eye.' 'Picton well knew,' wrote Siborne, 'that they had not lost that indomitable spirit, which, under his guidance, had immortalised them on that memorable field of battle ... What, then, might not be achieved by such innate valour – by such consummate discipline?'

They would need both qualities in abundance. Marshal Quiot's men from the 1st Infantry Division were heading for the farm of La Haye Sainte and for the sandpit held by the 95th Rifles; General Donzelot's forces and General Marcognet's were attacking the forward slope; further to the east, General Durutte's 4th Infantry Division moved forward, accompanied by a vast array of cavalry and light artillery batteries. Lt. Hope told Siborne: 'Everyone was now convinced that our affairs had approached an important crisis and that an attempt to resist the torrent must instantly be made, or the heights, and with them the victory, yielded to the enemy.' The battle had entered a critical phase.

East of the Brussels highway, the main French column was no more than forty metres from the Anglo-Allied line when Sir Thomas Picton, leading the 5th British Infantry Division, decided to act. Picton, who came from Pembroke, was a brave commander, as he had shown in the Peninsular War and at Quatre Bras, though he had only earned the reluctant loyalty of his troops through his courage, because he was irascible and foul-mouthed, his bitterness the greater because he had not been awarded the peerage he thought was his due. He had started his army career at thirteen, and now he was fifty-six he thought he was about to die. A few days earlier, in Belgium, he had even tried out a grave for size, declaring it a perfect fit. He ordered Maj.-Gen. Kempt's 8th British Brigade to move forward to join up with the skirmishers, towards a hedge which lined both sides of a nearby lane, which ran from east to west.

To the advancing French, the area appeared to be deserted. They saw that the Dutch-Belgian brigade had run, and there were gaps in the hedge through which it was easy to pass. Up to twelve thousand French infantry poured towards Picton's 5th Infantry Division, heading for the top of the ridge. Suddenly the British forces, hidden by the hedge and by the reverse slope, stood up. To the French they seemed to have appeared from nowhere. Then Picton, at close range, gave the signal to fire. Musket shots at a distance were notoriously inaccurate. But served up in a volley of fire and at close range against packed ranks of the enemy, they were deadly. Three thousand men were firing three thousand muskets, at point-blank range. As the balls flew hard and sharp into the enemy columns, Picton wasted no time in pressing his advantage. He screamed out the order 'Charge! Charge!' and his men burst yelling and shouting through the hedge, as if they were finally able to give vent to all their pent-up energy and nerves.

They were met with raking fire from the enemy skirmishers, which had fallen back to patrol the flanks of the French army. The ensign carrying the 32nd's colour was seriously wounded and Lt. Robert Belcher had to take the colour from him until another ensign could be called. Almost immediately, with the brigade still advancing, and the French infantry beginning to retreat, he found himself facing an enemy officer whose horse had been shot from under him. He told Siborne that 'when he extricated himself we were close on him. I had the colour on my left arm and was slightly in advance of the division. He suddenly fronted me and seized the staff, I still retaining a grasp of the silk. At the same moment he attempted to draw his sabre, but he had not accomplished it when the covering colour-sergeant, named

Switzer, thrust his pike into his breast, and the rank and file of the division, named Lacy, fired into him. He fell dead at my feet.'

There was little time for relief. As the Allied infantry advanced, a musketball hit Picton, passing through his right temple and penetrating his brain. His premonition had proved to be accurate. In the many histories of the battle, his death came to epitomise the courage of the British troops, for only later, when his body was removed from the field and laid out in Brussels, was it discovered that he had already been seriously injured. The wound was just above the hip, where the skin was badly bruised and distended, surrounded by dried blood. It became clear that Picton had been hit by a musketball at the Battle of Quatre Bras but had kept it quiet, refusing to tell anyone of his injuries. Two of his ribs had been broken, but he had secretly ordered his servant to bind him up so that he might still lead his men in battle without their questioning his strength or confidence. 'Such was Picton,' wrote Siborne, 'such his stern sense of duty; such his boundless zeal for the honour of his profession; such his complete devotion to the cause of his sovereign and country!' He was still wearing the civilian clothes and top-hat, which, quixotically, he had sported at Quatre Bras.

Despite their leader's death, Picton's troops charged on, tearing into the French with their bayonets, the British regiments and the Scottish Highlanders in the thick of the action. They had the upper hand, but they were in danger. The French heavy cavalry, the cuirassiers, were only moments away. But the French had reckoned without the Earl of Uxbridge. Uxbridge was a brave, strong, good-looking cavalry officer, who had led a dashing life. With eight children by his wife, Lady Caroline Villiers, he had scandalised society by eloping with the wife of Wellington's brother. He had survived both the scandal and the resulting duel with his wife's brother on Wimbledon Common. Now, as he watched the French advance, he decided to act impetuously, and bravely, again, by leading a charge of the heavy cavalry.

Uxbridge rode up to Lord Edward Somerset and ordered him to get his men into line, then galloped on to Sir William Ponsonby and ordered him to move against the French infantry. Uxbridge himself would lead the charge, by taking up a central position between the two brigades. In doing so, he was signalling a change of tactics. Instead of continuing to concentrate on defence, the Anglo-Allied army would take the fight to the French, to try to sweep them off the forward slope. To some officers, such as Captain Alexander Kennedy Clark, commanding the centre squadron of the 1st (Royal) Dragoons, it seemed the only option. He wrote to William Siborne: 'I ask you as an officer of experience how long the British Army could have held its position if the Count d'Erlon's Corps had been able to occupy the ridge of land that the head of their columns had gained? I may be in error but I cannot help thinking it the most critical moment of the day. The crest of the height had been gained and the charge of the cavalry at the crucial moment recovered it.'

The French cavalry had now reached the top of the ridge held by the Anglo-Allied infantry. It was as close as the French would get. At about 2.20 p.m., following Uxbridge's lead, Somerset's seven leading squadrons charged up the slope that had concealed them, manoeuvring through the ranks of the watching Hanoverian and King's German Legion infantry in Ompteda's brigade, posted north of La Haye Sainte. Then they crashed into the French cavalry near the ridge. It was an astounding sight. Despite the modest pace of their advance, they rode into the enemy horsemen with such force that the two sides seemed to bounce off each other, as if they were recoiling from the shock. The Earl of Uxbridge thought that the French had been completely surprised by the attack. 'I think the left wing of our infantry was partially retiring when I determined upon the movement, and then these nineteen squadrons pouncing down upon the hill upon them so astonished them that no very great resistance was made, and surely such havoc was rarely made in so few minutes.'

The conflict was brief, but bloody, the only clash of heavy cavalry of the entire day. Swords flashed and cut and thrust; horses galloped and reared and wheeled, or fell to earth, with their legs trembling and thrashing the air. The French had sabres which were longer than the British weapons but they were far less skilled as horsemen and soon they were driven off the ridge entirely and forced back down the slope, along with part of the left wing of infantry around La Haye Sainte, leaving behind the remains of two wrecked horse artillery batteries.

Cavalry Charge – The New Waterloo Model

Battlefield communication was hard, if not impossible, amidst the thunder of the guns and the horses' hooves, but, on the eastern side of the road, Sir William Ponsonby was determined that he would time his charge to perfection. So he asked Lt.-Col. Joseph Muter, of the 6th (Inniskilling) Dragoons, to ride in front of the central squadron, and not to advance until he had seen Ponsonby give the signal by waving his cocked hat. Ponsonby's makeshift system was nearly undone when his horse was startled by gunfire and reared up at the crucial moment. Instead it was left to Ponsonby's extra aide-de-camp, Major Evans, to raise his hat, and at that point, Ponsonby's Union Brigade, the alliance of the British, Scottish and Irish Dragoons, came galloping forward.

There were six squadrons of the Royals and Inniskillings in the first line, three more of the Scots Greys behind them. Such was their feeling of excitement that when the Scots Greys passed through the ranks of the 92nd (Gordon) Highlanders, some of the Highlanders grabbed their stirrups to be carried to the battle, crying out exuberantly 'Hurrah, 92nd! Scotland for ever!' Down the years which followed, Corporal John Dickson of the Scots Greys, who lived till he was ninety, told his relatives that it was 'a grand sight to see the long line of giant grey horses dashing along with flowing manes and heads down, tearing up the turf about them as they went. The men in their red coats and tall bear-skins were cheering loudly, and the trumpeters were sounding the charge.' It was hard for the cavalry to negotiate the road beyond the hedge, because it dropped away between high sloping banks, but there were very few accidents, to the men's surprise. The Royals and the Inniskillings cleared the road and hedges away to the right. 'As we tightened our grip to descend the hillside among the corn, we could make out the feather bonnets of the Highlanders, and heard the officers crying out to them to wheel back by sections. A moment more and we were among them.'

The cavalry had ridden straight into the infantry of both General Donzelot's and General Marcognet's Divisions, catching them so quickly that the French had no opportunity to form into defensive squares. Though the cavalry had probably not charged at speed, because it had to travel up the reverse slope, and then negotiate its way through its own infantry, the French had been expecting only infantry to appear. Lt.-Col. Muter thought the element of surprise had been crucial. 'I have always considered it a splendid illustration of the maxim that the attacks of cavalry against columns of infantry should be unforeseen and unexpected. The French infantry made good use of their musquets and fire, but had no time to throw themselves into square.'

The smoke from the continuous volleys of muskets mingled with that from the cannons, and only the occasional gust of wind cleared the air, enabling the soldiers on both sides to gain a tantalising glimpse of the battlefield, before the smoke would close in again, and the vision be taken from them. The undulating ground, and the height of the corn, made visibility all the harder. Captain Kennedy Clark remembered how the two sides did not see each other until they were about eighty or ninety yards apart. The French column fired, bringing down about twenty men, before realising, in a panic, that it was facing overwhelming odds. The men tried to pull back, but there were too many of them, and they were packed too close together, and behind them, at the rear, men were still advancing, so that the French army became a whirlpool of men moving forward and backward, a swirling tide so thick that the men could not even move their arms to fight, until the Dragoons had killed enough of them to free some space.

Captain Duthilt of the 45th French Regiment saw one of his men fall at his feet, killed by a sabre thrust. He and his men tried bravely to bayonet the Allied cavalrymen, but it was a hopeless cause, and the slaughter ran throughout the ranks, from the drummers and fifers to the officers. Packed closely together, the French did not know which way to turn as they fought for survival, aiming only to get back to the safety of the line. Artillery shells from their own guns landed among them, killing men from both sides. Captain Duthilt: 'In the bloody confusion our officers did their duty by trying to establish some sort of order and to reform the platoons ... just as I was pushing one of our men back into the ranks I saw him fall at my feet from sabre slash. I turned round instantly – to see English cavalry forcing their way into our midst and hacking us to pieces. Just as it is difficult, if not impossible, for the best cavalry to break into infantry who are formed up in squares ... so it is true that once ranks have been broken and penetrated, then resistance is useless and nothing remains for the cavalry to do but to slaughter at almost no risk to themselves. This is what happened ... our poor fellows could not reach far enough to bayonet those cavalrymen mounted on powerful horses, and the few shots fired in this chaotic mêlée were just as fatal to our own men as to the English. And so we found ourselves defenceless against a relentless enemy.'

In contrast, the Allied army, finally unleashed, was revelling in the thrill of battle. Lt. Robert Winchester of the 92nd Highlanders could not believe the speed of the destruction caused by the cavalry on a French column. 'In less than three minutes it was totally destroyed, 2000 ... of them having been made prisoners ... The grass field in which the enemy was formed, which was only an instant before as green and smooth as the fifteen acres in Phoenix Park, was in a few minutes covered with killed and wounded, knapsacks and their contents, arms, accoutrements, &c., literally strewed all over, that to avoid stepping on either one or the other was quite impossible; in fact one could hardly believe, had he not witnessed it, that such complete destruction could have been effected in so short a time.'

Just as damaging to French pride was the loss of two Eagles. To capture an Eagle was to steal a regiment's soul, and a guard party had been placed around the Eagle of the 105th which was inscribed with the names of the regiment's victories at Jena, Eylau, Eckmuhl, Essling and Wagram. Captain Kennedy Clark gave orders to his squadron – 'Right shoulders forward, attack the Colour,' and led the way to the Colour himself. 'On reaching it, I ran my sword into the Officer's right side a little above the hip joint. He was a little to my left side, and he fell to that side with the Eagle across my horse's head. I tried to catch it with my left hand, but could only touch the fringe of the flag, and it is probable it would have fallen to the ground, had it not been prevented by the neck of Corporal Styles' horse. I called out twice "Secure the Colour, secure the Colour, it belongs to me."'

So too Sergeant Charles Ewart of the 2nd Dragoons (the Scots Greys) captured the golden imperial Eagle of the 45th regiment, displaying the names of Austerlitz, Jena, Friedland, Essling and Wagram, the battles which had won it the proud sobriquet of 'The Invincibles'. In order to seize the trophy, Ewart had fought his own private bloody battle with two French soldiers. 'I cut him from the chin upwards, which cut went through his teeth. Next I was attacked by a foot soldier, who, after firing at me, charged me with his bayonet; but I parried it, and cut him through the head; so that finished the contest for the Eagle.'

D'Erlon's advance had been defeated, his corps pushed back in confusion, his battle-plan in pieces. It was not a terminal blow, not least as only half his men had been caught up in the worst of the battle on the ridge. But he had lost perhaps a quarter of his cavalry, as many as four or five thousand men. All he had to show for such losses was the capture by General Durutte's men of parts of Papelotte and Frischermont, seized from the Nassauers, in the east of the battlefield. It was a poor return for such heavy losses, a great and glorious blow struck by Wellington's men alone.

As for the Prussian troops, they were nowhere to be seen. Many miles away, the Prussian IV Corps, led by Bulow, had come to a standstill, to allow its rearmost units to catch up, while Ziethen's I Corps had only just begun its circuitous march to meet Wellington's left wing. But then who needed the support of the missing Prussian troops if this was what the British could accomplish on their own? And why should their hesitant advance be admired by Wellington or noted by the British veterans in their histories, when they and they alone had repelled the French so bravely?

VII

To the Chief Clerk in the Commander-in-Chief's Office
From Lord Fitzroy Somerset, Military Secretary to the Duke

Dover, 3 November 1834

My dear Lindsay,

I beg your attention to Sir W. Gordon's letter and to the memorandum by Colonel Ellicombe. You will see that they both concur with me in objecting to the circular and in thinking that it would lead to the production of a mass of contradictory information.

You had better communicate to Mr Siborne what they say.

Yours faithfully,

Fitzroy Somerset

The cavalry charge was captured by history in a way which made Siborne, too, its prisoner. While he was resolutely determined, in the face of the hostility of the military authorities, to make a model which showed the final moments of victory, he later decided to make a splendid new model of the heavy cavalry's attack. Thousands of model soldiers and hundreds of tiny horses populated the landscape of this battle, mixed up in a swirling mass, among their number the cavalry led by Sir William Ponsonby – the Royals, the Scots Greys and the Inniskillings. If Siborne had made this model first, instead of concentrating on the end of the battle, his difficulties would have been over, for the charge was seen as a brilliant, brave manoeuvre, a triumph of British courage that helped to turn the battle. William Siborne, a patriot at heart, was not one to disagree, even if the truth was more complicated than many veterans cared to admit.

For a while, it had been a glorious sight. Nearly two thousand men rode in a vast, spectacular line of heavy cavalry, galloping together in abandon as if they were on a fox hunt. Across the battlefield, above the creaking of leather saddles and the thunder of the hooves, came a distant sound of military music, the roar of heavy cannon, and the bang of muskets. Occasionally, a horseman was hit, tumbling from the saddle, his horse running on ahead, its load suddenly lighter. Occasionally, too, a horse was killed or wounded, collapsing on the ground with legs flailing, blood spurting from a chest or head or leg, its rider pitched helplessly from the saddle. Everywhere the cavalrymen looked the French were scattering, falling back towards their lines. The Allied army had the field to itself. The day was all but won. 'The plain appeared to be swept clean,' remarked the Earl of Uxbridge, 'and I never saw so joyous a group ... they thought the battle was over.'

But it was a disaster, a complete and utter disaster, the child of pride and excitement, born of the thrill of the chase, of exhilarating speed and freedom, of casting off the shackles which had been imposed on the Allied army for so long. How right Wellington had been to harbour such misgivings about the recklessness of cavalry! Major Evans of the 5th West India Regiment was an experienced Irish officer, who had distinguished himself in the Peninsula, and in the American War of 1812, capturing the Congress House with only a small band of infantry. He could tell straight away that the cavalry charge had gone awry: 'The enemy fled as a flock of sheep across the valley – quite at the mercy of the Dragoons. In fact, our men were *out of hand*. The helplessness of the enemy offered too great a temptation to the Dragoons ... It was evident that the enemy's reserves of cavalry would soon take advantage of our disorder.'

On went the King's Dragoon Guards, the 2nd Life Guards, the Royals, the Inniskillings, the Greys, on and on they charged, giving no thought to tactics, to discipline, to order, to securing a safe line of retreat. Only now did Uxbridge wheel around to look for support. To his horror, there was none. Nobody could hear him shout for help, nor the bugle calls he ordered. Nor was there any support on the left of the high road, behind Ponsonby's line, for the light cavalry brigades had moved up to support the charge, while Vandeleur's men, who could have acted as support, were too far back, slowed down by the sloping ground they had to cross. Only now, as the foremost line of Allied cavalry galloped up to the enemy's position, did the extent of the miscalculation become clear. They had advanced too far, too fast, and had been left without support, and were facing some 30,000 French infantry, cavalry and artillery, including the Imperial Guard. Infantry and artillery fire raked down on them. Major Evans, who was later to become the celebrated Sir De Lacy Evans of Crimean fame, rode over to Sir James Kempt to ask him to cover their withdrawal. But he knew it was too late: 'If we could have formed a hundred men we could have made a respectable retreat, and saved many; but we could effect no formation, and were as helpless against their attack as their infantry had been against ours. Everyone saw what must happen.'

Kempt replied that he could only advance by a couple of hundred yards, and that infantry alone could not save the day. The Allied cavalry was riding full-pelt into the enemy, a frontal assault into the very mouth of its guns. A brutal, horrible, bloody reckoning was upon them. Suddenly, inevitably, the French gun batteries sounded out, pounding their heavy balls into the path of the horsemen, accompanied by a hail of fire from the muskets of the infantry. The Greys and the Royals and the Inniskillings rode bravely into the batteries, wheeling round and leaning down to slash and cut at the gunners with the curved blades of their sabres, stabbing at their horses. But it was a hopeless cause. Not far away, they could see French lancers were approaching, their horses as fresh as the allies' were exhausted. Lt.-Col. Frederick Ponsonby was commanding the 12th Light Dragoons, part of Vandeleur's brigade, and had a clear view of the whole French position. The son of an earl, he had fought for Wellington for the best part of a decade, after joining the 10th Light Dragoons as a humble cornet. He feared for the safety of the Union Brigade led by his namesake Sir William Ponsonby: 'I saw considerable bodies of French infantry and cavalry in some confusion in the plain, and a good many scattered Dragoons in red nearly on the crest of the French position.

I felt that these were in the utmost peril.' The cavalry had tasted their moment of glory, but had lingered to enjoy it. Now they would pay the price.

Ten squadrons of cuirassiers were upon them, menacing in their breastplates, their great black horses charging forward. Then five squadrons of lancers arrived, and three of chasseurs à cheval, nearly 2500 horsemen in all. On the ridge, huge numbers of infantry in their tall fur hats were advancing too. Quickly and desperately the cavalry tried to charge the lancers. The horses reared, and some were killed by lances thrust into their flesh; riders fell, still trying to protect themselves from the lances with their bare hands.

Somerset's 1st Cavalry Brigade fought its way back to safe ground, taking heavy casualties, and the thirty guns the Allied army had seized in the giddying rush of the advance had to be abandoned. But Sir William Ponsonby's men, exhausted and exposed, were caught by the French lancers and chasseurs and Ponsonby, a distinguished officer who had fought in the Peninsular War, was killed. He lay on the ground, his cloak, edged with fur, blown to one side. By his outstretched hand lay a miniature portrait of a lady, and his watch. Other officers were dead, too, including the brigade major and a lieutenant. The Scots Greys, outnumbered and outfought, suffered terribly, and were charged repeatedly by the lancers who spread out over the field to pick off stragglers and the wounded. For the Allied army the defeat of its grand charge was a bitter blow, not least because it need not have happened.

As the Allied cavalry retreated in disarray, the horses ankle-deep in the mud, the French infantry was also drifting back towards its own line, shattered by the initial cavalry attack, so that the changing fortunes of battle were captured in this single moment, the remains of two attacks, one destroyed by the courage of the defenders, the other wrecked by over-exuberance. Uxbridge, manfully, owned up to the fact that he had made a ghastly error which had cost many of his men their lives: 'I committed a great mistake in having myself led the attack. The carrière once begun, the leader is no better than any other man; whereas if I had placed myself at the head of the 2nd line, there is no saying what great advantages might not have accrued from it. I am the less pardonable in having deviated from a principle I had laid down for myself.'

At last, however, reinforcements were arriving. On the eastern flank, Vandeleur's Light Cavalry Brigade was finally heading down the slope from the left flank towards the French position. But if the situation had been recovered, at least partially, by the support of the Light Dragoons, now it was to be thrown away again. Some of the cavalry disobeyed their strict instructions, and instead of waiting in the valley, dashed up the hill towards the French position, straight into fresh troops which had just been brought forward. Once more, ill-discipline would cost the Allied army dear. As the musketballs flew, there were scores of dead and wounded. The commander of the 12th Light Dragoons, Lt.-Col. Frederick Ponsonby, was seriously injured: 'I endeavoured to draw off my regiment, but being wounded and completely disabled, I soon fell to the ground upon the crest of the French position, and in the near vicinity of some guns which had probably been abandoned during the charge of General (William) Ponsonby's (heavy cavalry) brigade, as several men, I think of the Royals, were found in the same spot where I was picked up.'

Frederick Ponsonby was to suffer greatly. He lay injured on the ground for a day and a night, his agonies made all the greater by a passing enemy lancer who, seeing that the injured man was still alive, thrust his weapon into Ponsonby's back. Later, a French officer behaved in a more gentlemanly fashion: hearing Ponsonby complain of a raging thirst, he let him drink from his brandy bottle. Later still, two squadrons of Prussian cavalry galloped over Ponsonby, and it was not until the next day, long after the fighting had ended, that he was discovered, still alive. Ponsonby was made of stern stuff. He was carried in a cart to the village of Waterloo, where, to everyone's amazement, he gradually recovered from his terrible wounds, even though the cure must have been painful, too – it was said that he was saved by being bled. Ponsonby, who lived for another twenty-two years and became a major-general, was philosophical about the failure of the cavalry charge: 'I have said that a good many men fell on the crest of the French position. I know we ought not to have been there, and that we fell into the same error which we went down to correct, but I believe that this is an error almost inevitable after a successful charge and it must always depend upon the steadiness of a good support to prevent serious consequences.'

Others were less fortunate. Lt.-Col. James Hamilton, commanding the 2nd (Royal North British) Dragoons, the Scots Greys, was last seen alive as he led his men over the crest of the French position. Two families were to mourn him: the son of a sergeant-major, William Anderson, he had effectively been adopted by his father's former colonel, whose name he had taken. After the battle, Hamilton's body was found, with its arms cut off, and a bullet in the heart.

There were hundreds of wounded, too, lying in the valley, far from their own lines. One of the Scots Greys came round to discover that he was propped up below a French cannon, and that the explosion in his head was in fact the noise of the gun firing just above his ears. Not knowing what to do, he stayed still. A British officer discovered the body of a French hussar which, on inspection, was found to be that of a young girl who had died near the Allied line. It turned out she had been taken to battle by her lover, a French officer, who had kitted her out in military uniform in Paris. Several other bodies of women were later found lying in the mud, their reward for so faithfully following their men into battle, death in this bloody valley.

The weather was still dull and wet, and the cannon fire mingled with smoke from the muskets so that only occasionally, when the wind freshened and partially cleared away the smoke, could the charges of the cavalry and movements in both armies be distinguished. A direct shot from a French battery lit up the scene, hitting an ammunition box and causing a huge explosion. But the charge by Vandeleur's Light Dragoon regiments had finally succeeded in relieving the pressure on the retreating cavalry. As they straggled back to the Allied position, their return was covered by missiles from Captain Edward Whinyates's 2nd Rocket Troop.

Wellington, like Captain Mercer at Genappe, placed little faith in rockets, which he deemed as unreliable as cavalry. But compared with the cannons, they were light and mobile, and could be fired more quickly. They looked like, and were lit like, firework rockets and were fired either from a tripod, or stuck into the ground or a hedge. With a fair wind, they could travel a mile. Captain Dansey, from the rocket unit, who was severely wounded at Waterloo, remembered that the Troop had a 'great awkward lumbering carriage, with an apparatus called a Bombarding Frame for heavy rockets . . . I recollect our seeing it, with its great long frame cocked up in the air, at an angle of about forty-five degrees, firing away.' But the frame was too big to be taken to the front, and the rye was so high that the rockets had to be fired through it, without a clear idea of a target. In the event, the Rocket Troop fired more guns than rockets at Waterloo. The world was not yet ready for technology to replace the musket, lance or sabre.

At last, the battle quietened down, and the military calculations could begin. The cavalry advance had broken three divisions of French infantry, and had repulsed Napoleon's attack. The Allied army had survived a crisis and it had bought itself time to await the Prussian reinforcements. Certainly the dashing Uxbridge, despite accepting blame for getting carried away, thought the charge by the heavy cavalry had altered the battle's course, and, with proper support, might have won the day. 'Had I found only four well-formed squadrons, I feel certain that the loss the first line suffered when they were finally forced back would have been avoided, and most of these guns might have been secured, for it was obvious that the effect of that charge had been prodigious and for the rest of the day, although the cuirassiers frequently attempted to break into our lines, they always did it – as if they expected something more behind the curtain.'

It was scant consolation. Half of the men from the heavy cavalry brigades were casualties.

If it was a disaster, then to Siborne it did not appear to be one, for, like the men themselves, he saw only British courage and achievement, a patriotic view which would make his difficulties with the military and political establishment over the creation of his Model all the more remarkable. Indeed, in his meticulous factual history of the battle, he became quite carried away with his description of the 'glorious triumph' of the cavalry almost as if he too had taken part in Uxbridge's charge, only to be swept away by the passion of the moment.

'Thus terminated one of the grandest scenes which distinguished the mighty drama enacted on the ever-memorable plains of Waterloo,' he wrote. 'A scene presenting in bold relief, genuine British valour crowned with resplendent triumph; a scene, which should be indelibly impressed upon the minds as well of living British warriors, as of their successors in ages yet unborn. Britons! Before other scenes are disclosed to your view, take one retrospective glance at this glorious, this instructive spectacle . . .

'The dragoons are in the midst of the enemy's columns – the furious impetuosity of their onslaught overcomes all resistance . . . Their intoxicating triumph admits of no restraint. They heed not the trumpet's call to halt and rally, but plunging wildly amidst the formidable line of batteries ranged along the French position, they commence sabreing the gunners, stabbing the horses, and seem to clear the ground of every living being. But physical efforts, however powerfully developed and sustained, have their limit: exhausted nature yields at length; and their fiery steeds, subdued, not by force but by exhaustion, retire with lagging, faltering pace. You look in vain for support – there is none.

'But mark! A rescue is at hand – a gallant line of friendly cavalry throws itself against the right flank of infantry, the sole remaining column out of the entire attacking force that has yet kept together. The tide of destruction now sets in strongly against the lancers. Their pursuit is checked. The heavy dragoons are relieved from the pressure. A mêlée ensues: but you are not kept long in suspense; for in another moment this newly-arrived force, making good its way, succeeds in driving the lancers in confusion down to the foot of the valley. The arena in front is speedily cleared of both friends and foes – the discharge of rockets, which now attracts your attention, appears like a display of fireworks in celebration of the glorious triumph – the affair has terminated.

'But stay to witness the concluding part of the scene. Observe the splendidly attired group entering upon the right, just above La Haye Sainte. It is headed by one whom you cannot for a moment mistake – the illustrious Wellington. Lord Uxbridge, returning from his brilliant charge, now joins the Duke, while the whole *corps diplomatique et militaire* express in the strongest terms their admiration of the grand military spectacle of which they have been spectators. Among them are representatives of nearly all the continental nations, so that this glorious triumph of your valiant countrymen may be said to have been achieved in the face of congregated Europe. Honour, imperishable honour, to every British soldier engaged in that never-to-be-forgotten fight.'

If William Siborne was inspired by such patriotic fervour, how could his Model possibly offend 'the illustrious Wellington'?

VIII

Remarks upon Sir W. Gordon's letter and Colonel Ellicombe's memorandum

Dublin, 7 November 1834

Considering the number of accounts that have been published of Waterloo and the number of plans that have been drawn of the field, I must confess I do not see what novelty or interest a Model would possess if intended only to represent the positions occupied by the respective armies at the commencement of the action. At all events this was not the object I had in view when I undertook the work.

My idea was that so long as a sufficient number of surviving eyewitnesses of, and participants in, the Battle remained in existence, an excellent opportunity was afforded for the construction of a Model which by the grandeur of its scale, the minuteness of its finish, and the accuracy of its representation, should be at once novel and attractive and which by its depicting more particularly the eventful crisis of the Battle upon the issue of which hung the destiny of Europe, should at the same time possess that national interest and importance which we are accustomed to attach to works of art associated with deeds which constitute the glory of the Empire.

Siborne

In the valley, several thousand bodies lay in the mud. Wounded horses circled the dead and dying soldiers of both sides, while others grazed as if nothing untoward had happened. It looked as if the battle had already been fought and won, so that the great, calamitous noise of war, the clash of cavalry, the rattle of muskets and the boom of cannons, had been replaced by the shocked silence of its aftermath, a silence punctuated only by the groans of the injured and the panicked whinnying of horses. Smoke drifted slowly, like an afterthought, over the battlefield.

Still there was no sign of the Prussians. At La Haye Sainte and Hougoumont the garrisons were clinging on desperately. The Anglo-Allied army would not forget the awful time they had of it in the next few hours, but somehow, when the soldiers looked back on their suffering, it made victory all the sweeter. Whatever the Prussians had been through, their continued absence meant they would not be associated with the main battle seen by the survivors and reflected in the many instant histories.

There were many tales of bravery and of dreadful deaths before the contest was finally resolved. With the repulse of d'Erlon's attack, the battle for Hougoumont seemed to take on a new life, as if its capture was a prize which far outstripped its strategic value. The French had placed a howitzer in a corner of the wood, and it was shelling the buildings. Lt.-Col. Saltoun and his men had tried to capture it, but faced by three brigades, they had been forced to retreat into the Hollow Way. By three o'clock, Napoleon had ordered up a whole battery of howitzers, and soon Hougoumont and its occupants were caught in the middle of the heaviest bombardment of the war. Plenty of men had died on the battlefield from dreadful wounds; many had died after being hit by musketballs. Such deaths were bloody, and invariably instant, though some men had been terribly mutilated and were lying on the valley floor in the most appalling agony. But none of them had been subjected to the continual shelling which the defenders of Hougoumont now endured; none of them had been forced to wait, like men from the next century, for the next shell to land; none of them had been subjected to the torment of hearing a howitzer shell tearing through the air, fearing a direct hit as they tried to gauge from the deadly sound where it might drop next. Private Matthew Clay described his experiences inside the château: 'I was . . . posted in an upper room. This room was situated higher than the other buildings and we annoyed the enemy's skirmishers from the window. The enemy noticed this and threw their shells amongst us and set the building which we were defending on fire. Our officer placed himself at the entrance of the room and would not allow anyone to leave his post until our position became hopeless and too perilous to remain. We full expected the floor to sink with us every moment.'

A quarter of all the artillery employed by the three sides at Waterloo were howitzers. The French army had twelve which fired six-inch shells, six of them with the 'Grand Battery' and six with the Guard artillery reserve, and they had another fifty-eight which fired 5.5-inch shells. The howitzers looked like sawn-off cannons, their short barrels just over two feet long, which was barely a third the length of the twelve-pounder guns. Now, from long range, perhaps as far away as 800 metres, they were lobbing high-angle fire at the enemy. The gunners were firing common shell, a hollow iron sphere containing gunpowder, which flung out fragments of iron. Because the shells were designed to explode they could be deadly even against a hidden target, as long as they landed in approximately the right area. Against Hougoumont, the gunners simply had to aim for the roofs. The French were also firing carcass projectiles, incendiary devices fired by the howitzers, which were made from canvas, bound by iron hoops, and filled with flammable materials such as turpentine, tallow, resin, sulphur, antimony and saltpetre.

The projectiles, which could burn for up to twelve minutes, had found an easy prey. The straw and hay and wood which had been brought in from the rain caught fire rapidly, the flames licking at the feet of wounded soldiers who had been dragged into the outbuildings. Gradually, as the missiles dropped, a plume of smoke began to seep out of the complex of buildings. It started in the outhouses, on the north side of the château; it drifted out of the Great Barn; it wrapped itself around the farmer's house; and finally it curled out of the château itself. As the flames caught hold, there was one extraordinary event: they stopped at the feet of the life-size figure of Christ which hung above the door of the chapel. As Ensign George Standen put it: 'the anecdote of the fire only burning to the feet of the Cross is perfectly true, which in so superstitious a country made a great sensation.' Soon, however, the defenders found themselves unable to see for the billowing clouds of thick black smoke which enveloped them. The rest of the Allied army could only watch helplessly as smoke rose menacingly from the buildings and floated innocuously towards them on the breeze.

The defenders' plight was becoming desperate, surrounded by the enemy outside and threatened by a new enemy within the walls. Some of them managed to escape from the buildings, their uniforms on fire. But there were so few defenders inside the walls of Hougoumont that, as the ferocity of the attack intensified, few of them could be spared to care for the wounded, and several casualties of the howitzer bombardment, trapped by the flames, were burnt alive. Colonel Alexander Woodford of the Coldstream Guards remembered that the heat was so intense that neither he nor Lt.-Col. Macdonell could get into the stables where the wounded had been carried. Then a shell or carcass landed on the Great Barn, and smoke and flames burst out, spreading rapidly to the other outbuildings. 'Some officers attempting to penetrate into the stables to rescue some wounded men, were obliged to desist, from the suffocation of the smoke, and several men perished,' Woodford recalled. Woodford came from an ancient, well-connected family: his father was Governor of Trinidad, and a maternal relative, the Dean of Salisbury, had once saved the Countess of Derby and her house at Latham from Cromwell's army. Now Woodford himself was under siege, as he tried to staunch the flow of French attacks.

The gates of Hougoumont were still blocked by anything the defenders could lay their hands on – farming tools, ladders, wheelbarrows, even the trunk of a huge tree, long since felled. The officers had joined the lower ranks to fire muskets at the enemy forces. But still the shells continued to fall, and Corporal James Graham, a County Monaghan man, asked Lt.-Col. Macdonell for permission to leave his post in the garden, a move which would take him away from the gunfire. Graham was a brave man, one of the strongest in his regiment, and Macdonell was puzzled: why would Graham want to abandon his post? 'I would not,' replied Graham, 'only my brother lies wounded in that building which has just caught fire.' He managed to pull his brother Joseph to safety. After the battle, he was immediately promoted to sergeant, and was awarded a special gold medal for gallantry. He also won an annuity of ten pounds a year from a Norfolk rector, on the nomination of Wellington, although the rector soon went bankrupt.

Other survivors managed to crawl into one of the two courtyards, though even in the open air they found it hard to breathe because of the choking smoke. Ensign George Standen, the son of a banker, had seen the barn and cart house go up in flames, and watched as three or four officers' horses rushed out from the barn into the yard. In their confusion, only a minute or two later, they dashed back into the flames and were burnt to death. 'I mention this as I had always heard horses would never leave fire; perhaps some beam or large piece of wood fell and astonished them.' Many men sought refuge in the tiny chapel next to the château, crowding in among the dead who had been laid out on its floor, and in this place of sanctuary they listened to the crashing of timber and the explosion of shells, hell breaking loose outside. Some of them prayed they might be spared a fate which, it now seemed, must inevitably be theirs without divine intervention.

The defenders of Hougoumont had to stay put and fight for their lives. Short of ammunition, as the afternoon wore on, they were saved by an unknown soldier, who was ordered by Captain Horace Seymour, an ADC to Lord Uxbridge, to direct supplies to the beleaguered garrison. Seymour, who was reputed to be the largest and strongest man in the British army, remembered that 'I fell in with a private of the waggon train in charge of a tumbril on the crest of the position. I merely pointed out to him where he was wanted, when he gallantly started his horses, and drove straight down the hill to the Farm, to the gate of which I saw him arrive. He must have lost his horses as there was a severe fire kept on him. I feel convinced to that man's service the Guards owe their ammunition.' But at La Haye Sainte, too, the defenders were running short of ammunition, and no one had come to bring them fresh supplies.

*

The Anglo-Allied soldiers posted between the two main roads now came under intense bombardment from the enemy guns. The cannons of the French light batteries opened up; so too the twelve-pounders of the Imperial Guard, stationed on the heights above La Belle Alliance. Flash after flash leapt from the muzzles of the guns along the ridge occupied by the French, and clouds of smoke spewed into the air, an artificial sky of terrible construction. The earth shook beneath the feet of the Allied army, and great sound waves travelled through the air, making the men recoil from the percussive impact. It was an overwhelming display of fire-power, concentrated against one small section of the Anglo-Allied line, a blitz which was utterly shattering in its intensity. Shot after shot rained down upon the troops, a relentless barrage of missiles and noise, so that the earth felt as if it had been hit by a great black rolling wave of thunder, a shock-wave without end. William Leeke, the seventeen-year-old ensign who had rushed to join his regiment in Belgium, soup tureen in hand, may have been raw and naïve, but he had taken to army life like a veteran. 'The standing to be cannonaded and having nothing else to do,' remarked Leeke stoically, 'is about the most unpleasant thing that can happen to soldiers in an engagement . . .' The bulk of Wellington's army was still seeking refuge behind the reverse of the slope, so they were shielded from the worst of the onslaught, but they were nonetheless impotent to act or move or defend themselves.

For the infantry of the front-line the ordeal was even harsher, and they lay down flat on the ground to shelter as best they could from the deadly rain of iron which cascaded down upon them. At some point in the battle for Hougoumont, Sir John Byng's brigade had been moved forward to help the defenders, while the 14th Foot was moved into a gap in the line. For Ensign Keppel, the sixteen-year-old recruit whose ancestors had fought at Blenheim, coming under cannon-fire was a daunting experience: 'we halted and formed square in the middle of the plain. As we were performing this movement, a bugler of the 51st, who had been out with skirmishers, and had mistaken our square for his own, exclaimed, "Here I am again, safe enough." The words were scarcely out of his mouth, when a roundshot took off his head and spattered the whole battalion with his brains, the colours and the ensigns in charge of them coming in for an extra share. A second shot carried off six of the men's bayonets, a third broke the breastbone of Lance-Sergeant (Robinson), whose piteous cries were anything but encouraging to his youthful comrades. The soldier's belief that "every bullet has its billet" was strengthened by another shot striking Ensign Cooper, the shortest man in the regiment and in the very centre of the square. These casualties were the affair of a second.

'We were now ordered to lie down. Our square, hardly large enough to hold us when standing upright, was too small for us in a recumbent position. Our men lay packed together like herrings in a barrel. Not finding a vacant spot, I seated myself on a drum. Behind me was the Colonel's charger, which, with his head pressed against mine, was mumbling my epaulette, while I patted his cheek. Suddenly my drum capsized and I was thrown prostrate, with the feeling of a blow on the right cheek. I put my hand to my head, thinking half my face was shot away, but the skin was not even abraded. A piece of shell had struck the horse on the nose exactly between my hand and my head, and killed him instantly. The blow I received was from the embossed crown on the horse's bit.'

Still the roundshot tore into them, or ploughed into the ground beside them, while shells burst in the middle of their columns, killing, wounding, maiming or landing in the soil only to burst up again a split second later in a great avalanche of iron and mud and stones. The human cost was terrible to behold. Men were cut in two from direct hits, or were wounded by the glancing blow of a cannonball or from the fragments of shell. The surgeon John Thomson, reporting on the injuries for the Army Medical Board, saw a man whose leg had been torn off by a cannonball, and others whose shoulders had been ripped open. In one case, a cannonball had struck the outer part of a man's thigh, tearing off the skin, and exposing the muscles. There were 'several cases in which large portions of the buttocks and of the thighs had been removed by cannon-balls. These wounds had at first a gangrenous look, and passed afterwards into a state in which they shewed but little disposition to heal.' One soldier had been hit with such force by the splinters of a shell which had exploded near him that the feather-spring of a musket-lock was found inside his body, pressing down upon his femoral artery.

Marshal Ney had spotted what he took to be a weakness in the centre of the Anglo-Allied line, a retreat by some of its men, though it was probably some British battalions moving to the rear, carrying their wounded and pulling ammunition wagons, and he decided to mount a series of cavalry attacks. This was to become Ney's version of d'Erlon's infantry attack, a great sweeping advance of cavalry on a scale designed to make the enemy, already shaken by the bombardment, lose all confidence in its ability to fight, as if a display of overwhelming force alone would be enough to beat them. But Ney was taking a huge risk. Without any support from his own infantry, he was engaging well-armed infantry which was protected by cavalry and artillery, and by the position Wellington had chosen. Simply to reach the Allied front-line, his men would have to skirt around the fighting at Hougoumont and La Haye Sainte, and they would be forced to follow a path no wider than 800 metres, to avoid musket-fire from either farm, making the advance more vulnerable to attack. If they managed to scale the ridge, and get beyond the seven gun batteries of the front-line, they would find rank after rank of Allied infantry and artillery reserves waiting for them, and beyond them reserves of cavalry. To Wellington and his officers the French task looked impossible. Captain James Shaw, a staff officer attached to the 3rd British Division had anticipated a cavalry attack at some point of the day, but 'we had no idea that it would be made upon our line standing in its regular order of battle, and that line as yet unshaken by any previous attack by infantry.' Shaw, or Shaw Kennedy as he became known through marriage, would write the well-received *Notes on the Battle of Waterloo*, which was published in 1865, the year of his death.

If a spectacular show of strength could provide victory on its own, then the French would clearly win. No one in the Anglo-Allied army had seen such an array of cavalry. Sheltering from the fury of the gunfire were seven squadrons of lancers and a dozen of chasseurs. In all sixty-seven squadrons of cavalry, nearly 9000 horsemen, including 1200 chasseurs à cheval from the Imperial Guard, were readying themselves to bear down on the Anglo-Allied army over the course of the next two hours. 'Not a man present who survived could have forgotten the awful grandeur of that charge,' according to Ensign Rees Gronow, the fastidious Old Etonian in the 1st Foot Guards. First came the cuirassiers, in their steel body armour, with gilded copper rivets, twelve regiments in all, the straggling black fur of their helmets swaying in the breeze; then more than 800 lancers in their red tunics, with their lance-flags fluttering, and in the third line, the hussars, resplendent in their green and gold costumes and their black bear-skin shakos. Their weaponry was as vicious as their uniforms were colourful: the long straight, twin-guttered blades of the sabre, with which the cuirassiers had been trained to parry and thrust, by leaning over their horses' necks; the curved blades of the light cavalry sabres; the squat cavalry pistols and the long barrel of the Year XIII pattern musketoons; the shorter barrel of the carbines; and the long, thin, sharply pointed lances. Captain Mercer, of the Royal Horse Artillery, waxed poetic about the sight. 'I can compare it to nothing better than a heavy surf breaking on a coast beset with isolated rocks, against which the mountainous wave dashes with furious uproar, breaks, divides, and runs, hissing and boiling, far beyond up the adjacent beach. In a moment such shoals of lancers and others came sweeping down the slope that the whole interval between the lines was covered with them.' By 4 p.m., the first wave of 5000 French cavalry, in thirty-four squadrons led by Ney, was heading towards the right and centre of the Allied position, through the gap between Hougoumont and La Haye Sainte.

On the Anglo-Allied side, some 18,000 infantry and 56 guns, with 5000 fresh heavy cavalry behind them, faced the charging enemy. When the batteries opened fire, it was as if the horses had hit a hidden trip-wire. Captain Mercer, in charge of half a dozen guns which he had galloped into position near the centre of the line, saw nearly the whole leading rank fall at once, making the ground impassable for those behind. 'The discharge of every gun was followed by a fall of men and horses like that of grass before the mower's scythe . . . many cleared everything and rode through us; many came plunging forward only to fall, man and horse, close to the muzzles of our guns.' Most of the French front-line fell, among them Marshal Ney who lost his horse and had to find another.

Still the cavalry came forward in vast numbers, despite the casualties they had taken, and it was with some confidence that they neared the enemy position. The ground was so soggy that their horses could not work up pace, so they arrived at a slow but steady trot. 'A deliberate advance, at a deliberate pace, as of men resolved to carry their point,' recalled Mercer. 'They moved in profound silence, and the only sound that could be heard from them amidst the incessant roar of battle was the low thunder-like reverberation of the ground beneath the simultaneous tread of so many horses.' The Allied guns opened fire again when they were only forty metres away, inflicting terrible damage on their ranks, but, undaunted, the French pressed forward and rushed the batteries.

Wellington had anticipated the cavalry attack, and knew that the worst outcome would be for his army to lose its artillerymen. So he had given strict instructions that they should not stay to fight if their position was overrun and, now that they found themselves surrounded by enemy cavalry, they followed his orders to the letter, abandoning their guns to seek refuge in the protection of the squares formed by the infantry. Soon Mercer could see 'only the deserted guns still in position on the ridge. Every living soul seemed to have been swept away by this terrible burst.' The cuirassiers had succeeded in capturing a whole line of gun batteries. It was a moment of high elation, especially for the French veterans of the Peninsula who had failed to hold on to a single cannon from the Duke's army. Without thinking, they charged on, convinced that they had the enemy on the run. It was if they had learned nothing from the ruins of the Allied cavalry attack, as if there was some innate failing in the minds of horsemen of whatever national-ity which tempted them to ignore the reality of battle, so that, carried away by the power of their animals and the thrill of the moment, they were unable to calculate the likely consequences of their actions. Over the top of the slope they went, along the length of the Allied ridge, only to find that Wellington's men were waiting for them, drawn up in tight defensive squares. For a young soldier like Ensign Wheatley it was a frightening experience: 'No words can convey the sensation we felt on seeing these heavy-armed bodies advancing at full gallop against us, flourishing their sabres in the air, striking their armour with the handles, the sun gleaming on the steel. The long horse hair, dishevelled by the wind, bore an appearance confounding the senses to an aston-

Forming Square – The New Waterloo Model

ishing disorder. But we dashed them back as coolly as the sturdy rock repels the ocean's foam.'

Napoleon's cavalrymen may have been brave enough to attack a square, but no horse would dare challenge such an imposing obstacle, and there were more than twenty of them. Ensign Gronow remembered the 'overwhelming, long moving line' of cavalry and as the horsemen rushed down upon the squares, 'the very earth seemed to vibrate beneath their thundering tramp. One might suppose that nothing could have resisted the shock of this terrible moving mass. In an almost incredibly short period they were within twenty yards of us, shouting "*Vive l'Empereur!*" The word of command "prepare to receive cavalry" had been given, every man in the front ranks knelt, and a wall bristling with steel, held together by steady hands, presented itself.' But still the squares held their fire. 'Our men had orders not to fire unless they could do so on a near mass,' recalled Gronow. 'The object being to economise our ammunition, and not to waste it on scattered soldiers.' Finally, when the horses were only thirty paces away, the soldiers fired their guns. The effect was instantaneous. Lieutenant Macready of the 30th – the actor's brother – could see 'helmets falling, cavaliers starting from their seats with convulsive springs ... horses plunging and rearing in the agonies of fright and pain.' Bullets clattered against the breastplates of the cuirassiers, a noise the men likened to a violent hail-storm beating upon panes of glass. Some cavalry officers even tried to back their terrified horses into the squares, so that the creatures could not see the enemy.

The squares were charged not once, but three, four or even five times, as wave after wave of cavalry attacked, seemingly without any regard to their own safety. The squares took many casualties, but if an infantryman fell from a sabre cut or a bullet from a cavalryman's carbine, another stepped forward from the reserve to take his place. Still the squares would not break. The men had orders to fire low so that on the first discharge of muskets, the ground was quickly covered by fallen horses and their riders, halting the advance of those behind them and breaking the shock of the charge. One officer, watching the cavalrymen fall to the ground, thought the effect similar to a spoiled child crushing squadrons of brightly coloured toy soldiers. 'The thing was impossible,' thought Captain Mercer, pitying the French. Lieutenant Edward Sumner watched as a horse's head was split open by a shell, reduced in an instant to a burst of crimson and orange pulp. Fragments of shell and canister shot sliced into the horses, cutting open their sides and backs and legs, reminding him of freshly slaughtered cattle he had once seen on display in London. But inside the squares, the infantry, too, were suffering, suffocated by the smoke and the smell of burnt cartridges. It was impossible to move without treading upon a wounded comrade, or upon the bodies of the dead; and there were loud groans from those who lay injured. Ensign Gronow remembered that 'our square was a perfect hospital, being full of dead, dying and mutilated soldiers.'

A great plume of black smoke hung over the battlefield, as Hougoumont continued to burn, but the Allied army was winning the engagement on the ridge. While more than sixty Allied cannon had been over-run, they had not been spiked, to put them beyond use. Nor had the charge on the squares been successful. Every army trained its horses to run at infantry, usually at special field days, but they were also taught to pull up before impact, or to swerve round the flanks, and there was no horse in existence that would charge at bayonets. So the first line of French cavalry had simply opened up, pouring right and left as it sought to avoid the raking fire from the squares. The following line had done the same, so that it appeared to the men as if a fast-flowing river had been divided by a great rock which lay in its path, swirling around the obstacle where it had been cut in two. 'Not a single individual set an example of soldier-like devotedness by rushing upon the bristling bayonets,' noted the future battlefield tour guide, Private Edward Cotton of the 7th Hussars.

For the French the consequences were disastrous. They lost all order, and as each line of cavalry charged forward they crashed into the men in front, a collision of men and horses, caught up in the intersections between the Allied squares. 'It was pitiable to witness the agony of the poor horses, which really seemed conscious of the dangers that surrounded them,' Ensign Gronow noted. 'We often saw a poor wounded animal raise its head, as if looking for its rider to afford him aid.' By the time they had reached the rear of the squares, men from different cavalry regiments had become mixed up, leaving themselves unsure of what to do and where to go, under fire from all sides and vulnerable to an Allied counter-attack. Every time the Allied squares fired, men and horses would fall, and Captain Mercer saw survivors struggling with each other, using the pommels of their swords to fight their way out of the mêlée, intent only on saving themselves.

The Anglo-Allied cavalry, in perfect order, now charged at the leading units of the enemy. Uxbridge rallied regiment after regiment to drive the French back through the squares, over the ridge and down the slope. This time the Allied cavalry charge was disciplined, and most men heard the order to return. 'On this memorable day the 1st Light Dragoons, King's German Legion, attacked enemy cavalry a total of nine times,' remembered Lieutenant William Fricke, a Peninsula veteran who was badly wounded at Waterloo, 'whereby the enemy were prevented from forming a breakthrough three times.'

At Hougoumont, then La Haye Sainte, and now on the ridge, the Anglo-Allied had held firm. The Duke of Wellington, pleased with the success, asked Lt.-Col. James Stanhope of the 1st Foot Guards for the time. It was twenty-past-four and he claimed he had every reason to be confident. 'The battle is mine,' he concluded, 'and if the Prussians arrive soon, there will be an end of the war.' Perhaps to encourage his men who had withstood such punishment, Wellington was being optimistic. The battle was finely poised, and it was unclear how much more his army could take before its defences finally cracked.

For the Anglo-Allied soldiers, it would be a long afternoon. They had taken heavy casualties and would doubtless take more before the day was done. But it was their battle, a great and glorious defence which was theirs and theirs alone. At the time, and when they came to look back on it, the Prussian advance, though desperately needed, was of little or no consequence at all. Against the infantry and cavalry, and at Hougoumont and at La Haye Sainte, they had beaten back the French. No wonder the high command thought that William Siborne could have chosen any of these, very British, scenes to model – if only he had not already made up his mind.

IX

Further remarks upon Sir W. Gordon's letter and Colonel Ellicombe's memorandum

Dublin, 7 November 1834

I cannot persuade myself that there are not to be found, among the mass of surviving Waterloo officers, more particularly among those who held important commands on the day, many, who even supposing them not to retain a vivid recollection of *all* the distinguishing features of *the last great action in which they were engaged*, are fully able to answer the simple question 'What was the formation and position of the regiment or battery at the moment the French Imperial Guards reached the crest of the right of our position' – a moment so definite, so distinct, and so critical.

Nor can I conceive how an attempt to illustrate more in detail the main feature of the Battle 'must in a great measure tend to weaken the high authority of the Duke of Wellington's Despatch', for it will contain nothing at variance with one syllable of that document, and moreover, I do not intend to fasten a single figure upon my Model until I shall have submitted for His Grace's approval and correction, a plan of the action, showing the manner in which I propose to distribute the troops at the moment in question.

Siborne

William Siborne was so impressed by the bravery of the infantry squares that he chose to model the cavalry charge as one of 'the other prominent parts of the Battle' – though he never completed the task. Of all the scenes from the battle that he could have chosen, apart from the 'last great action', the defeat of the French cavalry was the most spectacular. True, it was achieved, as was the defence of Hougoumont, by obduracy rather than brilliance, but it was entirely down to the courage and resolve of Wellington's men, without Prussian help, in the face of an overwhelming, thunderous charge of horsemen. Obduracy is not easily depicted on a model, but it required strong nerves and character to hold the ridge against the French attacks. Both these qualities the soldiers showed in abundance, and they were proud to look back on what they had endured, with extraordinary stories of survival.

As the French again rode out across the valley, with artillery shells passing overhead, Captain Mercer watched 'a cloud of skirmishers' attack his battery with 'a fire of carbines and pistols from only forty yards away.' Mercer knew that to return fire too early would merely bring the cavalry down upon them before they had time to reload. So, absurdly, to encourage his men, he jumped on his horse in front of his own battery 'and began a promenade up and down' as if he was on a gentle country trot. He saw that an enemy cavalryman was far too close for comfort, but could not betray his anxiety in front of his own men. The cavalryman fired at him, and missed. Mercer was so relieved to have survived that he wagged a finger, as if in admonishment, then realised how ridiculously he was behaving. The cavalryman had a second chance. Mercer heard the shot as his enemy reloaded and fired again. The ball sped past the back of his neck and went straight into the head of Private Miller, the leading driver of one of his guns.

A fresh cavalry charge was approaching. The men still had to ride through a fusillade of canister from the Allied artillery, and death for some was certain. But this time they would be less exposed to a counter-attack from the Anglo-Allied army because Ney had been careful to keep some of his horsemen in reserve. In the course of the second hour of the attacks, an additional 4000 horsemen were thrown into the battle, another ten regiments and thirty-three squadrons, including a heavy cavalry division. Otherwise, it was as if the two sides had decided upon a replay of the first hour of the assault.

Mercer saw an officer in rich uniform, his breast covered in decorations. Both sides drew breath, the artillerymen waiting as the cavalry moved closer. Finally, Mercer gave the order for the guns to fire. The Allied artillery was double-shotted with both canister and roundshot, or with a double round of canister, causing carnage among the advancing cavalry. The front rank of horses again collapsed, and men and animals fell to the ground where they joined the victims of the first, failed attack. 'I allowed them to advance unmolested until the head of the column might have been about fifty or sixty yards from us, and then gave the word, "Fire!" The effect was terrible. Nearly the whole leading rank fell at once; and the roundshot, penetrating the column carried confusion throughout its extent. The ground, already encumbered with victims of the first struggle, became now almost impossible. Still, however, these devoted warriors struggled on, intent only on reaching us. Those who pushed forward over the heaps of carcasses of men and horses gained but a few paces in advance, there to fall in their turn and add to the difficulties of those succeeding them.'

For a while, across the front, the French appeared to have the upper hand. Even in a lull in the fighting, there were casualties. 'An ammunition cart blew up near us, smashing men and horses,' Ensign Wheatley noted in his diary. 'I took a calm survey of the field around and felt shocked at the sight of the broken armour, lifeless bodies, murdered horses. Shattered wheels, caps, helmets, swords, muskets, pistols, still and silent. Here and there a frightened horse would rush across the plain trampling on the dying and the dead. Three or four poor wounded animals standing on three legs, the other dangling before (them). We killed several of these unfortunate beasts and it would have been an equal charity to have performed the same operation on the wriggling, feverish, mortally lacerated soldiers as they rolled on the ground.' But each time, the defenders managed to close ranks, covering the gaps.

Between each cavalry charge, the French artillery fired endless rounds into the Allied squares, rounds which might tear three or four bodies apart with a single shot which might then bounce into a nearby square to wreak as much destruction again, while shells exploded to destroy six or seven lives at a time. The shots came in 'as thick as hail' according to Private Tom Morris, of the 73rd Foot, who wrote a minor classic, *Recollections of Military Service in 1813–15* which was first published in 1845. Morris saw men falling all around him, blood streaming from an eye wound, or a shredded leg. Morris was a twenty-year-old Cockney who always thought he knew best, and he was invariably critical of anyone in command, especially his veteran company commander. On this occasion, there was no one he could blame. A howitzer shell landed in front of his battalion, and the men could only watch helplessly as its fuse burned down, then try to take shelter against the explosion. Morris himself was hit by a shell fragment that cut his left cheek so that the blood poured out over his clothes. He was lucky: seventeen of his colleagues were wounded more seriously, or were already dead. 'The carnage was frightful,' Edmund Wheatley wrote in his diary. 'The balls which missed us mowed down the Dutch behind us, and swept away many of the closely embattled cavalry behind them. I saw a cannonball take away a colonel of the Nassau regiment so cleanly that the horse never moved from under him.'

Wellington sent forward Adam's infantry brigade, the strongest in the British army, to protect the squares of Brunswick infantry, which were held to be in panic, by forming a new front line near Hougoumont's Great Orchard. There was good reason for him to do so. Captain Mercer saw that 'the Brunswickers were falling fast – the shot every moment making great gaps in their squares . . . every moment I feared they would throw down their arms and flee; but their officers and sergeants behaved nobly . . . managing to keep their squares closed in spite of the carnage made amongst them.'

Adam's brigade was made of sterner stuff: his men were mainly veterans of the Peninsula. In this position, they were an obvious target for the French guns. Ensign William Leeke saw a French artilleryman go through the whole process of sponging out one of the guns and reloading it. He could see that the gun was pointing at him. 'When it was discharged I caught sight of the ball, which appeared to be in a direct line for me. I thought, shall I move? No! I gathered myself up, and stood firm, with the colour in my right hand. I do not exactly know the rapidity with which cannonballs fly, but I think that two seconds elapsed from the time I saw this shot leave the gun until it struck the front face of the square ... It was fired at some elevation and struck the front man about the knees, and coming to the ground under the rear man of the four, whom it most severely wounded, it rose, and passing within an inch or two of the colour pole, went over the rear face of the square without doing further injury.'

If the French had been able to maintain the intensity of their attacks, then it is possible that defenders would have cracked. But the attacks, uphill on soft ground, lacked pace and the cavalry charges lacked coordination against a resolute infantry in squares. The tide was beginning to turn. With every repeated charge, little by little, and almost imperceptibly at first, the strength of the assault was beginning to wane. The horses were exhausted from the long charge, and stood still, blown, refusing to move any further. Once again, the French had seized the British guns, but once again they had failed to spike them, and the pointlessness of their capture stood as a metaphor for the futility of the cavalry charges themselves, a magnificent, brave, irresistible spectacle, which was ultimately flawed.

From the smoke which hung over the crest of the Allied ridge emerged the survivors of the charge, broken squadrons, shattered divisions, a straggle of dejected men on foot. Among them was Marshal Ney who stood, resolute, next to a captured British gun, hitting its muzzle again and again with the blade of his sword. But for all his defiance, he could not turn the course of events, nor mask the truth of what was happening. He tried, of course, finding a fresh horse after a fourth was shot from under him and he led his men over the ridge again. Each time, and there were perhaps half a dozen such charges in all, the horses were slower than before. Each time the squares held firm and each time the Anglo-Allied gave chase when the French retreated. And each time, the heap of dead and dying on the ground, of both men and horses, grew larger. Captain Rudyard of the Royal Artillery: 'The cuirassiers and cavalry might have charged through the battery as often as six or seven times, driving us into the squares ...

In general, as a squadron or two came up the slope on our immediate front, and on their moving off at the appearance of our cavalry charging, we took advantage to send destruction after them, and when advancing on our fire I have seen four or five men and horses piled upon each other like cards, the men not having even been displaced from the saddle, the effect of cannister.'

Ney's dream of a glorious cavalry victory was coming to an end. The great assault was failing.

Despite the failure of the cavalry charges, Napoleon was certain that Wellington's line would crack. He told Ney that the farmhouse of La Haye Sainte held the key, and that with its capture the rest of the enemy's defences would crumble. Once again the fiercest fighting would be for a key outpost held by a handful of men against overwhelming odds, the farm of La Haye Sainte, so that, once again, the stories from the battle would concentrate on the heroics of the beleaguered Anglo-Allied army in the face of almost certain defeat.

La Haye Sainte was more vulnerable than it had ever been, despite the bravery of the men inside. For hour after hour, they had resisted French attacks. Eighteen-year-old George Drummond Graeme, a Scottish lieutenant with the 2nd Light Battalion of the King's German Legion, noted that 'the ground was literally covered with French killed and wounded, even to the astonishment of my oldest soldiers, who said they had never witnessed such a sight. The French wounded were calling out "*Vive l'Empereur*", and I saw a poor fellow, lying with both his legs shattered, trying to destroy himself with his own sword, which I ordered my servant to take from him.'

The farm of La Haye Sainte was strategically important to Wellington because it was only 200 metres from the ridge which his men were holding. Like Hougoumont, it was a fastness which could be used to break up enemy attacks, but which, if captured, could be turned into a base from which the French could advance. It was built on a far smaller scale than Hougoumont, around three sides of a square, and it was harder to defend. On the north side, facing the Allied forces, was the farmhouse itself, with some stables and a kitchen garden; on the west side there were the rest of the stables and cow-houses; on the south side, facing the French, was a large barn and an orchard. A brick wall, running alongside the Brussels road, linked the main buildings, to complete a quadrangle. Near the centre of the wall was a lean-to which was called the 'piggery'.

Despite the wall, there were several obvious weak points to La Haye Sainte's defences: there was a large gate, opposite the barn, which opened through the boundary wall onto the road, and a doorway close to the dwelling-house; there was another gate at the end of the stables, and a large door in the barn, both of which opened out into the fields. There was also a passage which ran right through the house, and led from the farmyard into the kitchen garden. So little thought had been given to the farm's defences, unlike Hougoumont, that the vast barn door had been broken up for firewood the previous evening. But as at Hougoumont, the defenders had managed to build an abatis, an obstacle made from the branches of trees, to block the Brussels to Charleroi road at the south end of the boundary wall.

La Haye Sainte was held by Major George Baring and six companies

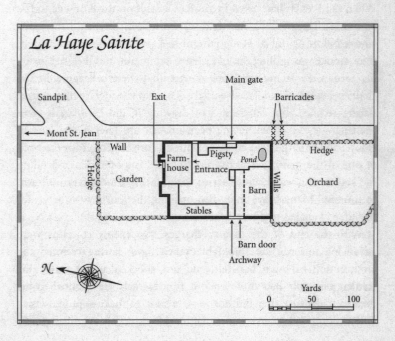

of the 2nd Light Battalion of the King's German Legion, part of Colonel Ompteda's 2nd KGL Brigade, with several companies posted in the orchard, and one in the garden. Baring was a veteran of a decade's fighting abroad, including six years in the Peninsula where he had been wounded in the bloody battle of Albuera. But he had never been in a tighter spot.

By about five o'clock, the defenders were dangerously short of ammunition, despite Baring's repeated pleas for supplies to be sent through from the British lines. Baring had instead received a stream of reinforcements, a hundred and fifty men from a Light Company of Nassauers. Welcome as the extra troops were, they were not what Baring wanted, and he had become impatient. 'It could not compensate for the want of ammunition, which every moment increased, so that after half an hour more of uninterrupted fighting, I sent off an officer with the same request.'

With every passing hour, the battle for La Haye Sainte had come to resemble the fight for Hougoumont, in both intensity and tactics. When the French had failed in another assault on the entrance to the barn at La Haye Sainte, they had set the roof on fire, as if the black smoke billowing out of Hougoumont had given them the idea. Soon, thick smoke was spilling out of La Haye Sainte too, and the men inside the farm were facing the same danger that their colleagues in the château complex had faced earlier. 'There was water in the court,' Baring recalled, but 'all means of drawing it and carrying it were wanting – every vessel having been broken up. Luckily the Nassau troops carried large field cooking kettles; I tore a kettle from the back of one of the men; several officers followed my example, and filling the kettles with water, they carried them, facing almost certain death, to the fire.' Many brave men died, making the journey to the pond, but they managed to douse the flames.

With the end of the cavalry charges, two enemy columns were advancing towards the smoke-blackened farm. Baring counted the ammunition his men had left, and was shocked at the result: his soldiers had only had three or four rounds each. He shouted to his men to make sure they did not waste a shot, to make sure that every bullet counted. 'I received one unanimous reply: "No man will desert you – we will fight and die with you!" Never had I felt myself so elevated: – but never also placed in so painful a position, where honour contended with a feeling for safety of the men who had given me such an unbounded proof of their confidence.' For Baring knew it was inconceivable that the defenders could continue to hold out, unless fresh supplies came through.

No ammunition could be spared to help Baring's tiny garrison. Yet his men were about to face a French attack which was more furious than any they had experienced that day, and the open entrance to the barn was still vulnerable. As the columns moved towards the farm, the defenders tried to heed their leader's instruction not to waste a bullet. They were down to three or four cartridges each. But it was impossible to defend the garrison without firing, and yet for every shot which rang out, the defenders' chances of survival were diminishing, even as the bullets hit their targets. Once more, Baring sent a desperate request back to his own lines: 'every shot that was now fired increased my uneasiness and anxiety. I sent again to the rear with the positive statement that I must and would leave the place if no ammunition was sent me. This was also without effect. Even the officers, who, during the whole day, had shown the greatest courage, represented to me the impossibility of retaining the post under such circumstances.' Once more, La Haye Sainte's barn was set on fire, and once more the flames were put out. But soon the weight of numbers deployed by the French began to tell, and suddenly the enemy had reached the gates, and then just as quickly the infantrymen were wielding great axes and the axes were crashing down upon the timber, almost as if the battle for Hougoumont had transferred itself to La Haye Sainte but this time with a greater prospect of success. The axes did their job and the gates were collapsing. The French had smashed their way into the stables. The door to La Haye Sainte lay open. It was six o'clock.

Only a few hours before, the weight of numbers in the tightly packed columns had caused such a loss of life at La Haye Sainte that French bodies had been put to use as a grisly barricade; now, as the attackers filed through an opening which had been narrowed by a barricade, all that stood in their way was fifteen inches of triangular metal on the end of the defenders' guns,. For a few minutes the garrison held firm, but it was clear that the men were making a last, defiant stand. The French climbed the outer walls, and captured the roof, from where they picked off the exhausted defenders. Reluctantly Baring gave the order to withdraw. 'Inexpressibly painful as the decision was to me of giving up the place, my feeling of duty as man overcame that of honour, and I gave the order to retire through the house into the garden.'

The French, bolstered by a brigade from Durutte's 4th Infantry Division, swarmed into the farm, passing through its narrow alleyways, into its rooms and across its courtyard, slaughtering the defenders in revenge for the heavy casualties they had taken during the day. Lt. George Drummond Graeme was scrambling to get into the back garden: 'We all had to pass through a narrow passage. We wanted to halt the men and make one more charge, but it was impossible; the fellows were firing down the passage . . .' A Frenchman had Graeme in his sights. 'He was about five yards off, and levelling his piece just at me, when the officer stabbed him in the mouth and out through his neck; he fell immediately. But now they flocked in . . . and some wounded soldiers of ours who lay there and cried out "pardon" were shot, the monsters saying "Take that for the fine defence you have made . . ." An officer and four men came first in; the officer got me by the collar, and said to his men, "*C'est ce coquin.*" Immediately the fellows had their bayonets down, and made a dead stick at me, which I parried off with my sword, the officer always running about and then coming to me again and shaking me by the collar; but they all looked so frightened and pale as ashes, I thought, "You shan't keep me," and I bolted off through the lobby; they fired two shots after me, and cried out, "*Coquin,*" but did not follow me.'

After more than eight hours of fighting, after countless infantry and cavalry attacks on the Anglo-Allied line, the French had finally gained a victory. They moved quickly to secure their prize, making good its defences. Engineers moved in to erect firing platforms; more loopholes were carved into the walls; gates and doors were strengthened and barricaded. The main gate leading to the Genappe road was smashed with an axe, like Hougoumont's north gate before it, except this was a gesture of finality and not a temporary triumph. The survivors gave up hope of recapturing the farm, and trailed back to the ridge. Hour by hour, about four hundred men had fought four thousand, and the greater force had won. The battle was now 'a wild one', recalled John Kincaid. 'It was a sort of duelling post between the two armies, every half-hour showing a meeting of some kind upon it ... men's lives were held very cheap.'

The capture of La Haye Sainte was perhaps inevitable: its strategic importance had not properly been recognised by the Anglo-Allied army, which seemed to give greater priority to Hougoumont. Five times its defenders had asked for ammunition and five times they had been denied. Now Wellington would pay the price. The farm's capture moved the French front-line forward, giving them the chance to launch a wave of fresh attacks against his defences from close range, placing the centre of the Anglo-Allied army in jeopardy. Among the soldiers who saw the danger unfold over the next two hours was the Cheshire officer Lt.-Col. William Tomkinson, who wrote in his diary: 'The occupation of La Haye Sainte enabled the enemy to form a considerable body of troops close in its rear, and from that point to commence attacks on the troops in position immediately above the house. Parties of cuirassiers, from two to three squadrons and frequently less, occasionally supported by a few infantry, and in many instances without infantry, rode up to the hill occupied by our troops.'

At six-thirty, Ney moved his men around the sides of the building, less than a hundred metres from the enemy, and he moved a horse artillery brigade to fire on the Anglo-Allied lines from an advanced position, protected by the garden hedge and the small hills which lay alongside the farm. From here, the guns could fire canister at Kempt's brigade behind the Wavre road. As the bullets flew down on them, the men of the 95th Rifles, stationed on the knoll near the sandpit, could also feel the instant impact of the French success. Captain Jonathan Leach, who took command of the 95th when two senior officers were wounded, told Siborne that he thought the capture of La Haye Sainte had been 'highly disastrous ... The French instantly filled the house with swarms of sharp-shooters, whose deadly fire precluded the possibility of our holding the knoll and the ground immediately about it, and they established also a strong and numerous line of infantry, extending along the line of Kempt's brigade.'

Across the battlefield, the situation for the allies was now critical. All Wellington could do, like Blücher before him at Ligny, was to use attack as a form of defence. Lt.-Gen. Charles Alten, the commander of the 3rd British Division, ordered a battalion led by Colonel Christian von Ompteda, which was in square, to move against the infantry. Ompteda was no coward, but he knew from his own observations that enemy cavalry were lurking in a hollow in the ground behind the front line of sharp-shooters. He was in the middle of explaining his reservations to Alten, when the Prince of Orange gave him the order to attack. Again Ompteda expressed his unhappiness, but the Prince refused to listen, and not only repeated the order but told the colonel he was not allowed to argue. Ompteda was sure what his fate would be, but he gathered together the 5th Line Battalion of the King's German legion, put himself at its head, and led it towards the tirailleurs whose fire was posing such a menace. Edmund Wheatley, the battalion's ensign, remembered that 'Colonel Ompteda ordered us instantly into line to charge, with a strong injunction to "walk" forward until he gave the word. When within sixty yards he cried "charge", we ran forward *huzzaing*. The trumpet sounded and no one but a soldier can describe the thrill one instantly feels in such an awful moment.'

At first, it seemed as if the Prince of Orange had been right. The enemy ran away in the face of the attack, with Colonel Ompteda leading the way on horseback, seeking refuge behind the hedges near the garden of La Haye Sainte. Captain John Berger of the 5th Line Battalion thought the French 'seemed astonished at the extraordinary calm approach of the solitary horseman, whose white plume showed him to be an officer of high rank.' Ompteda jumped the garden hedge and drew his sword, but disappeared from sight, swallowed up by a throng of enemy infantry and cavalry. Among the advance party was Edmund Wheatley: 'I found myself in contact with a French officer but . . . he fell by an unknown hand. I then ran at a drummer, but he leaped over a ditch through a hedge in which he stuck fast. I heard a cry of "the cavalry, the cavalry!"' The next moment, as Ompteda had feared, the ranks of cuirassiers appeared, attacking the right flank of his men, rolling up his line in an instant, so that there was no escape. Only thirty men made it back to the relative safety of the Hollow Way.

Wheatley, who had been knocked out, came to and saw that Ompteda was among the dead, shot through the neck at close range. 'On recovering my senses, I looked up and found myself, bareheaded, in a clay ditch with a violent headache. Close by me lay Colonel Ompteda on his back, his head stretched back with his mouth open, and a hole in his throat. A Frenchman's arm across my leg.' The powder marks on Ompteda's collar showed he had been shot at close range.

Battalions had shrunk in size to a mere handful of men; cavalry brigades had been reduced to less than the strength of a regiment; raw recruits had taken the place of captains. There was nothing the men could do, except pray, or send messages to Wellington begging for reinforcements which never came because none could be spared. All day they had been ordered to wait, a deliberate tactic punctuated by occasional Anglo-Allied attacks, but now the strategy declined into one of immobile passivity, in place of which there was no alternative and from which there seemed to be no escape. But theirs had been a vital contribution to the glorious victory. By the same token, the Prussians could not be credited with helping out at all.

By late afternoon, the main Prussian army had in fact moved closer to the battlefield. In doing so, the history of the battle, and Siborne's Model of its climax, became more complex, for no longer could events at Waterloo be seen as the exclusive preserve of the Anglo-Allied army. The soldiers of IV Corps had crossed the Lasne stream, and the right flank of the French line was now within their sights. Their plan was to attack when the whole Corps had gathered behind the woods near the hamlet of Frischermont, which lay to the east of Napoleon's line, but almost level with it, some 1500 metres south of Wellington's left wing. Lt.-Col. William Tomkinson thought it was a decisive moment, albeit a strange one, for neither he nor the Duke was accustomed to relying on an ally: 'We saw a column advance out of a wood beyond Frischermont, and anxiously waited to ascertain by the fire whether it was a corps joining the enemy or the expected Prussians. They had artillery with their advance, and ere long we saw them forming to their front, and their guns open against the enemy. Such a reinforcement during an action was an occurrence so different from former days in the

Pensinsula, where everything centred in the British army, that it appeared decisive of the fate of the day.'

The leading Prussian columns had emerged from the woods, to be rewarded with a spectacular panorama of the battle, when Blücher saw that, with Napoleon's attack on the Anglo-Allied centre, the balance of the conflict was shifting. The key to the battle would be control of the village which lay a mile and a half downhill to the south, Plancenoit. If Blücher could capture it, then he would control the roads which ran south and east, and with it the French army's line of retreat. A Prussian infantry brigade, virtually the size of a division in Wellington's army, advanced along the straight road which led to the village. Belatedly, the French realised the danger and tried to shore up their position, sending one of General Lobau's brigades from the 6th Corps to occupy the village and, slightly to its north, three more brigades, two cavalry divisions, and nearly forty guns.

In the centre of Plancenoit, the church was the strongest defensive position, occupying the highest point in the village, so that its spire could be seen across the battleground. It was encircled by a low stone wall, which faced onto a steep bank, and on the lower ground, by

Plancenoit – The Great Model

houses and hedges. In this corner of the battlefield, as at La Haye Sainte and Hougoumont, the battle would be fought in a confined space, with little room for the two sides to manoeuvre, but with plenty of room for bloodshed. Shortly before six, the Prussians attacked the village from both sides, two battalions to the right and two to the left. Two columns of the 15th Regiment advanced to the church, although it cost them dear, as the French gunfire rained down on them. There is no clear account of how long the fighting lasted, or of how long it took the Prussians to capture the village. But the consequences of their success were clear. Napoleon was forced to divert all eight battalions of the Young Guard to come to Lobau's aid, men he could ill-afford to spare.

Napoleon's action had a swift effect, and as the contest tilted, his Young Guard quickly ejected the Prussians from the village. In each sector of the battlefield, therefore, the contest was on a knife-edge. Though he had been supported by the arrival of some of Ziethen's men, Wellington was so hard-pressed by Napoleon's frontal assault that it seemed as if his line must give at any moment; away to the east, Lt.-Gen. Thielemann and his III Corps were heavily outnumbered at Wavre; and at Plancenoit the battle could go either way. Blücher made his mind up: he would not send reinforcements to Thielemann but he would make his stand among the hedges, stone walls and houses of the village. The outcome of the battle would be decided not with a great military manoeuvre, like the infantry and cavalry charges on the fields of Waterloo, but by bloody, brutal, vicious hand-to-hand fighting in a country churchyard.

Three brigades from the Prussian IV Corps moved forward, the 14th, 15th and 16th, to prepare for another assault on the village centre. From behind the churchyard wall, a heavy fire of canister and musket forced them to withdraw, taking heavy losses. Again they rallied, and again they charged, and again they were compelled to pull back. Encouraged, the French skirmishers decided to advance from their protected positions. It was a crucial error. It enabled the Prussians to counter-attack with cavalry, encircling the village in a pincer attack from both left and right, and, as a regimental history makes clear, 'the village was recaptured and a large number of enemy guardsmen were

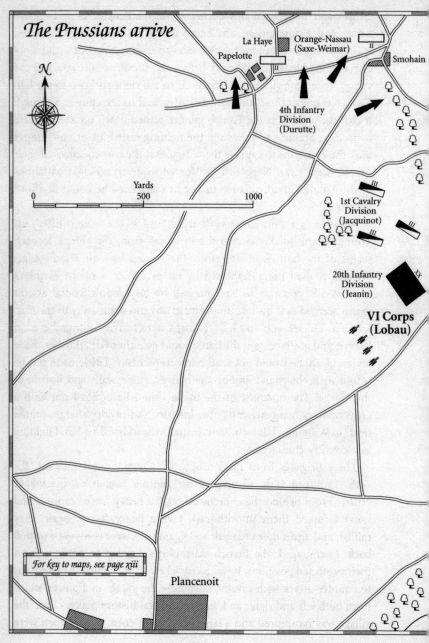

The Prussians arrive

La Haye
Papelotte
Orange-Nassau
(Saxe-Weimar)
II
Smohain
II

4th Infantry
Division
(Durutte)

N

Yards
0   500   1000

1st Cavalry
Division
(Jacquinot)

20th Infantry
Division
(Jeanin)

**VI Corps
(Lobau)**

For key to maps, see page xiii

Plancenoit

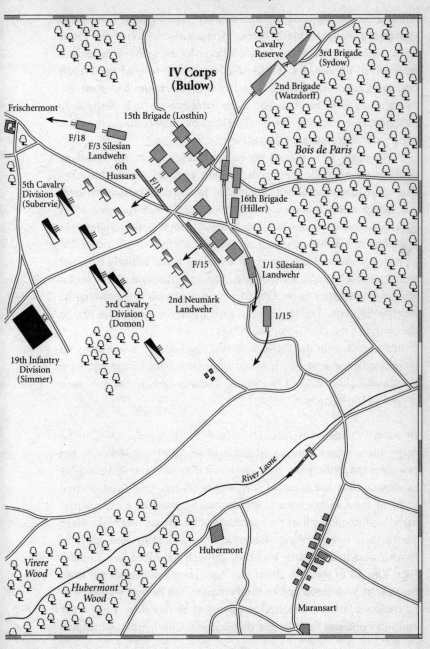

IV Corps (Bulow)

Cavalry Reserve

3rd Brigade (Sydow)

2nd Brigade (Watzdorff)

Frischermont

15th Brigade (Losthin)

F/18

F/3 Silesian Landwehr

6th Hussars

Bois de Paris

F/18

5th Cavalry Division (Subervie)

16th Brigade (Hiller)

1/1 Silesian Landwehr

F/15

1/15

3rd Cavalry Division (Domon)

2nd Neumârk Landwehr

19th Infantry Division (Simmer)

River Lasne

Hubermont

Virere Wood

Hubermont Wood

Maransart

either killed or captured in close combat.' The fighting around the churchyard was particularly fierce. 'Here a vicious, bloody and bitter battle took place.' The cavalry took heavy losses, and two brigadiers were killed. All day, the Anglo-Allied army had resisted the French onslaught, and countless men had died as the hours had gone by, hours in which the Prussians were confidently, then desperately expected. Now they too were spilling their blood liberally on the same battleground occupied by the two armies.

If Napoleon were to lose the battle for Plancenoit, the Prussians could attack his right wing from behind and could prevent his army from retreating, and already roundshot fired from Prussian batteries was falling among his men on either side of his vantage-point at La Belle Alliance. He could still win the Battle of Waterloo, indeed his prospects still looked as strong as Wellington's line looked weak. But he had to make sure of victory, for if he lost, it was unlikely his army would survive to fight another day. Almost in desperation, he sent a mere two battalions of the Old Guard to Plancenoit. Extraordinarily, barely a thousand French veterans, their drums beating, again turned the course of the contest for the village.

But overall, with the Prussian arrival, the odds on a stalemate, an inconclusive outcome which would allow both sides to regroup, were lengthening, like the feeble evening shadows cast by the sun as it dipped to the horizon.

By now, Wellington desperately needed Prussian help. Out on the ridge, many Allied guns stood unattended, silent memorials to the casualties the artillerymen had taken. Not only were the soldiers short of ammunition, but many of their senior officers were dead, leaving some of the infantry squares under the command of inexperienced men. With the French in the ascendant, after the capture of La Haye Sainte, there was no respite. Casualties were mounting, and scores of injured were making their way back through the Allied line. Captain John Kincaid of the 95th Rifles may have been battle-hardened from his time at Walcheren and in the Peninsula, but he was worried that he could see little but the dead and dying of his own side: 'I felt weary and worn out, less from fatigue than anxiety. Our division, which had stood upwards of five thousand men at the commencement of the battle, had gradually dwindled down into a solitary line of skirmishers. The twenty-seventh regiment were lying literally dead, in square, a few yards behind us. The smoke still hung so thick about us that we could see nothing. I walked a little way to each flank, to endeavour to get a glimpse of what was going on; but nothing met my eye except the mangled remains of men and horses, and I was obliged to return to my post as wise as I went.'

The defenders of Hougoumont, too, were coming under the most intense pressure, forced to withstand a renewed French onslaught, from an enemy which believed that now La Haye Sainte had fallen, the château, too, would be toppled. By now all Hougoumont's outhouses were on fire, except those near the wood. The men inside were slowly suffocating from the smoke, which choked their lungs, and blurred their vision, so that the buildings which had afforded them such protection became gradually indistinct, as if the battle was becoming an hallucination, an event which was becoming gradually unreal the more the battle threatened. But the château's blackened fortifications continued to protect the men from their fate.

It was half-past-six in the evening, and Wellington, it was noted, kept glancing anxiously to the east, looking for the help of the Prussians which was needed more than ever. For the greater part of the day the Duke had expected, believed and hoped for their arrival. Now, frustratingly, men from Ziethen's I Corps were within sight of the main battlefield, engaged in clashes on the far right of the French line. Wellington sent an aide-de-compte, John Freemantle, a lieutenant-colonel in the 2nd Foot Guards, along the Namur road towards the Prussian forces. 'Sir Horace Seymour came and reported to the Duke of Wellington that he had seen the Prussian column. The Duke called upon me to go to the head of their column and ask for 3000 men to supply our losses . . .' It seemed to Ziethen as if the Anglo-Allied effort was failing and he began to wonder if he should make good his retreat before he too was swept away by the overwhelming tide.

Ziethen was pulled by conflicting military demands. His chief of staff arrived back from a meeting with Wellington's officers: the position of the Nassauers on the left wing of the Anglo-Allied army had worsened, and Ziethen's men were needed there more urgently than ever. But his own commander, Blücher, was desperate for support against the Young Guard at Plancenoit, and had demanded that the 1 Corps move to support him there. Ziethen could not disobey an order, so he started to move his men towards the tiny village.

Marshal Ney could see that victory was within his grasp. The centre of the Anglo-Allied line had been thinned out by the continual bombardment. French artillery had been manoeuvred further forward so that from only a short distance away the barrels of their guns were facing two squares of infantry, formed by the 3rd Battalion of the 1st Foot Guards, under Maj.-Gen. Maitland's leadership, and by the 30th (Cambridgeshire) and 73rd Regiments which had come together to create a single corps. The guns opened fire, sending their shot directly into the two squares, and carving wide gaps in the ranks. Wounded men, with ghastly injuries, staggered back through the lines, or were carried on stretchers by the bandsmen towards the field hospitals at Mont St Jean or Waterloo.

One man's intervention helped to change the course of the battle. General Muffling rode furiously along the ridge occupied by the Anglo-Allied army, his role as Blücher's liaison officer in Wellington's headquarters making him anxious about the apparent lack of progress by his countrymen. What he saw, when he arrived at the farm of Papelotte, appalled him: Ziethen and his I Army Corps were moving away from the battlefield. Muffling rode on alone, and stopped him in the valley below the farm. The centre of the Anglo-Allied line was so fragile, he said, that Ziethen had to send his men. 'The battle is lost unless you come back at once.' Finally, Ziethen accepted that the exigencies of the battle took precedence over the orders of his commanding officer, and within quarter of an hour, his advance guard, four lines of his men, the 1st Brigade, reserve cavalry and three batteries, took up their positions in battle order at La Lavette, the hussars on the right wing joining up, at last, with Wellington's army.

It had taken him a full day, but unwittingly Blücher had at last fulfilled the promise he had made to Wellington to come to his support. On the rolling fields of Waterloo, the contest had finally become the battle of three armies. And in becoming so, its history, for William

Siborne, became dangerously complicated. How could Wellington be accorded the full share of victory that he and his supporters demanded, when the Prussians had finally joined the battle?

X

Dublin, 7 November 1834

After all . . . there are insurmountable obstacles to an abandonment of my original design. More than a hundred of my circulars have already been issued and I continue issuing them daily. I have made application to the French and to the Prussian military authorities for information with respect to the 'Crisis.'

I have made and have in hand, houses represented as on fire, others as shattered with shot and shell. I have several thousands of figures, representing men in the act of firing and such, and as any alteration now would be attended with incredible inconvenience, sacrifice of labour, great loss of precious time and very heavy expense, I trust that in expressing my earnest wish to complete my work upon the plan with which I at first set out I may not be deemed deficient in proper deference and submission to the military authorities or undeserving of their favourable countenance and support.

Siborne

The problem William Siborne faced, as he sifted the evidence about the Crisis of the Battle and examined the different roles played by the three armies, was that as the fighting neared its climax, no soldier could tell clearly what was going on. 'I ask you to consider how little we knew of the actual overall circumstances and conditions,' wrote

Captain Albertus Cordemann of the King's German Legion, to Siborne. 'And also to consider how fierce and desperate the enemy attacks were . . .' It was probably the most acute observation Siborne was to receive. No single soldier could say definitively how the battle ended, and why Napoleon's men had suddenly turned and run. All they knew was that it was a great and glorious victory, and that it had been won by the Duke of Wellington's army alone. 'With respect to your present inquiry,' wrote Lt.-Col. Dawson Kelly, of the 73rd Foot, to Siborne, 'it is fully within my memory that the fog and smoke lay so heavy upon the ground that we could only ascertain the approach of the enemy by noise and clashing of arms which the French usually make in their advance to attack, and it has often occurred to me from the above circumstance (the heavy fog), that the accuracy and the particulars with which the *Crisis* has been so frequently and *so minutely* discussed, must have had a good deal of fancy in the narrative.' Dawson Kelly, from County Armagh, was a highly respected observer: towards the end of the battle, a sergeant of his regiment told him that all the officers in the 73rd had been killed or wounded, and although he was a staff officer, he had immediately taken charge.

The final stages of the battle were all the more confusing because victory occurred after a terrible final hour for the Anglo-Allied army. As Napoleon pressed home the attack, no unit suffered more than the 27th (Inniskilling) Regiment, whose ranks were thinned, and thinned again, by the continual French bombardment. The Inniskillings were a stationary, standing target at a range where it was almost impossible for the enemy gunners to miss, across a distance at which the devastation caused by canister, as it spread wickedly through the air, was terrible to behold. Even when reduced to statistics, rather than recalled as flesh and blood, the toll it took was shocking. The 27th Regiment had started the day two short of seven hundred men, and of these 480 had become casualties. Sixteen of their nineteen officers were killed or wounded. Within a few minutes, the Inniskillings had been shredded.

Along the ridge, some gun batteries lay disabled, and the artillerymen were exhausted after six hours of loading and firing their guns. On the Allied right of the high road, the guns in front of Ompteda and Kielmansegge's brigades were out of action, and two artillerymen could be glimpsed vainly trying to fire them, though they did not have enough ammunition to succeed. A French battery near La Haye Sainte opened up on Captain Mercer's troop: 'We suddenly became sensible of a most destructive flanking fire from a battery which had come, Lord knows how, and established itself on a knoll somewhat higher than the ground we stood on, and only about 400 or 500 yards a little advance of our left flank. The rapidity and precision of this fire were quite appalling. Every shot almost took effect, and I certainly expected we should all be annihilated. In some instances the horses of a gun or ammunition waggon remained, and all their drivers were killed. The whole livelong day had cost us nothing like this ... I sighed for my poor troop – it was already but a wreck.'

But thirty guns remained, double-shotted with canister, conserving their ammunition, waiting until the enemy was upon them. When asked, the Duke would simply say that it was the duty of the men to stand firm, not to retreat and not to attack, and that no reinforcements could be spared to replace any men who died, although they were dying in their hundreds, some with appalling injuries. Captain Sempronius Stretton of the 40th (2nd Somersetshire) Regiment: 'Towards the evening, whilst the regiment was in open column, a roundshot from the enemy took off the head of a captain near me, and striking his company on the left flank, put *hors de combat* more than twenty-five men. This was the most destructive shot I ever witnessed during a long period of service.' If any regiment epitomised the tactics Wellington had adopted throughout the course of the long, bloody day it was the 52nd. Its men had fought little, but they had been subjected to constant cannon-fire, and now they had been forced back some forty metres behind the ridge, behind the low bank that Mercer's men had used during the cavalry charges. Quite possibly Ensign William Leeke of the 1/52nd wished he had followed his father into the church. 'The roar of roundshot still continued, many only just clearing our heads – others, striking the top of the position and bounding over us – others, again, almost spent and rolling down gently towards us. One of these, when we were standing in line, came rolling down like a cricket-ball, so slowly that I was putting out my foot to stop it, when my colour-serjeant quickly begged me not to do so, and told me it might have seriously injured my foot. Exactly in front of me, when standing in line, lay, at a distance of two yards, a dead tortoise-shell kitten. It had probably been frightened out of Hougoumont, which was the nearest house to us, and about a quarter of a mile off.

'In front of our left company were several killed and wounded horses; some of the latter were lying, some standing, but some of both were eating the trodden down wheat or rye, notwithstanding that their legs were shot off, or that they were otherwise badly wounded. There was a peculiar smell at this time, arising from the mingling of the smell of the wheat trodden flat down with the smell of gunpowder.'

Leeke could see hundreds of his dead colleagues, scattered about him; below the bank there were more dying men wrapped in blankets, and then, grotesquely, he saw the ghastly mirror image of two men stumbling back together through the lines: 'To the right lay some twenty of our badly and mortally wounded men, covered by their blankets, which some of the poor fellows had got out from their knapsacks. I particularly remember at that time two poor fellows passing through the line to the rear, who, I think, must have had their arms carried away by the same cannon-shot, for they were both struck exactly in the same place, about four inches below the shoulder, the wounded arm being attached to the upper part by a very small portion of skin and flesh, and being supported by the man taking hold of the hand of that arm with his other hand.'

But Wellington had done what he could to strengthen the line in readiness for the French attack, bringing in the few reserves available to the centre, where the gunfire from La Haye Sainte had caused most damage; with the first Prussian reinforcements arriving, Sir Hussey Vivian started to move from the left wing to the rear of the centre with his cavalry brigade, to be followed by Sir John Vandeleur's. None of this could prevent the French from keeping up their fire from around La Haye Sainte, making the most of their captured possession. The consequences were appalling. The left square of Maj.-Gen. Kielmansegge's 1st Hanoverian Brigade, in particular, suffered dreadfully from the fire of two guns which the French had stationed in the northwest corner of the garden of La Haye Sainte, only a hundred paces away. The infantry could do nothing other than take the punishment, unable even to return fire because they feared hitting their own cavalry. More French guns were brought forward and they opened up on the right square of the same brigade, and within minutes an entire side of the square had been blown away, leaving the remaining men standing in a triangle. Their commander and many other officers fell, until finally the unit was reduced to a handful of men.

The Prince of Orange, Wellington's nominal deputy and a man who had not covered himself in glory through his military decision-making so far, could see that Wellington's centre was in danger of buckling, and so he ordered the Nassau Battalions to charge, and led the advance himself. In doing so, he was showing both bravery and determination, and independence too, for his tactics did not meet the demands of the Duke of Wellington's strategy. Whether he was wise to make such a manoeuvre was another matter. Very quickly, he was struck by a bullet in his left shoulder, and was invalided out of the remaining contest. His attack failed, and the Nassauers were forced to fall back. 'Through- out the whole of the two great battles of the 16th and 18th of June the Prince of Orange had displayed the greatest gallantry and the most ardent devotion to his country,' wrote Siborne. 'His conduct was the admiration of all, and the whole Anglo-Allied army rejoiced to find that the life which he had so freely exposed, had been spared for the future benefit and service of his native country, over which he now reigns in the hearts of his people.' It was another sign that Siborne's sympathies lay with the establishment, which made his fall from favour all the more puzzling to him, for his tribute was wide of the mark, given the Prince's misjudgements during the battle which had caused the loss of so many men.

The situation had become desperate by the time Wellington moved five battalions of Brunswick infantry to patch the centre of his line. They came under such heavy fire as soon as they arrived that they lost all shape and retreated, along with the brigades of Kruse, Kielmansegge and Ompteda, a hundred paces back. From the thick smoke, which hung like a fog over the battlefield, Wellington himself emerged to rally the Brunswick battalions, who were bolstered too by the arrival of Sir Hussey Vivian's fresh brigade of cavalry. Hussey Vivian was shocked by what he saw: 'I arrived in the rear of the infantry just at the time that several small squares of foreign troops were giving way. In fact my wheeling into line in their rear and cheering them actually halted two of them, and gave them confidence. Lord Edward Somerset with the wretched remains of the two heavy Brigades, not 200 men and horses, retired through me, and I then remained for about half an hour exposed to the most dreadful fire of shot, shell and musketry that it is possible to imagine. No words can give any idea of it (how a man escaped is to me a miracle), we every instant expecting through the smoke to see the enemy appearing under our noses, for the smoke was literally so thick that we could not see ten yards off.'

But if Wellington's men were suffering then the Prussian deployments at Plancenoit were having an impact on Napoleon's army, too, draining him of men, sucking out the energy and initiative which they needed if he was to succeed in his object of breaking the centre of the Anglo-Allied line. The danger for the French, which the Emperor clearly saw, was that after its repeated attacks, his army would become so tired that it would lose the battle by failing to win it, as if it had begun the task of demolishing a wall with energy and commitment, but when its repeated blows had failed to remove more than a few bricks, it had been left slumped and exhausted on the ground.

Napoleon, like Blücher before him at Ligny, had to gamble. He decided to deploy the Imperial Guard, never before defeated, the very men whose ability and loyalty could not be questioned, whose imperial pampering and protection had added to their legend, so that it looked, to any detached observer of the scene, as if their summons was less the throw of the gambler's dice, and more the cool, rational use of forces who would put the day beyond doubt. On receiving the order, their acting commander, General Drouot, gathered together the crack units in front of La Belle Alliance, while General D'Erlon, leading I Corps, and General Reille, leading II Corps, were ordered to advance upon the enemy again with the whole of the remaining French army. It was, effectively, a general advance of the French army, led by the Guard, but supported by infantry, the remaining cavalry, and crucially the artillery, with a battery under the Old Guard's artillery commander, Lt.-Col. Duchand, in the first line.

Napoleon's deployment of two battalions of Old Guard infantry to

Plancenoit, to try to shore up his eastern flank, had, however, deprived Drouot of men, leaving him with just eight battalions for the final attack, five from the Middle Guard, and three from the Old Guard. Five battalions were placed in the front line, and three in the second. When they were ready, the leading battalions moved down to a hollow in the ground near the southeast corner of Hougoumont, from where they were to support the attack by the first column. Behind them lay the remains of the once-splendid cavalry, the only cavalry reserve left to Napoleon after the destructive forces of the battle, and all that he could call on to support the new push, or, though he dared not think of it, to reinforce his retreat.

The battle was reaching its crisis, its point of no return. If Wellington could hold the ridge, the battle would be over, because by now, with the Prussian intervention growing stronger, Napoleon was fighting not just the Anglo-Allied army but the clock. At around 7.30 p.m., as the sun dipped down to the horizon, the Imperial Guard appeared through the smoke, moving confidently forward as if the day-long fighting that had preceded their advance had been the act of underlings, work which was somehow beneath their exalted status. While the fact that Napoleon rarely deployed them until it was safe to do so was a source of some jealousy within his own army, it was a tactic which at the same time gave great heart to his own forces for no greater signal could be given that a French victory was at hand. While they advanced, the whole of the French artillery boomed out, so that the Imperial Guard moved forward to the sound of thunder, as if they were powerful enough to create their own storm to match the one which had heralded the battle.

Victory or defeat depended upon the strength of Napoleon's veterans. But, as if he knew that the success of their deployment depended as much upon their image as the reality of their power, the Emperor spread the word that Marshal Grouchy had finally arrived from the east with his thirty thousand men. Up and down the lines the message went, giving encouragement to men who had fought bitterly all day with little but a farmhouse to show for their endeavours. The Guard's band began to play triumphantly, and the music mingled with cries of '*Vive l'Empereur*', and swords and bayonets were pushed into the air, muskets were shouldered, and even some of the wounded were moved to join in the advance, along with the remaining squadrons of cuirassiers and the artillery of the Guard. In ten minutes, they would be within firing range of the Anglo-Allied line.

Napoleon himself led the men towards battle, but not into it, for after appearing at the head of the columns for the initial part of their journey, he suddenly pulled to one side at the bottom of the valley, and turned into a quarry by the side of the Charleroi road, just south of La Haye Sainte. From there, he watched the Guard go past. His sudden withdrawal was a surprise to some of the soldiers who had been told that the Emperor himself was leading them in the final assault on Wellington's position. If they were unhappy with his decision, then they did not show it, and marched past with rigid discipline. But then they were the Immortals, and nothing less was expected of the best the French army had to offer: 'that sacred cohort', Siborne called them, the better to emphasise the magnificence of the triumph. Sacred they may have been, but Napoleon prudently kept a ninth battalion in reserve, between La Haye Sainte and Hougoumont, and two battalions of grenadiers in a square south of La Belle Alliance.

Wellington had placed his infantry, not in squares, but in ranks which were four deep, strong enough to tackle an enemy on foot, and still robust enough to withstand the remains of the French cavalry. He was ready for the attack, as Lieutenant William Sharpin of the Royal Artillery recalled: 'A few minutes before the French Imperial Guards made their appearance the Duke of Wellington rode up to our battery and hastily asked me who commanded it; I replied that Bolton did, but that he was just killed, and that it was then under Napier. His Grace then said, "Tell him to keep a look to his left, for the French will soon be with him," and then he rode off. I had scarcely communicated the Duke's message, when we saw the French bonnets just above the high corn, and within forty or fifty yards of our guns.'

The advance began at around 7.30 p.m., when the noise of battle was intense. Captain Cordemann of the 3rd Line Battalion, King's German Legion, could not hear the orders of his commanding officer partly because of 'the uninterrupted thunder of cannon' and partly because there had been so many fatalities that 'the battalion often did not know who the actual commanding officer was.' Soon, Marshal Ney's men were nearing the steep rise in the ground which led to the Anglo-Allied position, but they were marching into a hail-storm of fire, with canister and grape raining down on them from only forty metres away. Lt. Sharpin: 'I believe they were in close columns of grand divisions, and upon reaching the crest of our position, they attempted to deploy into line, but the destructive fire of our guns loaded with canister shot, and the well-directed volleys from the infantry, prevented their regular formation.'

The French refused to halt their advance, even as their men fell, and they reached the summit, clouded in smoke from the British gun batteries, with nothing to bar their progress towards the Anglo-Allied line. For the seventeen-year-old ensign of the 30th Foot, Edward Macready, it was a daunting sight: 'The Imperial Guard was seen ascending our position in as correct order as at a review. As they rose step by step before us, and crossed the ridge, their red epaulettes and cross-belts put on over their blue great-coats, gave them a gigantic appearance, which was increased by their high hairy caps and long red feathers, which waved with the nod of their heads as they kept time to a drum in the centre of their column.' Dimly, through the smoke, the French could make out the cocked hats of the British officers, and they pressed on until only forty or fifty paces separated them from their enemy. 'The fire was very heavy,' recalled Captain Thomas Taylor of the 10th Hussars. 'I saw their men through the smoke apparently not fifty paces from our infantry.'

Duchand's horse artillery had wheeled its cannons towards the top of the slope and now it did terrible damage to two squares, jointly formed by the remains of four battalions, from the 30th (Cambridgeshire) and the 73rd Regiments, and the 33rd (1st Yorkshire West Riding) and 69th (South Lincolnshire). These survivors came under point-blank fire from the French gunners who carved great gaps in the squares, and so dire was their predicament that the Colours of the 30th and 73rd were sent to the rear. If Wellington's army was to lose, then the French would not be able to celebrate their conquest with such a prize.

As if to put an end to his men's suffering, the brigade commander,

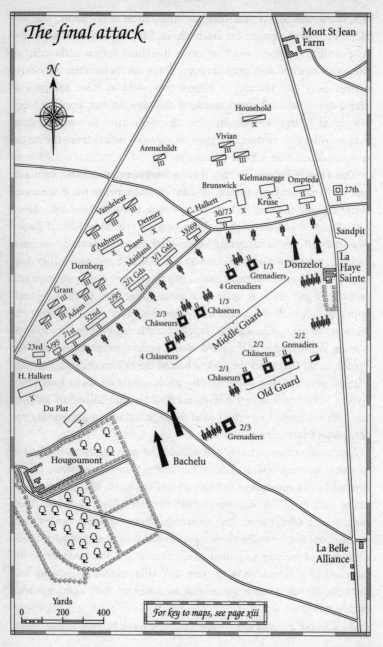

The final attack

N

Mont St Jean Farm

Household
X

Vivian
III

Arenschildt
III

III   III

Kielmansegge   Ompteda
II   II

Brunswick   X   27th
X   II

Vandeleur   C. Halkett   Kruse
III   30/73   X

III   Detmer   X   Sandpit
III   X   La
d'Aubremé   33/69   Haye
X   Chassé   Sainte
Dornberg   Maitland   II   II   1/3
III   2/1 Gds   II   Grenadiers   Donzelot

Grant   Adam   3/1 Gds   4 Grenadiers
III   III   II   II   II
III   52nd   2/3   1/3
2/95   Châsseurs   Châsseurs
23rd   71st   Middle Guard   2/2
II   3/95   4 Châsseurs   2/2   Grenadiers
II   II   Châsseurs   II

H. Halkett   2/1
X   Châsseurs   Old Guard

Du Plat
X

Hougoumont   2/3
Grenadiers

Bachelu

La Belle
Alliance

Yards
0   200   400

For key to maps, see page xiii

160

Sir Colin Halkett, gave the order to fire at the enemy troops, the 1/3 and 4th Grenadiers, as they came up the last few steps of the slope. Then something extraordinary happened. The first wave of the enemy began to retreat. 'Our surprise was inexpressible,' he reflected afterwards, 'when through the clearing smoke we saw the backs of the Imperials flying in a mass. We stared at each other as if mistrusting our eyesight. Some guns from the rear of our right poured in grape among them, and the slaughter was dreadful.' 'The column seemed to burst,' said Lt. Charles Parker Ellis of the 1st Foot Guards. Just in time, a Belgian horse battery led by Captain Krahmer had arrived to send canister flying through the air at the Guard, from barely a hundred metres away. 'Nowhere did I see carcasses so heaped upon each other,' recalled Edward Macready. 'Their grand metallic bang, bang bang, bang, with rushing showers of grape were the most welcome sounds that ever struck my ears – until I married.' His view obscured by the thick gunsmoke, Halkett was unsure what had happened: 'I never could account for their flight . . .' he concluded. Captain Weyland Powell, of the 1st Foot Guards, was equally unclear what had happened. 'Whether it was from the sudden and unexpected appearance of a corps so near them, which must have seemed as starting out of the ground, or the tremendously heavy fire we threw into them, *La Garde*, who had never before failed in an attack *suddenly* stopped. Those who from a distance and more on the flank could see the affair, tell us that the effect of our fire seemed to force the head of the column bodily back. In less than a minute above 300 were down.'

The confusion on the Anglo-Allied side was as great as if they had been defeated. Halkett gave the order for his men to about-face, perhaps to seek the protection of the crest. But Duchand's gunners had not retreated and fired shot after shot into their ranks. The four Anglo-Allied battalions which had formed themselves into two squares became completely entangled with each other, as they rushed to find safe ground. Lieutenant Edward Macready: 'There was a hedge in our rear, to which it was deemed expedient to move us, I suppose, for shelter from the guns. We faced about by word of command, and stepped off in perfect order. As we descended . . . the fire thickened tremendously, and the cries from men struck down, as well as from the numerous wounded on all sides of us, who thought themselves abandoned, were terrible. An extraordinary number of men and officers of both regiments went down almost in no time. (Lt. Edmund) Prendergast of ours was shattered to pieces by a shell; (Captain Alexander) McNab killed by grape-shot, and (Ensigns) James and Bullen lost all their legs by roundshot during this retreat, or in the cannonade immediately preceding it.' Fifty cuirassiers, thought Macready gloomily, would be all that was needed to annihilate the brigade. He was not to know that Napoleon's cavalry was spent, destroyed by its failed efforts during the course of the long day.

Now another wave of the Guard reached the top of the ridge, the 1st and 2nd Battalions of the 3rd Châsseurs à Pied, even though they had taken heavy casualties on their journey. Their task was almost impossible: not only had the troops to climb the steep slope which led to the Anglo-Allied position, they had to do so in the face of the artillery which lined the ridge. The French could not even see their enemy because Wellington had ordered Maitland's Guards to lie down, pressed flat against the ground, hidden by the neck-high corn. The French were only twenty-five metres away when Wellington reportedly gave the order: 'Up, guards; make ready!' (Whether Wellington actually said this is a moot point: Lord Saltoun, of the 1st Foot Guards, wrote to Siborne: 'Your last point is whether the Duke made use of the words "Up, Guards, and at them." I did not hear him, nor do I know any person, or ever heard of any person that did. It is a matter of no importance, has become current with the world as the cheering speech of a great man to his troops, and is certainly not worth a controversy about. If you have got it I should let it stand.') More than 1400 men stood up suddenly, so that it appeared to their enemy as if they were springing out of the ground, and sent out a dense volley of fire. They were aided by angled fire from two battalions of the 33rd and 69th Regiments, which Sir Colin Halkett had pushed forward to the left of the Guard to attack their flank. The impact was instantaneous, as dramatic and as shocking as the gunfire which had caused the French cavalry to falter in the afternoon, so that the men in the front line of the attacking force fell in their hundreds, as if the ground under them had suddenly given way. Now it was the turn of the French soldiers to suffer as harshly as Wellington's men had done from the effects of enemy fire.

But the French were not to be denied. Encouraged by their officers, they tried to deploy over a wider front, to get away from the devastating effects of the Anglo-Allied gunfire. Again and again they were driven back. Captain Weyland Powell recalled that the Imperial Guard 'now wavered, and several of the rear divisions began to draw out as if to deploy, whilst some of the men in their rear beginning to fire over the heads of those in front was so evident a proof of their confusion, that Lord Saltoun holloaed out *"Now's the time, my boys."* We charged down the hill till we had passed the end of the orchard of Hougoumont.' But Maitland quickly became aware that the last square of the Imperial Guard, the 4th Châsseurs, was advancing on his right, and saw that his flank was in danger of being turned. He gave the order to halt and face about, but his left wing misheard the command over the noise of the gunfire and the shout went up that they should form square, perhaps not just a misunderstanding in the heat of battle, but a reflection of the fact, too, that the men still feared that they were in a position where they would be hopelessly exposed to an enemy cavalry charge. Saltoun tried desperately to remedy the error, but he was too late, and, to sort out their confusion, the battalion was forced to head back to the crest of the ridge. Once more, the momentum of an Anglo-Allied attack had been lost and the 4th Châsseurs pressed forward.

The final desperate moments of the battle were approaching, though some of the army did not know it. Wrote Captain Cordemann of the King's German Legion, to William Siborne: 'You may perhaps have some concept of how great was our amazement when, after this serious strain, the sudden order came from the Duke of Wellington to all squares and corps immediately to "Form line! Four deep and advance!!"' The key intervention seems to have been led by Sir John Colborne, commanding the 1/52nd, who was watching the enemy advance from the ridge and decided that the chasseurs looked vulnerable to a counter-attack. When Adam rode up to ask Colborne what he was going to do, he replied he would 'make that column feel our fire' and acting on his own initiative, ordered his light infantry battalion to advance. As the remains of the 4th Châsseurs pressed forward, they suddenly came face to face with the strongest battalion in Wellington's army, more than a thousand bayonets, on their left flank.

Colborne considered that his intervention had been crucial: 'I have no doubt that the fire on the flank of the French column from the 52nd skirmishers, and the appearance of a general attack on its flank from Sir F. Adam's brigade and Sir H. Clinton's division generally, was the cause of the first check received, or halt made by the Imperial Guards.' Marching, not charging, in perfect order, four lines deep, the regiment wheeled left on command, to face the flank of the Imperial Guard, and forced the advance to come to a halt while the French column turned to face the attack. For several minutes, the two sides exchanged fire and more than a hundred men from the 52nd were killed.

Colborne now ordered his men to stop firing and gave the order to charge with bayonets. Lt. George Gawler of the 52nd was determined to claim the credit for his regiment, and spent the succeeding years giving Siborne the benefit of his views: 'When the 52nd was nearly parallel to the enemy's flank, Sir John Colborne gave the word, "Charge, charge." It was answered from the regiment by a loud steady cheer and a hurried dash to the front. In the next ten seconds the Imperial Guard, broken into the wildest confusion, and scarcely firing a shot to cover its retreat, was rushing towards the hollow road in the rear of La Haye Sainte.'

The mounted officers led the line, including Colborne himself and also Major William Chalmers, who placed his cap on the point of his sword, and stood up in his stirrups, to cheer the regiment forward. But their casualties were mounting. 'I consider that about 140 of our men were killed or wounded at this time, in the course of five or six minutes,' recalled William Leeke, who was still carrying the regimental colours of the 52nd. An adjutant was badly wounded in the head, and brought back by his horse through the line, the blood streaming down him; Captain Diggle, commanding No.1 company, was hit by a bullet near his left temple. Lieutenant Dawson was shot through the lungs; another officer lost a leg. Major Love was severely wounded in the head, and, as he lay on the ground, in the foot and in two other places;

General Adam was severely wounded in the leg; Sir John Colborne's horse was killed from under him, and he himself was grazed in the hand and foot.

The men were paying a heavy price for their success. But now the Prussians were alongside them and the day was nearly theirs.

XI

To William Siborne
From Sir Hussey Vivian, Commander-in-Chief in Ireland

Royal Hospital, 7 November 1834

My dear Siborne,

I regret much of your continued indisposition and especially as it prevents your coming to me, as I was desirous of having an opportunity of saying a few words to you on the subject of your Model and in reference to Sir Willoughby Gordon's remarks upon your proposition to place the troops as they stood at the Crisis and his own proposition to place them as they stood at the commencement of the Battle.

My opinion decidedly is that it is preferable to place them as they stood at the Crisis.

You will exhibit an infinitely more interesting part of the day (and) . . . the troops will convey some notion of the Glorious Victory which would not be the case if the two armies were simply posted in their original position.

Lastly, and it is of all the most important consideration and which does not appear to have occurred to Sir Willoughby, if you describe the commencement of the battle or rather the period before the fight commenced – *what are you to do with the Prussians?* The advance of the Prussians and their attack on Plancenoit and on the right flank & rear of the French was one of the most important features, if not the most important in the whole day.

In haste,

Ever yours very faithfully,

H. Vivian

Despite the confusion of battle, Sir Hussey Vivian, for one, was certain that the Prussians should take their full share of the glory: 'In truth, I care not what others may say, we were greatly indebted to the Prussians, and it was their coming on the right and rear of Napoleon that gave us the Victory of Waterloo.' At around 7.30 p.m., the time when the Middle Guard was making its final attack on Wellington's army, the main body of General Ziethen's I Corps poured onto the battlefield near Smohain, from a hollow in the ground, driving a wedge between the French forces in the east, under General Lobau and General Durutte. Nearly 2500 infantrymen headed straight for d'Erlon's men and for Lobau's left flank. Behind the infantry came more than a thousand cavalry led by Col. von Lutzow, and another two thousand men from General von Treskow's brigade. Together they attacked the French line from the rear, while Ziethen's artillery fired on the enemy from the crest of the hollow. The French advance was being cut in two by the Prussians, while on the ridge its spearhead, the Imperial Guard, was fighting for its survival against Wellington's men. 'Treason!' came one cry. 'Save yourselves' was another. 'The Prussians!' The French retreated, rapidly, behind the heights of Smohain. Only at Papelotte, among the houses and high ground, did the French put up any resistance, staging a firefight which lasted half an hour. Ziethen, the man who had dared to disobey Blücher, was rolling up the French line with impunity, safe in the knowledge that the enemy had pushed so far forward that there was no danger of attack by any reserves.

Out on the ridge, Wellington ordered a general advance. Unsupported by cavalry on either flank, the remaining French soldiers had no recourse to help from the rest of their army. They could not move right, for that was where the line of British guards were firing at them; nor could they move left, because of the advance of Adam's brigade. Either they went forward, and won the day, despite the terrible losses they were enduring, or they turned and accepted defeat. For a soldier in the middle of one of the columns, imprisoned in a stationary mass of men with no means of escape, it must have been a terrifying experience, even for Napoleon's veterans. Blinded by the thick smoke of battle, assailed by weaponry and noise, pressed by men to the front and back and sides, with seemingly no control over their own fate, many of the men could not fully understand what was happening, except that they were caught in a death trap. The officers began, slowly at first, and then with increasing speed, to lose control of their men. Their men would not wait for the next, inevitable bayonet charge. They had had enough, and they turned and ran. William Leeke: 'As we closed towards the French Guard, they did not wait for our charge, but the leading column at first somewhat receded from us, and then broke and fled; a portion of the rear column also broke and ran; but three or four battalions of the Old Guard, forming part of this second column, retired hastily, in some degree of order, towards the rising ground in front of La Belle Alliance, with a few pieces of the artillery of the Guard.'

With the Guard's failure, the battle turned, the unprecedented humiliation eating into French morale. All day the army had pounded at Wellington's position, all day, like Wellington, it had taken heavy casualties. But, unlike Wellington, they could not claim that the status quo, the retention of a defensive position, was a victory. The only triumph had been the conquest of La Haye Sainte. And now the Guard had found the heat of battle to be too fierce. What future was there now in this desperate, bloody business if the Guard could not make headway? The incredulous shout went up, '*La Garde recule! La Garde recule!*' The words reverberated around the army like the drumbeats which had accompanied the morning's advance.

Wellington determined to seize the moment, and to show, as if in contrast, that his troops, though shattered by the battle, were still confident and brave. Vandeleur's 6th British Cavalry Brigade, the 11th, 12th and 16th Light Dragoons, was ordered to descend into the plain and pursue the enemy. Captain William Tomkinson rode with the 16th Light Dragoons: 'They were in complete deroute and confusion . . . we made a rush and went into their column with the companies which were stationed in their front, they running away to the square for shelter. We completely succeeded, many of their infantry immediately throwing down their arms and crowding together for safety. Many too ran away up the next rising ground.'

Wellington also sent forward Hussey Vivian's 6th Cavalry Brigade to attack Napoleon's cavalry reserves at La Belle Alliance. As Hussey

Vivian's men emerged through the smoke, they could see, all across the valley, the enemy scattering in confusion, columns of infantry hurrying back in disorder, different units all mixed up together. Half-way towards the French position, however, Vivian noted the two squares of Imperial Guard infantry that Napoleon had posted protectively to the side of La Belle Alliance, with cavalry and artillery mounting guard on the flanks. But Napoleon's deployments could not camouflage the depredations of the day. The cavalry screen was but a shadow of its proper self, regiments, and even brigades, reduced to the size of mere squadrons. Lieutenant-General Jean-Martin of the French army: 'the whole army was in the most appalling disorder. Infantry, cavalry, artillery – everybody was fleeing in all directions. Soon no unit retained any order except the two squares formed by this regiment's two battalions posted to right and left of the main road . . .' For the first time in the battle, it appeared as if the polarity of the engagement had been reversed, with Wellington, so long the keeper of the ridge, committed to attack, and Napoleon relying on the defensive precautions he had cautiously put in place while he tried to rally his troops.

Wellington, watching the success of Vivian's advance against Napoleon's reserves and the retreat of the French army, now ordered the advance of his infantry. He stood on a rise of ground, near Maitland's brigades, and doffed his hat, waving it high into the air as a signal for his troops. For the first time in the battle, except for their postings in the outposts of the line, such as Hougoumont and La Haye Sainte, his foot-soldiers were allowed licence to move from out of the cover afforded by the ridge. The French were on the run; and the Anglo-Allied line was advancing, chasing, harrying, released from their tortoise-like existence, the battle finally in their favour. 'To see in this manner the rapid movements of the cavalry, artillery and infantry – in a race – forwards, and to see the enemy fleeing in all directions, was and remains for me a pleasurable and unforgettable vision,' noted Captain Cordemann. 'For us at the time all the more so because we heard or perceived of no visible reason for it.' The battle had turned into a rout. It was just a question of how quickly the Allied armies could finish off their task.

In the village of Plancenoit, too, barely a thousand metres from Napoleon's main line of communication, the contest had swung back towards the Prussians, though the battle still raged fiercely. The village was burning and flames were licking at the windows and doors of the church. As the flames rose higher, the Prussians defeated a battalion of the Old Guard in a nearby wood, enabling them to attack the village from three directions. More than 35,000 Prussian troops, from IV Corps and II Corps, moved forward to encircle the 13,000 French defenders, and wave after wave of fresh troops were thrown into the fight. Suddenly, the occupiers' resolve broke and they ran for their lives. 'The remnants of the Guard left in a great rush,' the Prussian 25th Regiment reported, 'leaving behind large masses of artillery, equipment and ammunition waggons.' There was only one item the troops refused to abandon, their Eagle, and the chasseurs formed a square to protect it as far as the main French line of retreat. In doing so, many of them lost their lives. 'Unlike other parts of the battlefield,' the regiment concluded, 'there were no cries of "*Sauve qui peut*" here. Instead the cry "*Sauvons nos aigles*" – let's save our eagles – could be heard.'

It was a forlorn gesture of defiance. Within the hour, Napoleon's eastern wing was lost.

The day had dawned with shafts of light shining through the overhanging cloud, and now that it was ending the setting sun was struggling to penetrate the smoke of battle. Many of the survivors of the battle noted how the light, where it managed to break through the smoke, was so intense that it appeared to highlight, in almost lurid fashion, individual sections of the battlefield. 'The sun gave a lurid sort of glare,' remembered Captain Thomas Taylor of the 10th Hussars, twenty years later. It 'made such a picturesque battle piece that I . . . wished I could paint it. I can still shut my eyes and see it.' But then, as if to signal that the battle was nearly over, and at a terrible cost, the sun sank below the horizon and cast a red, bloody glow over the sky. To match it, the blood-letting continued. Lord Uxbridge, on the point of leading the British cavalry in their final, glorious attack, was hit by canister in his right leg, a wound which was so severe that, given the surgery of the times, it could have caused his death: he was helped away by men from the 23rd Light Dragoons and before the day was out his leg had to be amputated in the village of Waterloo.

The battle was, at its end, a confusion of infantry and cavalry, ally and enemy, advance and retreat. 'The terrain was so soft and deep that the people could only get through with great difficulty,' recalled Captain Cordemann, 'and some of them lost their shoes in the process; the field before us was so covered with killed and wounded enemy soldiers and cuirassiers, horses and weapons of all sorts that we could not keep our ranks closed, but continually had to split up to avoid humans and horse.' Previous contests became mixed up with the later clashes, with units returning to their own line only to find themselves embroiled in a new battle which had developed in their absence.

The remainder of Vivian's 10th Hussars, chasing the routed French cavalry, found themselves riding through the remains of the French infantry as it fled from the battlefield, and then they came across a new pocket of resistance, half a battalion of the Guard which had decided to put up more of a fight. But once the word had spread through the French army that the Guard had been defeated, there was no prospect of their resistance taking hold. Captain Pierre Robinaux, who had taken part in the assault on Hougoumont, found that it was impossible to rally his troops: 'What did we see? Our troops in full retreat at every point. The cavalry followed the example of the infantry, and I saw dragoons galloping off and knocking down the wretched foot-soldiers, even riding over their bodies. This happened to me once. Furious at this disorder, and exhausted with running, I realized that we had been hurrying across the plain without being pursued at all, so I kept shouting in a loud voice: "Halt! We must rally. Nobody is after us."' It was useless. Napoleon had no reserves to draw on which might stem the haemorrhage from the front line, or provide a rallying point to stop his army becoming a disorganised mob. On either side of the Charleroi road, the French retreat was in full flight. Captain Cordemann noted that 'in our first half-hour of our advance, between fifty and sixty abandoned enemy cannon lay behind us on the terrain we had passed, and a large number of men were running about leaderless.' The Anglo-Allied advance recaptured, triumphantly, the one possession the army had lost in the day's fighting, when Lambert's brigade occupied La Haye Sainte, abandoned by the French and inhabited only by the wounded and the dying. There were so many French soldiers on the run that the advancing Prussian cavalry of Ziethen's corps, and the cavalry of Vivian and Vandeleur found themselves caught up in a great tide of men. In the middle of all the confusion, only one French cavalry regiment, the grenadiers à cheval, retained its composure, retreating slowly but surely, walking away from the battlefield, as if it was beneath its dignity to rush.

Slowly, deliberately, the remaining French squares retreated, taking terrible losses from the infantry guns and from the artillery which fired canister into them at point-blank range, stepping over the bodies of their fallen comrades, pausing every fifty metres or so to close up, before continuing on their long, bloody retreat. They were the only organised part of the army; all around them, the once-disciplined force had evolved into an anarchic creature, which bore only a faint, if recognisable, military resemblance to its previous self; artillerymen cut themselves free from their weaponry, overturned the ammunition wagons, and rode off without their guns, and cavalrymen threw away their weighty body armour to make their escape on foot. Though ungallant, it was a tactic more likely to ensure survival than adhering to discipline, for inexorably, step by step, the remnants of the old order, the inhabitants of the squares, were dying. By the time the Guard reached La Belle Alliance, many of them were dead. But the allies' advance was not without its own cost. One of Bulow's batteries opened fire into Adam's brigade, as it climbed the high ground behind La Belle Alliance. And in the gathering gloom, Prussian cavalry charged at their British allies in the 18th Hussars; the 1st Hussars of the King's German Legion charged two units of Vandeleur's brigade, thinking they were French.

Wellington's men had fought to the point of exhaustion, and they had little appetite for a prolonged chase. When Blücher led men from his IV Corps to meet Wellington, the Duke explained that his army was too tired to continue. It fell to the Prussians to lead the chase into the night, and in the commitment they displayed it is impossible not to admire their endeavour. For three hard days they had fought and marched, marched and fought, and now they still had the energy to harry the French to the bitter end. In doing so they ensured the completeness of the Allied victory: without the fury of their pursuit Napoleon could, perhaps, have reunited his broken army and steadied himself for another day.

The Prussians were unrelenting in their determination to eliminate the remnants of their shattered enemy. Blücher sent Bulow's corps down the Charleroi road, with Ziethen's corps in support. Pirch's corps was sent back across the River Dyle to intercept Grouchy's troops, still fighting at Wavre, and still ignorant of the outcome of the main battle As the Prussians passed the final position of Wellington's army, near La Belle Alliance, their musicians struck up 'God save the King' and they moved on to the sound of British cheers. The Prussian advance was led by troops from Plancenoit, under Gneisenau, who entered into the chase with a spirit and energy which had seemed so conspicuously lacking in his initial march towards the battlefield. His men had been up since dawn, and they were tired and hungry, but still he spurred them on, placing a drummer boy on a horse so that the retreating French might hear the noise and think that the infantry was on their heels.

Heading south down the Charleroi road, the chasing Prussians found the wreckage of the French army in Genappe. Colonel Lavasseur, an aide-de-camp to Marshal Ney, was astonished to find the town so full of vehicles 'that it was impossible to walk upright in the streets and the infantry were obliged to crawl under the waggons in order to get through.' There were hundreds of vehicles, many of them over-turned, the vital equipment of an army at war which had become an encumbrance to an army in retreat, baggage waggons and carts, ammunition waggons and guns.

Just as Wellington had found in his retreat north after the battle of Quatre Bras, Genappe was a bottleneck, its main river-crossing too narrow to cope with a rush of troops, and now thousands of them were crushed together as they tried desperately to cross the river. Thousands of men were hemmed into the narrow streets, and in their fear they used their weapons on each other, swords, and guns, and bayonets. In the crowd of panic-stricken soldiers was the Emperor himself, his passage this far protected by the two remaining squares of the Old Guard. Now he found he could not move, with his coach hemmed in by the fleeing mob his army had become. He jumped on his horse and escaped, just in time, before the Prussians arrived in force with their lances and sabres. The French, desperately, tried to construct a makeshift barricade, but the Prussians brought up their artillery and destroyed it. Then they plundered the Emperor's coach, stealing anything of value, his hat, his court sword and two scabbards, perhaps designed for his triumphal entry into Brussels, the imperial toothbrush, his gold-mounted pistols, his monogrammed dinner service, his collapsible spy-glass, a cane, a gold dinner service, a writing desk, medals and even, it was said, a million francs worth of diamonds sewn into the lining of a spare uniform. The Prussians struck with a savagery that, even now, took the French by surprise, according to Fleury de Chaboulon, the secretary to the Emperor: 'The capture and pillage of the army's baggage had momentarily halted the enemy's advance, but at Quatre Bras he caught up with us and fell upon our vehicles . . . Five other carriages immediately behind us were attacked and sabred, but by a miracle ours managed to escape . . . The Prussians, in savage pursuit, treated the wretches whom they overtook with unparalleled barbarity . . . Most of the soldiers had thrown away their weapons and now found themselves defenceless. They were nonetheless massacred without mercy.' It was not until Gneisenau had cleared the road as far south as Frasne that he called a halt for the night, satisfied that the remnants of the French army had been put to the sword, and its survivors forced across the Sambre.

Wellington rode slowly back from his meeting with Blücher, across the battlefield, now dark, picking his way through the detritus of the contest between La Belle Alliance and La Haye Sainte – the abandoned guns and wagons, the bodies lying in the mud, including four complete squares of French guardsmen, still in military formation. The Duke returned to his headquarters in the inn at Waterloo, speaking little, and though he was bone-weary he could not go to sleep in his own bed because it had been taken by his aide, Colonel Gordon, who was dying. Instead he sat down, and in silence, began to write his official despatch to London.

That night, Blücher too put pen to paper. 'I have been true to my word,' he wrote, in a letter to his wife. 'On the 16th I was compelled to withdraw before superior forces; but on the 18th acting with my friend Wellington, I have annihilated the army of Napoleon.'

XII

To confine yourself to one period of the battle, is to lose the point of your labour; and many regiments who bore a conspicuous part of that day, will be entirely left out. So complicated an action as that was, never can be represented by one plan. It occurs to me, that it would be much more satisfactory to yourself and also to the public, to place the respective armies in order of battle at its commencement on your model, accompanied by three separate plans, showing the progressive stages of the action.

Captain George Miller, letter to William Siborne, 2 December 1834

For all their amity in the first glow of victory, the two allies could not even agree on what the battle should be called. Despite Blücher's suggestion that it should be called La Belle Alliance, it became Waterloo when the Duke insisted on naming the battle after the small village north of his position which had housed his headquarters, even though it did not lie on the battlefield itself. Perhaps the decision was appropriate, despite its geographical infelicity. The alliance which had served the two armies so well in war was soon unravelled by history which, in England, placed the laurels, uncompromisingly and unhesitatingly, on the Duke of Wellington's head.

This made life even more difficult for William Siborne in the years which followed. The details of victory were as disputed as they were celebrated, as each of the allies tried to cast their actions as the deciding factor. At what time had the Prussians launched their attack? Had they cut Napoleon's army in two by breaking through at Plancenoit before, during or after Wellington's defeat of the Imperial Guard? Within the Duke's own army, too, there was dissent over which units should take the credit for repelling the Immortals. Until the last participants had died, the 1st Foot Guards and the 52nd Foot would dispute their precise role in events, and the exact share of glory which should be apportioned to each.

The truth was that few, if any, of the participants had been granted a clear view of events. Some men, such as Ensign Dirom of the 1st Foot Guards, were sure of what they had seen: 'with regard to our formation, that of the Imperial Guard, and what took place, I feel as certain as if it had only occurred yesterday.' Others knew only that such certainty was misplaced. Lieutenant Browne, of the 4th (King's Own) Regiment, told Siborne: 'I fancy that regimental officers, and more particularly company officers, have little time or opportunity of knowing anything beyond their own division or brigade, and that the smoke, the bustle, which I fear is almost inseparable to regiments when close to the enemy, and more particularly the attention which is required from the company officers to their men, intercepts all possibility of their giving any correct accounts of the battles in which they may be engaged.' The smoke was a crucial factor in obscuring the finer details of the battle. Some men, such as Captain John Kincaid of the 95th Rifles, could barely see anything at all: 'The smoke hung so thick about, that, although not more than eighty yards asunder, we could only distinguish each other by the flashes of the pieces . . .' The result is that, in the swirling, hectic, bloody, confused, fast-moving moments of the Crisis of the Battle, it was impossible to be sure whether the main Prussian intervention came before, during, or after the defeat of the final French attempt to scale the ridge.

Wellington had no time for any of these eyewitness accounts, because he felt history was the sole preserve of the army's leaders. He was himself certain of what he had witnessed, and from his position under the elm tree at the crossroads he had galloped around the narrow battlefield, particularly the centre and right of his line, encouraging his men and issuing his orders. So his view of the battle was more wide-ranging than the men in his service who came to write their own accounts, but, nevertheless, he was not in a position to weigh the respective contributions of each army. What he knew, for sure, was that his men had paid a terrible, bloody price, whereas his allies had not been on the battlefield until the afternoon was spent. Who, in these circumstances, would expect him to praise the Prussian army as much as his own troops in the account he wrote for London – his Waterloo Despatch?

Letter from the Duke of Wellington to Lord Bathurst, Secretary for War
Waterloo, June 19, 1815

The enemy repeatedly charged our infantry with his cavalry, but these attacks were uniformly unsuccessful, and they afforded opportunities to our cavalry to charge . . .

These attacks were repeated till about seven in the evening, when the enemy made a desperate effort with the cavalry and infantry, supported by the fire of the artillery, to force our left centre near the farm of La Haye Sainte, which after a severe contest was defeated; and having observed that the troops retired from this attack in great confusion, and that the march of General Bulow's corps by Fischermont upon Plancenoite and La Belle Alliance, had begun to take effect, and as I could perceive the fire of his cannon, and as Marshal prince Blücher had joined in person, with a corps of his army to the left of our line by Ohain, I determined to attack the enemy, and immediately advanced the whole line of the infantry, supported by the cavalry and artillery.

The attack succeeded in every point; the enemy was forced from his position on the heights and fled in the utmost confusion . . .

I should not do justice to my feelings, or to Marshal Blücher and the Prussian army, if I did not attribute the successful result of this arduous day to the cordial and timely assistance I received from them.

The operation of General Bulow upon the enemy's flank was a most decisive one; and even if I had not found myself in a situation to make the attack which produced the final result, it would have forced the enemy to retire, if his attacks should have failed; and would have prevented him from taking advantage of them, if they should unfortunately have succeeded . . .

I send, with this despatch, two Eagles, taken by the troops in this action, when Major Percy will have the honour of laying at the feet of His Royal Highness.

I have the honour, &c.

WELLINGTON

Wellington, while recognising the Prussian contribution to victory, asserted that his attack had produced 'the final result' and that only afterwards had the Prussian advance begun to have an impact. But from the Prussians' point of view, a subtly different battle had taken place. Their role had not just been one of 'cordial and timely assistance'. Two battles had been fought that day, at Wavre and Waterloo, and they had distracted thousands of Napoleon's men for the greater part of the day. More than this – upon their arrival they had instantly laid waste to his troops. The contest for Plancenoit had been vital, draining Napoleon's army of men and guns, weakening d'Erlon's flawed attack and Ney's final, bitter charge. Their advance had been the decisive ingredient, the crucial factor, the catalyst for victory. At the very least, by forcing Napoleon to fight on two fronts, they had divided his army, weakening the strength of his assaults on Wellington's position. When Plancenoit was lost, the battle was lost. The Prussians could not have won the day without Wellington, but in turn it was inconceivable that he could have won it without them.

Above all, the Prussians considered Ziethen's men had defeated the Emperor by breaking through his line in overwhelming numbers during the final French attack. The Prussian commanders filed a despatch which gave an entirely different emphasis to their role in breaking Napoleon's army, suggesting that Wellington's defeat of the Imperial Guard, and their advance, had happened at one and the same time.

General Gneisenau, by order of Field-marshal Blücher:
The French troops fought with desperate fury; however, some uncertainty was perceived in their movements, and it was observed that some pieces of cannon were retreating. At this moment the first column of General Ziethen arrived on the points of attack, near the

village of Smouhen, on the enemy's right flank, and instantly charged. This movement decided the defeat of the enemy.

The right wing was broken in three places: he abandoned his positions. Our troops rushed forward at the *pas de charge*, and attacked him on all sides, *while at the same time* the whole English line advanced. Circumstances were entirely favourable for the attack formed by the Prussian army: – the ground rose in an amphitheatre, so that our artillery could freely open its fire from the summit of a great many heights, which rose gradually above each other, and in the intervals of which the troops descended into the plain, formed into brigades, and in the greatest order, while fresh corps continually unfolded themselves, issuing from the forest on the height behind us. The enemy, however, still preserved means to retreat, till the village of Plachenot, which he had on his rear, and which was defended by the guard, was, after several bloody attacks, carried by storm . . .

Few victories have been so complete; and there is certainly no example that an army, two days after losing a battle, engaged in such an action, and so gloriously maintained it.

In the middle of the position occupied by the French army, and exactly upon the height, is a farm, called La Belle Alliance.

There it was that by a happy chance Field-marshal Blücher and Lord Wellington met in the dark, and mutually saluted each other as victors. In commemoration of the alliance which now subsists between the English and Prussian nations, of the union of the two armies, and their reciprocal confidence, the Field-marshal desired that this battle should bear the name of La Belle Alliance.

By order of Field-marshal BLÜCHER,
General GNEISENAU.

Three days after the battle, Major Henry Percy of the 14th Light Dragoons finally reached London with Wellington's despatch, after a race through the Brussels countryside and a sea-crossing to Dover. He found Lord Bathurst chairing a cabinet meeting, and told him the good news; then he delivered the same message to the Prince Regent, who was at dinner. Wellington's triumph, and his version of events, had reached London. 'I lose not a moment in communicating to you the fullness of my joy and admiration at the unparalleled triumph of your last and greatest achievement,' wrote George, the Prince Regent, to Wellington. 'Greatest, my dear Lord, not only in military glory, but in political importance; and not only in this proof of what all believed, that even the consummate skill of the Corsican could not withstand the superior genius of our own hero, but in the now nearly realised expectation, resulting from this victory, that England, under the auspices of her transcendent General, is again destined to rescue the world from tyranny and oppression.'

William Siborne, who was anxious to place thousands of toy soldiers in their exact positions at the moment of victory, had to reconcile the differing versions of events so that he might depict, with the accuracy of a topographer, the Crisis of the Battle on the vast tableau that would become his extraordinary legacy, the Great Model of Waterloo.

In the years that followed, to the end of his long life, Wellington never again described the battle in any detail. He scorned all histories, and simply stood by his Waterloo Despatch. On 19 June 1815, he had effectively written history himself. In doing so, he and his supporters cast a long shadow over Siborne. Either British bravery, and Wellington's skill, had won the Battle of Waterloo, or the victory had been down to the Prussians. There was no possibility, in their minds, that the one had been dependent on the other. The Duke had, effectively, won the battle on his own and the authorities were adamant that, in building his Model, Siborne would be in danger of assigning the wrong position to the Prussian troops at the moment of victory, and in doing so would give them too much credit for the famous victory.

But while Wellington stayed silent, Siborne gathered the evidence for his Model. Throughout the 1830s he was in contact with scores of survivors of the battle, starting with officers from the Anglo-Allied army, and he kept a diligent record of all the material he acquired. He listed, alphabetically, all his correspondence, starting with Lieutenant-General Sir Frederick Adam, and ending with Lieutenant-Colonel H. Wyndham of the Coldstream Guards, an A to W of the battle. There were major-generals, captains and colonels, lieutenants and sub-lieutenants, ensigns, aide-de-comptes, adjutants, sergeants, surgeons and staff officers. In addition to his circular, Siborne noted that he had sent twenty-seven letters to twenty-five different Waterloo officers asking for information. He wrote their names, one on each line, in his notebook: for example, 'to M Genl Macdonell, 19 Nov 1834; Col The Hon H Murray 18 Jan 1835; Lt Colonel G Hunter Blair, 12 March 1835; Lt Col the Hon E Stanhope, 23 March 1835; Lt Col CP Ellis 1 April 1835; Lt General Byng, 31 March 1835; Major Pratt 6 April 1835. M Genl Lord Saltoun 4 Jan 1838.'

Siborne read the accounts of the battle that had already been written, both at home and abroad, and he even engaged a member of the Prussian General Staff in a long correspondence. Sifting through the different, and differing accounts, weeding out inaccuracies and reconciling discrepancies, took years. Nearly every day there was a reply to his circular, and sometimes half a dozen. 'We know that every moment of time that he can employ, without interfering with his official duties, is sedulously devoted to the model,' said the *United Services Journal*. 'He is to be found at work by day-break, and he admits of no interruption beyond that which duty imposes upon him.'

All the time, Siborne was cross-referencing the replies to his circular, seeking to iron out contradictions between eyewitnesses, trying to establish the time of the final French attack, and scrupulously marking up maps of the battlefield with the positions of each unit. 'You are supposed to have taken the direction of the line *a-b* in your charge,' he wrote to Cornet Thomas Marten of the 2nd Life Guards, seeking clarification over the nationality of some riflemen in the foreground of the Model. 'The Germans say that while they were in the dip or hollow between the Wavre road and the little hedge with three trees in it (near the sandpit) *British* cavalry advanced . . . Perhaps these little circumstances may tend to refresh your recollections.' To another officer: 'when the General advance took place, (did) the 51st in extended order move forward along with a portion of the Guard and Brunswickers by *the right of Hougoumont* . . . ?'

Like the topographer he was, when Siborne received the answers to his questions he plotted the historical contours they provided, but he was not content to ink them in as fact until he had surveyed them from every conceivable angle, checking them from another vantage-point just as he had surveyed the battleground itself. On and on went the questions and the replies came back to him in microscopic detail:

'With respect to query No. 1 – the general answer may be that the 23rd Royal Welch Fusiliers was formed in square . . .'

'In answer to your letter of the 27th instant, I beg to state to you, to the best of my recollection, the following details regarding the positions and movements of the 5th Line Battalion K.G. Legion during the battle of Waterloo.'

'I have marked thereon with a pencil the position I occupied with the Light Company of the 14th Regiment . . .'

'My dear Sir, In reply to your note of the 2nd instant I regret to state that the officers of the 42nd, 79th and 92nd did not wear plaid on the memorable field of Waterloo . . .'

By the end of 1834, Siborne had completed the first stage of his task, receiving answers from nearly every unit, and he wrote up an account of the British view of the positions of the armies in a memorandum. He then tried, not surprisingly without success, to get the French to provide their view of the Prussian attack on Plancenoit, and with more luck, he contacted officers of the King's German Legion. In 1835, he received his first reply from the Prussian Minister of War, and later he even received the exact details of the colours carried by the Prussian infantry. But still Siborne wasn't satisfied; on and on the correspondence went, for another three years. Eventually, there was no doubt about it in his mind: the Prussians had reached the main battlefield before the moment of victory, and both their arrival and Wellington's repulse of the Imperial Guard should be shown on his Model of the battle.

Siborne had promised to submit his plans to the military authorities for their editorial approval and, six years into his project, he kept his word. On 6 September 1836, he wrote to Lord Fitzroy Somerset to announce that the first stage of his work was over: he had prepared a plan of the Crisis of the Battle, showing where the different forces stood. He sent the plan of the Model to Fitzroy Somerset, the Duke's military secretary, asking for Wellington's view on the positions he had allotted to the troops at the Crisis of the Battle.

My dear Lord,

  At length I am enabled to transmit to your Lordship a plan, carefully prepared according to the result of the information in my possession & to the best of my judgement of the disposition which I propose to make of the troops upon the Waterloo Model, and I shall feel greatly obliged by your having the kindness to submit it with the enclosed explanatory memorandum to the Duke of Wellington for any corrections or alterations which His Grace may feel disposed to make, and in particular to bring under His Grace's notice the '*doubtful points*' which I have enumerated and which without the Duke's great assistance I feel myself quite unable to clear up in a satisfactory manner.

There is no doubt that Fitzroy Somerset did, indeed, place Siborne's plan in the hands of the Duke of Wellington, and there is no doubt, either, that the Duke examined it and reflected upon the proposed deployment of the model troops. At the same time, for reasons which are unclear, the Duke's reaction was not relayed to Siborne, and we only know of Wellington's views from an edition of his Supplementary Despatches, which were published after his death. According to his memorandum on William Siborne's plan, Wellington was not over-enamoured with the Model, primarily, it seems, because of his traditional resistance to any historical analysis of his battlefield actions. His reaction was the somewhat weary response of a national hero who wished to distance himself from the project without being drawn into either overt criticism or praise of the Model. If anything, Wellington was impressed by Siborne the topographer, and his praise, faint though it may have been, was for the less controversial aspect of the Model, the layout of the fields and crops. On the success of Siborne the military modeller, he did not wish to be drawn, and, apart from a broad hint that he was not pleased, he left the fight to others:

'I have looked over the plan of the ground of the battle of Waterloo, which appears to me to be accurately drawn. It is very difficult for me to judge the particular position of each body of troops under my command, much less of the Prussian Army, at any particular hour.'

For most of the 1830s, the authorities had tried to dissuade Siborne from portraying the Crisis of the Battle but he had ignored their requests to represent a less controversial moment. It had become clear to them that he had been obtaining information directly from the Prussian General Staff, and that he proposed to show how thousands of Prussian soldiers had been placed in forward positions at the precise moment of victory, as if contradicting the Duke's official record of events, in his despatch after the battle, that his attack upon the Imperial Guard had produced the final outcome.

As far as the authorities were concerned, Siborne had to be brought back into line. At first, they were prepared to go softly. Just over a month after he wrote his letter to the Duke, he received a letter from a chief clerk in the commander-in-chief's office, F.H. Lindsay, offering a clandestine meeting to discuss the Model, and particularly the role the Prussians had played at Waterloo.

CONFIDENTIAL

> Horse Guards
> 26 October 1836

My dear Siborne,

Lord Fitzroy Somerset appears to have placed your papers in the hands of the D. of W. – and from what I can gather, it is clear he is solicitous to converse with you upon some points which are very material to the perfect accuracy of your plan. Especially touching the share the Prussians actually had in deciding the Battle. I therefore write – *earnestly* – to press your coming here – and as it may lead to your having an interview with the Duke, it will be as well that you should be prepared accordingly.

Let me hear by return of Post that it is convenient for you to come – and the sooner the better as you may catch the Duke either on his way through town – or at Walmer where you might have the assistance & advice of Lord Fitzroy before hand.

Keep the object of your journey quiet – but believe me you will do well to come.

Yours very sincerely

Lindsay

But Siborne was not going to be caught by any half-promises of a meeting with Wellington. After three years of managing and paying for the project on his own, the model-maker knew more about the battle than anyone. So Siborne rejected the olive branch that Lindsay had proffered. In his reply, he elides two issues into one, complaining about the treatment that had been meted out to him financially, and insisting that the accuracy of his Model was beyond doubt. A new, even more plaintive tone entered his letter-writing, a sign, perhaps, of the enormous stress that he had placed himself under. His salary in Ireland was just over £330 a year, and he had become so obsessed with the need to complete his Model that he had under-estimated the toll it would take on his health and his family finances.

29 October 1836

My dear Lindsay,

Be assured that I am most fully sensible of your kindness & of your attention to my interests evinced by your proposal that I should immediately proceed to London ... but you will I fear scarcely believe me when I tell you that it is quite out of my power to do so simply from my want of means. The truth is I am completely *ruined* by my undertaking that it is very doubtful whether the small sum I have remaining in hand will suffice to enable me to transport the Model to London when completed ...

It is with regret I must confess I am at this moment writing this to you suffering with extremely ill health and the utmost depression of spirits.

William Siborne simply refused to travel to discuss the issue at hand, the disposition of the Prussian troops. Although, throughout his project, he had given every indication that the authorities would find his Model to their liking, he was proving as obdurate about the rectitude of his research as he had been about showing the precise moment of victory. Perhaps he had simply had enough of the financial stress of making the Model, after the withdrawal of government funding, and thought, however misguidedly, that he might use the request as a lever to get his money; or perhaps he was so convinced of the accuracy of his historical research that he simply did not see why he should change his mind. Would he have changed the basis of his Model if the government had offered him money at this point? It did not, and Siborne was unmoved by Lindsay's suggestion of a secret meeting. Bolstered by the constant support of his mentor, Sir Hussey Vivian, Siborne insisted that the Prussians had played a crucial role at the climax of the battle, and should not be removed from the rolling fields that he had painstakingly modelled. He stood his ground, as if he had had enough of all the financial difficulties he had been placed under, but also as if the topographer in him railed against the forces of inexactitude which were seeking to persuade him to gainsay the facts he had so carefully compiled. In the face of such pressure, Siborne's wish to court establishment approval, or at least not to offend his political and military masters, proved to be less powerful, at this stage, than his desire to stand by the findings of his eyewitness accounts.

> Although my going to London is quite out of the question, I think it right to remark that I am most ready to supply answers to any questions respecting the proposed disposition of the troops on the Model. With respect to the Prussians, I may observe *in justification* that the distribution of their 4th and 2nd Corps which was in support coincides generally with the best French accounts & that the disposal of the 1st Corps, is strongly confirmed by corroborating evidence in my possession.
>
> PS More especially as regards the most advanced Prussian cavalry Regts. *in rear* of the British left wing, *before* the general advance of our line

The conflict between Siborne and the military rumbled on into 1837. On 6 February Sir Hussey Vivian sent Siborne a map on which he had drawn the Prussian deployments he had witnessed, and a week later he repeated his view, by letter, that Ziethen had begun to join up with the left wing of Wellington's army well before the Crisis of the Battle, enabling Wellington to move reinforcements, including Vivian's own cavalry, to shore up the centre of his line. On 23 February, Siborne wrote to Fitzroy Somerset to announce that he was making some minor alterations to his Model, changing the position of the troops attacking Plancenoit, which he had 'thrown somewhat less forward than they appeared upon the Plan which was submitted for the Duke of Wellington's inspection.' But again he stood by the positioning of the leading Prussian troops, declaring that they 'emanate solely from rigid adherence to historical truth.'

Siborne wrote that he hoped Fitzroy Somerset would give him 'full credit' for trying to remove the impression 'of any apparent inclination on my part to attach more weight to the information furnished me by the Prussian Military Authorities than what is fairly due to it after a careful investigation and comparison of the best authenticated French accounts of the operation that took place on the right flank of the Army of Napoleon, as well as of such collateral evidence in my possession from officers of our own service.' Somewhat optimistically, he added: 'I enter-tain high hopes that a perusal of the accompanying manuscript will satisfy your Lordship that the positions which I have assigned to the several Prussian corps are not so much at variance with the true history of the Battle as you were first led to imagine.' The Model, Siborne added for good measure, was a work of art, or an historical memorial of one of the greatest events of modern times, and it was impossible for him 'to contemplate without pain and concern' the prospect of losing the patronage previously extended to him, 'from no other cause than that arising from the most conscientious adoption on my part of certain views founded upon the evidence of which I have been put in possession.'

At the same time, Siborne was still trying to extract money, either from the government or from the army, to pay for the spiralling cost of his Model. He informed Fitzroy Somerset that while three officers had lent him one hundred pounds each, he still needed another four hundred to complete it. He hoped that Fitzroy Somerset or Lord Hill might lend him the money, if he could convince them 'that my views as to the operations of the Prussians are not the result of any perverse opinions of my own.' It was the worst possible set of circumstances in which to operate: he had, however unwittingly, offended the establish-ment, and yet he desperately needed its financial support, and whether through naïveté or desperation, he was still clinging to the hope that he would be offered the lifeline that he thought was his due.

Siborne now wrote a long letter to the Secretary at War, Lord Howick, who had taken office in 1835, in which he again outlined the tangled history of the funding of the Model, and once more asked the government to intercede, a plea which was accompanied by a covering letter from the faithful Hussey Vivian. The strain of trying to complete the Model while holding down his proper job as assistant military secretary was clearly proving too much. He was nearing the end of his financial resources. 'Your Lordship may readily conceive that holding as I do, an Appointment demanding the daily performance of very important duties, it can only be by the devotion of every moment that can be spared from those duties, to the most laborious occupation entailed upon me by so great an undertaking, amounting, I may truly say, to a state of slavery, which has proved most injurious to my health, that I can possibly hope to arrive at a completion of the work.

'It is, however, most disheartening to find that at the moment when I have every reason to anticipate a conclusion of my labour in the approaching summer, my work must again be suspended for want of further funds, and that should I not succeed in obtaining them, the Model must be abandoned even when so very near its completion, and a pecuniary embarrassment must follow which can only end in the ruin of myself and my family.'

Siborne proposed that the government should lend him the money to finish the Model, and that the interest on the loan should be met from his pay. This would see him through to the public exhibition of the Model, which, he confidently anticipated, would enable him to pay off the debt outright. But the sums he needed were still huge: there was four hundred pounds to transport the Model in a finished state from Dublin to London, and another three hundred to erect a temporary building large enough for its exhibition. Once again, Siborne's appeal for help concentrated on the unfairness of the government's initial decision to back the project and its sudden withdrawal of funds. He concluded: 'I trust that the circumstance of my having undertaken it in the first instance with the whole sanction and authority of the Government, of my having been so very unexpectedly deprived of the advantage of such sanction and authority as far as regarded its necessary expenses, and of my having, out of my great anxiety to complete a work of such national interest and importance, made the utmost possible sacrifice of my time, health, and all available resources – will satisfy your Lordship that in venturing upon this appeal to the Government, I am supported by a fair and reasonable claim upon its generous consideration.'

Siborne, by this stage, probably had no trust at all in his ability to win the government round, but if he was truly confident, rather than simply desperate, then such optimism was misplaced. Howick gave a short reply, which gave no ground at all, and used Siborne's assertions about the intrinsic merit of his Model to reject any claim on the Treasury. The government had washed its hands of the project and, like the military itself, probably wished it had never helped to unleash such an expensive and unnecessarily democratic project.

War Office

5 January 1837

PRIVATE

Dear Sir Hussey,

I received your note of the 3rd enclosing Lt. Siborn's letter, and it would have given me great pleasure if in consideration of the strong recommendation you have given him I could have complied with his request, but I have no authority to do so, and it would have been quite in vain for me to recommend the application to the Treasury where the case has already been decided.

I cannot conceive that if the work is really so good and if Lt. Siborn has grounds for expecting that he could repay the advance he wants he would have any difficulty in obtaining a loan to this amount from private individuals.

I am Sir,

Howick

Events were now colliding in a way which spelled disaster for William Siborne. Once more, he approached Fitzroy Somerset to help win government funds for the construction costs of the model. But he found that Fitzroy Somerset was less concerned with Siborne's financial predicament than with the issue of the Prussians.

Horse Guards
7 March 1837

My dear Sir,

I return the confidential memorandum ... I am very much obliged to you for letting me see it as also for the details which your letter affords.

Knowing how much time and labour you have bestowed on the Model of Waterloo, how ably you have executed the work and how important it is to your interests that no time should be lost in exposing it to view I feel great reluctance in acknowledging to you that I continue of the opinion I before specified and that I still think that the position you have given to the Prussian troops is not the correct one as regards the moment you wish to represent, and that those who see the work will deduce from it that the result of the Battle was not so much owing to British Valour, and the great generalship of the chief of the English Army, as to the flank movements of the Prussians.

Believe me very faithfully yours,
Fitzroy Somerset

Somerset had summed up the controversy perfectly. Either British valour and Wellington's superb leadership had won the battle of Waterloo, or the victory had been down to Prussian 'flank' movements. There was, in his mind, no possibility that the two events had been inextricably linked, that the one could not have happened without the other and that the Prussians, though late onto the stage, had played a central role in the events, rather than a tangential one as Fitzroy Somerset's dismissive description of their contribution had suggested. Even without the key issue of the time of the arrival of thousands of Prussian troops, the battle for Plancenoit had clearly forced Napoleon to divert more than ten thousand of his men, weakening the impact of Ney's final assault. Correctly, Somerset observed that 'the time of the advance of the Prussian armies varies much in the different accounts' and he was adamant that the Duke had been unaware of any forward movement made by the Prussians in large numbers. Then he indirectly referred to the Duke's own account of the battle. 'I have always understood that the Duke's movement in advance arose from his observing the confusion of the Enemy after the failure of their last attack.' Finally, and unsurprisingly, and in the cold manner in which a gentleman might dismiss a servant from his employ, Fitzroy Somerset declared that he would not back the project, implicitly suggesting that the cause for his reluctance was Siborne's insistence that the Prussian should share the field of battle at the moment of victory. 'I regret to say that it would be very inconvenient to me to subscribe at this moment and I am therefore obliged to relinquish the idea of assisting in the completion of the Work.' The two issues had, effectively, become one. Siborne would certainly receive no official help in recovering his money unless he fell into line with the army's view of the battle.

Throughout his troubles, however, Siborne could still rely on the full support and encouragement of Sir Hussey Vivian, who had seen firsthand the crucial role played by the Prussian army. On 19 April 1837, Vivian wrote to Siborne to stress the importance of the Prussian advance against Plancenoit. 'I care not what one may say to depreciate the importance of Prussian aid. My own opinion always has been and always will be that but for that aid our own advance would not have taken place ... we could not have thought of it had not the Prussians carried Plancenoit and had not the enemy in consequence began to leave. I saw some part of their force move towards the rear, which was observed by the D. of Wellington (I apprehend) before he gave the order to move.' Then, perhaps sardonically, as if he knew his man, Vivian added: 'I know not what high authority may object to giving due credit to the Prussians – certainly not the D. of W. I should think.'

Bolstered by Hussey Vivian's support, Siborne again sent a list of points for Fitzroy Somerset to clarify, a sign both of his assiduity and of his continuing desire to win over the opinion of his superiors. But it was a lost cause. Three years earlier he had rejected the idea that subscribers should be allowed to give the Model to the Duke of Wellington because it would 'deliberately deprive myself of the honour and gratification of presenting in my own name, as the author, the results of my labours either to the Duke of Wellington, or to the government.' Now he was given the cold shoulder by the very army leaders he was most keen to impress. Certainly Fitzroy Somerset was unmoved by the request for information. The Duke of Wellington had not commented publicly on the battle since 1815 and he would not change his mind now. If he could not control history, he would say nothing. Once again, Siborne was dismissed with ruthlessness, couched in the icy language of bureaucratic politeness.

28 August 1837

My dear Sir,

I return the Memorandum which you sent me on the 14th instant and regret to say that it is not in my power to afford you any information upon the several points to which your queries are directed.

It appears to me that the Duke of Wellington could not fairly be called upon to speak to any separate or specific operation of the Battle without going at the same time into the whole question and having his opinion received as entirely conclusive.

Very faithfully yours,

Fitzroy Somerset

Siborne had lost his battle to win over the opinion of the establishment. Much like the battle fought by the commander he so admired at Waterloo, it had been a strange, obdurate affair, marked by the dogged defence of an entrenched position against almost overwhelming odds. He had marshalled his arguments as doughtily as the Duke had deployed his troops, but, like the Duke on the battlefield, he had made tactical errors too. His refusal to treat with the Duke of Wellington when summoned to a clandestine meeting had been as cavalier as the charge by the heavy cavalry on the afternoon of Waterloo. In the end, Siborne's obsession with accuracy had so consumed him that, instead of fighting cleverly, he had revealed his position too openly, showing, on the one hand, how importunate he was, while refusing, on the other, to alter his view of history. In the end, it was inevitable that an opponent as politically skilful as Fitzroy Somerset might see that Siborne's need for money might end the crisis of the Model once and for all.

Unfortunately for Siborne, however, he was not just fighting the

Château de Hougoumont – detail

establishment. As Major Basil Jackson, of the Royal Staff Corps, put it: a military historian 'who has a loftier aim than merely to amuse his readers, rarely meets with much encouragement in England; so that unless he can contrive to blend entertainment with instruction, his work must be a dead weight on the publisher's shelves.' So too for William Siborne. If he was to recoup his investment, the public would have to pay.

Public opinion held that it had been a very British victory, not least because the story of the battle had become a popular entertainment. True, its horror had been captured by a bleak painting called 'Château de Hougoumont, Field of Waterloo', by Denis Dighton, a former ensign in the 90th Foot, who made accurate drawings of the clearing of the battlefield in 1815, the year in which he was appointed Military Painter to the Prince of Wales.

In front of the bullet-scarred walls of the château two men are seen tipping a body into a pit, observed by two waiting officers. The landscape is bare and blasted: the branch of a tree lies on the ground. Half a dozen hats and rifles lie discarded on the ground. Naked limbs sprawl, tangled, over the edge of the freshly dug mound. But it was the romantic view of the battle which soon prevailed, for most artists preferred to concentrate on the glory of the battle, rather than its bloody consequences, and in doing so they paid little attention to accuracy, least of all to the grim reality that had so impressed Dighton.

The largest and most popular painting of them all was also one of the most stylised, and while its elephantine size was in itself a reflection of the scale of the victory, its vast acres of canvas had little room for more than a scant acknowledgement of its grim reality. Specially printed handbills drove thousands of paying spectators to see the enormous picture, making it, within a year of the battle, one of London's most popular attractions.

The Panorama of Leicester-Square was the invention of Robert Barker, an itinerant portrait-painter, who, it was said, had been struck by the potential of a vast 360-degree painting as he walked on Calton Hill in Edinburgh, and saw the city at his feet.

To create the illusion he required, he bought a plot of land in London, and paid an architect to design a rotunda on two levels. Each level was a different size, and on each a vast panoramic painting could be hung. In the roof there were two windows, one to shed light on the lower level, and one on the upper. To enter the world of the panorama, spectators walked along a dark corridor, to prepare themselves for the scene which awaited them. Finally, they reached an observation platform, which kept them at a distance from the canvas, with a canopy concealing the lighting overhead. Before them lay a continuous circular picture, hung in such weak light that it was impossible to see beyond the upper edge of the canvas. Its dimensions were simply enormous – some fifteen metres wide by one hundred and twenty metres long. So powerful was the illusion it created that, as they stared in the half-light, the audience felt as if it was in the centre of the picture.

The whole effect of the panorama depended on trickery, as well as on a degree of artistic accuracy. Even the name of Barker's enterprise managed to combine reality and falsehood – he called it La Nature à Coup d'Oeil. The secret lay in eliminating the outside world, by removing all the boundaries or reference points by which a spectator could judge size and distance, or compare art with reality. To this end, the

DESCRIPTION
OF THE
FIELD OF BATTLE

AND DISPOSITION OF THE
TROOPS engaged in the ACTION

FOUGHT ON THE
18TH of JUNE, 1815

NEAR

WATERLOO

ILLUSTRATIVE OF THE
Representation of that great Event

IN THE
PANORAMA,
LEICESTER-SQUARE

'Rivers of blood I see, and hills of slain,
An Iliad rising out of one campaign.'
Addison's Campaign, 11th and 12th lines.

PRICE SIXPENCE

1816

picture was hung without a frame and seemingly without any support. At the royal inauguration of the Leicester-Square Panorama in 1794, it had worked too well. 'The View of the Fleet at Spithead' made Princess Charlotte feel sea-sick.

The Leicester-Square Panorama was a great success and more than a hundred productions were held there until its closure in 1861. After Spithead came the 'Battle of Aboukir'; then Robert Barker's son, Henry

Aston Barker, displayed the result of his first study tour of Constanti-nople and in 1802 a panorama of Paris after the Peace of Amiens was shown. But it was the 'Battle of Waterloo' which would make Henry Aston Barker's fortune: he took more than £10,000 within a few months of its opening, and it proved so popular that it was exhibited across England and even in North America.

Barker's panorama of the battle was painted 'on the largest Scale from Drawings taken on the Spot' and it showed conspicuous British gallantry during the advance of the French Imperial Guards, at the end of the battle. In the painting, long since lost, an ensign who had been wounded in the knee was portrayed dropping the King's Colour, only for it to be bravely rescued. Sir Peregrine Maitland was mounted near the centre of the line, with his hat off, cheering his men. In the foreground, some drummers were carrying away the body of Lt.-Col. Charles Thomas, who had been killed in the final charge. A troop of the mounted rocket-brigade was firing rockets into the enemy from a sand-bank on the left of the Genappe road near La Haye Sainte. Near the village of Mont St Jean, an ammunition wagon had blown up.

The panorama claimed it was showing fact not fiction. In its adver-tisements and in the booklets which it sold to spectators it emphasised that its artists had made their studies and sketches on location. Henry Aston Barker had himself visited the battlefield to sketch the landscape and talk to officers, as the guide to his panorama made clear: 'he respectfully informs the public, that, in order to give a correct Rep-resentation of the Battle of Waterloo, he went to Paris, and, from the Officers at Head-quarters, procured every possible Information on the Subject.'

But the panorama had to balance conflicting demands – whilst it had to be accurate, in case anyone complained, it also had to entertain the public and make money. Indeed, it constantly strove to perfect its design to eradicate awareness and achieve total illusion. So while it sought to portray a moment of truth, it deliberately confused fiction and reality to heighten the effect on spectators, and to involve them in the action to such a degree that they actually felt as if they were there.

The result was that Waterloo was presented as a romanticised ideal, a portrayal of heroism and the national character which had forged such a splendid victory. In depicting the moment of victory, Barker's vast painting took artistic licence to play with the known facts. The Duke of Wellington was represented in the foreground, near the Guards. But this was merely illustrative, not factual. 'To say where he actually was, at this period, is impossible,' the guide to the painting remarked. 'His Grace, in the course of the day, went to every part of the line, animating the troops with his presence; and in some cases, leading them on.'

Nor did Barker have any compunction about tinkering with the final advance of Wellington's army, although he was scrupulous enough to admit it. 'This is the period represented, generally, in the Panorama,' declared his brochure, 'though a liberty has been taken, as to time, in introducing the glorious charge made by the Highlanders, and General Ponsonby's brigade of cavalry, upon the enemy's corps, commanded by Count d'Erlon, consisting of 20,000 infantry, who were all dispersed, killed, or taken prisoners; losing two Eagles in the conflict. The charge was made a few hours before the general advance of the British army.'

If the panorama took liberties, then so did other artists and actors. A highly theatrical version of the Battle of Waterloo was re-enacted at the Royal Amphitheatre of Arts, with cannons blazing and horses charging. At Vauxhall Gardens, more than a thousand spectators watched a re-enactment of the attack on Hougoumont, their view of the epic contest spoiled only by the smoke used by the production as muskets cracked out and the château set on fire. Scores of instant history books were written, of variable quality. 'Buonaparte was equally astonished and chagrined at the obstinate resistance of the British troops,' wrote the novelistic author of *A Full and Circumstantial account of the Memorable Battle of Waterloo*. 'He incessantly took snuff in large pinches from his waist-coat pocket, violently sniffing up part, and throwing the rest from him. "These English are devils!" he exclaimed; "will they never be beaten?"'

To compound the nationalistic fervour, a universal loathing of foreigners seemed to settle over the land. With the future of Europe settled by the great battle, and with Napoleon safely in exile, a new balance of power existed, so that, in the place of the lost Emperor, it was

The Panorama of the Battle of Waterloo

200

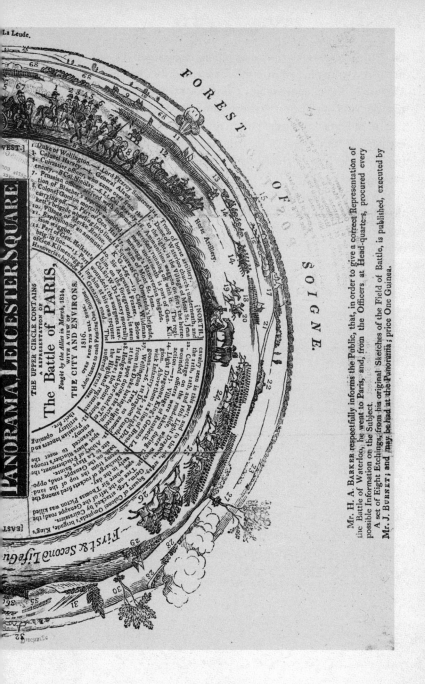

Mr. H. A. BARKER respectfully informs the Public, that, in order to give a correct Representation of the Battle of Waterloo, he went to Paris, and, from the Officers at Head-quarters, procured every possible Information on the Subject.

A set of Eight Etchings, from his original Sketches of the Field of Battle, is published, executed by Mr. J. BURNET; and may be had at the Panorama; price One Guinea.

the Prussians whose territorial ambitions cast a shadow over England's newfound strength, and over the peace established by the Congress of Vienna. In the circumstances, it was not surprising to find that the rejoicing over Wellington's victory soon turned into a national celebration of a heroic encounter from which the Prussians were all but excluded. Within a year of the fighting, and with all the imperfections implicit in its hurried transition from fact, the Battle of Waterloo was passing into legend.

It was from this half-remembered world of make-believe and glory that William Siborne had determined to salvage the true history of the day.

XIII

He is attempting the impossible! May his compatriots have the firm intention of telling the truth, the whole truth and nothing but the truth, and may they also tell only what they know from personal experience and leave out everything they know from hearsay. Otherwise there will be such a confusion of time and sequence of the individual movements that he who collects and orders the data will be faced with insurmountable difficulties.

Captain Kristofe Heise, King's German Legion,
letter for William Siborne, 18 September 1837

The work-load must have been staggering. As Fitzroy Somerset had found out to his cost, Siborne was carrying out meticulous military research. But he was also making his Model to impossibly high standards. First, he told students of his methods, he surveyed the ground from its highest points, then moved on to the villages and farms of the battlefields, where he noted their main features, a church spire or a tall chimney. Then he drew a map, and coded it with symbols to represent pasture, meadowland, heath, cornfields, trees and woods and roads. At Waterloo, he also drew a detailed plan of Hougoumont, and he spoke to the local farmers about the state of their crops on the day of the great battle. He labelled objects he found hard to represent, such as houses, churches, mills, walls and bridges.

When it came to making the Model itself, Siborne explained that the first difficulty he faced was in choosing an appropriate relationship between the horizontal scale and the vertical. Visitors to the Model would be viewing it as if they were several miles above the battlefield, rather than seeing it as if they were walking along it, with their eyes only five or six feet above the ground. Because of this difference in perspective, the terrain would look unnatural if the two scales were identical: it would turn a model of a gently undulating surface into an undeviating plain, and a mountainous region into hills. For drawing a map of an entire country, Siborne found that the best scale was six inches to a mile, or 1 to 10,000, because it would enable every battalion, squadron and battery to be shown in the exact proportion to the area of ground it occupied. This scale was fine for the horizontal scale of a model too, but Siborne had calculated that the vertical scale should increase, over and above this, by a third if the ground was mountainous, a half again if it was hilly, and by two thirds more if the countryside was gently undulating. Only if the model was small enough to be picked up could this rule be ignored, and the Great Model was certainly not going to be pocket-sized. On the vast tableau that he planned, Siborne's scale was nine feet to the mile along the horizontal, or 1 to 600, and, because of the rolling countryside around Waterloo, he chose as his vertical scale, 1 to 180.

To make his preparatory model, Siborne fixed a tracing of the ground on a slab of plaster of Paris. He preferred to use a base of plaster, rather than a well-seasoned board, because if he left the work for any length of time, he could put a wet cloth underneath it, and it would keep his modelling clay moist, without warping the base. Into this he fixed pins, with pointed pieces of wire for the highest parts, which he tapped into place with a small hammer along the principal bends of the horizontal lines, and along the bends of roads and other boundaries, cutting all the pins and wires to the right length with a small wire-cutter. He used fine clay to fill in the spaces between the pins, until their tops could barely be seen, so that he had created a rough model of the ground, ready for him to craft it more finely with small pieces of box-wood or ivory, of various shapes, some turned and flattened, others squared or pointed.

To make the mould, he made a wooden frame about an inch thick, and an inch higher than the highest point of the Model, and he fixed it to the clay so that it met the side of the Model perfectly. With a camel-hair brush, he painted the surface of the Model with 'sweet oil', taking care not to get any on the sides of the frame. Then he poured plaster of Paris, mixed with water, over the clay, waiting a quarter of an hour or twenty minutes for it to cool. The oil would have made it easier to remove the mould which had formed, which was then put aside to dry. This was then given several coats of drying oil, and it was then put aside for a few days.

To make the cast, he brushed the mould with more sweet oil, and the inner sides of the frame, and again poured plaster into the mould. When this, too, had dried, he tapped the upper side of the frame all over with a hammer to remove the cast. He replaced any broken pieces with glue, or papier-mâché, which he shaped and glued into place, and then he keyed the whole surface with a special liquid called isinglass so that it was ready to take paint.

Siborne made another wooden frame, and fixed it to the cast, and then started to divide up the cast into smaller squares, using a pencil and a ruler, to match the way he had marked up the plan of the Model. By breaking it down into these smaller areas, he could then mark the places where he was going to fix objects to the Model. He used green silk chenille or green cotton for the hedges, laid along his pencil lines, and glued firmly in place; narrow slips of white card represented walls; but trees were more complicated to make. Siborne again used chenille, which he cut into small pieces according to the scale of the Model. He then put six or seven patches of glue onto the Model, and dampened a small piece of wood with his tongue, so that a piece of chenille would stick to it, and then pushed it gently down onto one of the spots of gum. If he was modelling on a very large scale, he bunched the chenille together with fine wire, which he twisted with a wire-cutter to form a stem and fixed the trees into narrow holes with a pointed instrument, and held the whole structure together with gum.

Houses were made out of cork, their sides coloured white and their roofs red, streams were coloured pale blue, road, lanes and paths were painted to look drab or dusty; but with fields, Siborne was anxious to avoid a uniformity of colour. In one of his books on topography, which included a section on model-making, he advised that light and dark green should be contrasted together, and that 'a few browns should be introduced' to represent fallow land. For rocks, the dark ground should be laid on first, and then the other colours, such as grey, red, light brown, 'slightly and delicately with a brush almost dry'. There were instructions, too, on how to make the colours of the model – they should be ground with very weak gum water – for, said Siborne, 'the selection and disposition of them of course depend greatly upon the taste of the artist, who must adhere as closely to nature as the materials at his command will admit.' Finally, he insisted that models should be provided with cases to protect them from dust and should never be exposed to the sun.

By 1833, Siborne had prepared the groundwork of the Great Model. It measured exactly 21 feet 4½ inches by 19 feet 8¼ inches, and Siborne, perhaps with one eye on posterity, was taking no chances with its durability. The base was divided into more than thirty compartments joined firmly by brass plates and screws, and the plaster of Paris which he used to model the terrain had been 'very carefully prepared in a particular manner', he told the *United Services Journal*, to render it impervious to the influence of heat or moisture. Siborne detailed every meticulous preparation he had made: for example, the plaster would give the Model 'a degree of hardness and solidity by which it becomes infinitely more durable than wood, and totally exempt from the risk of warping, to which models constructed of the latter material are so extremely liable.'

Siborne's skill as a topographer and the eight months' hard work he had put into surveying the battlefield were fully acknowledged by the magazine which stated that he had 'carried his labours to such a degree that he has, with the greatest mathematical precision, ascertained not only the position and extent of every object and enclosure, but the nature and level of the surface and its undulations.' In fact, Siborne had done far more than this. He told the magazine that he had felt that it was 'incumbent' on him to create 'the most rigid imitation' of nature. To effect this, he declared, he had acquainted himself, as far as possible, with the state of cultivation in every field on the day of the battle.

To do this was hard enough, but to create a realistic model with the information at his disposal was a task of an entirely different order. Siborne was aware that carving the different fields from solid material over a surface area of 420 square feet would be an immense undertaking, and he concluded that, in any case, the end result would not be worth the effort. He thought the crops on the ground would simply look stiff when they were contrasted with the tens of thousands of tiny model soldiers with which he intended to populate his Model.

Instead, Siborne went to great lengths to make the ground as realistic as possible. Partly, this was because he was concerned that the Model should be approved by the military authorities that had commissioned it, and partly it was because, like the owners of the Leicester-Square Panorama, he wished his portrayal of the battle to appeal to the general public too. But, most of all, he wanted to appeal to the soldiers, and their commanders, who had fought at Waterloo. So, unlike the panorama, Siborne did not award himself licence to stretch the facts, to appeal to popular imagination through presenting a romanticised ideal of war. He desperately wanted his Model to be a success, and there would soon come a time when he needed it to be one for financial reasons, and in that regard he had more in common with the Barker family than he would have cared to admit. But he would achieve his ambition through his scrupulous devotion to accuracy. 'In this he has succeeded,' said the *United Services Journal*, 'so as to be able to exhibit the different kinds of grain, such as wheat, oats, rye, barley; also beans, peas, potatoes, clover, together with trees and hedges – in all of which, colour, form and general appearance, are imitated as closely as possible.'

Siborne's modelled fields were so flexible to the touch that he was able to raise or press down any part of the crops, according to the information provided by the soldiers who responded to his circular letter. In this way, Siborne was able to alter the landscape of his Model to match the devastation caused by the battle and the continual movement of troops. This was important because it gave him the freedom to make changes, which, as a devotee of accuracy, he thought he needed in case the information with which he was working turned out to be incorrect.

Siborne did not make the toy soldiers himself and to this day, it is unclear where they were modelled. The main industry was based in Germany, emerging from the lively business carried out by pewterers and tinsmiths who made miniature religious charms, before discovering that more bellicose, and less saintly, creations could be even more profitable. The father of the toy trade was one Johann Gottfried Hilpert, who from his factory in Nuremberg, produced flat tin figures which were inspired by the campaigns of Frederick the Great. By the end of the eighteenth century, the industry had spread throughout Europe, but Germany remained its home, leading the way in both quality and quantity. The years when Siborne was making his Model coincided with a surge in the tin soldier industry and German soldiers were being exported across Europe and the United States. As there was no such history of modelling toy soldiers in England, and we know that Siborne paid a tradesman to make his army, it is likely, but not certain, that he bought his soldiers from Germany.

Even with such help, however, the Model took a year longer to make than Siborne expected, and it was finally ready to be exhibited in October 1838. But he had clearly run out of funds again, and based on later correspondence, it looks as if Siborne had decided to mortgage its future, and his own, by raising money against the exhibition profits he was sure he would make. He had consistently maintained in his battle with the government, that the Model was bound to be a success, and that it would recoup any money it chose to give him. Now he had taken on a heavy debt, in addition to the costs he had already incurred, to enable him to finish the project. Effectively, he had pawned the Model, and the only way he could recover it for himself would be if it captured the public's imagination, as he was sure it would.

Even if he had fears for the future, however, he must have been a happy man. He had completed his life's work, despite all the hostility to his project. He had come through financial crises and survived. He had braved military resistance, and faced it down. He had seen off opposition in the higher circles of government, and lived to tell the tale. Those forces were still ranged against him, but they had failed to prevent him from achieving his goal. It had taken him eight years of dedicated research and model-making, but he had done it. He had produced the finest, largest, battlefield model the world had ever seen.

What a moment it must have been for him, when at long last the Model was ready to be advertised on the front page of the *United Services Gazette*.

The **MODEL** of the **BATTLE** of **WATERLOO**,
covering a space of 420 square feet,
and containing 190,000 **figures,**

IS NOW OPEN for EXHIBITION,
at the EGYPTIAN-HALL, PICCADILLY

Admittance One Shilling.

Open from ten till five in the morning, and from
six till nine in the evening, brilliantly illuminated.

Siborne, in the teeth of the opposition of the establishment, had put his Model on display. Now, however, it was at the mercy of an even more fickle constituency, the ticket-buying public, in the exhibition hall of a strange building which looked as if it had been transplanted from a foreign land.

The Egyptian Hall, or Bullock's Museum, was a nineteenth-century curiosity, as incongruous an adornment to the London scene as it was spectacular. It had been built in the style of ancient Egypt to the specification of one William Bullock, to house his natural history museum. Bullock was a traveller, a naturalist and an antiquarian, and at the turn of the century he had founded a Museum of Natural Curiosities in Sheffield, where he had been a jeweller and goldsmith. He moved his museum first to Liverpool in 1801 and then in 1812, the year Napoleon invaded Russia, to London. The new museum, at 22 Piccadilly, cost £16,000, and was built in a passable imitation of the temple of Tentyra in Upper Egypt. Hieroglyphics festooned its exterior, and above the papyrus columns of the entrance, flanking a window on the first floor, stood the carved figures of the deities Osiris and Isis.

The Egyptian Hall quickly won itself a reputation as the centre for spectacular shows, and William Bullock became one of London's most successful and commercially-minded showmen. Over the later course of the century the diminutive Tom Thumb would take to the stage here, in front of crowds of hundreds, and here too the magician Maskelyne nightly cut off the head of his fellow-illusionist, Cooke. Under Bullock's stewardship, however, the museum mainly contained arms and armour, and artefacts brought back from the South Seas by Captain Cook. An engraving of the time shows a large room, lit from above by a cupola, in which, in the centre, stands a collection of animals, including, among others, an elephant, a rhinoceros, a bear and a zebra, grouped as if they had been corralled together on the Ark. Shields and swords lined the walls, while a dozen or so visitors are shown viewing the exhibits.

Within the eclectic, even eccentric, range of exhibitions in the Egyptian Hall the benchmark for judging the success of Siborne's exhibition had been set by a single display which was held during Bullock's ownership of the space. His most sensational and lucrative investment had been an exhibition of Napoleon's relics, including the carriage, captured on his retreat from Waterloo, which made Bullock the staggering sum of £35,000 for an outlay of £2500. While the former Emperor languished on St Helena, his coach drew such great crowds to the Egyptian Hall that an engraving was made of the crush which daily surrounded the vehicle. Nearly a quarter of a million visitors paid a shilling to see the coach, and another half-million saw it when it went on tour: eager eyes took in its dark blue bodywork, complete with the Imperial arms which were emblazoned on its bullet-proof door panels, the vast wheels and the undercarriage, painted in vermilion, edged with blue and gold, and the sabre cuts aimed at the coachman when the carriage was captured at Genappe, but which had sliced its springs instead.

Inside the coach, a mahogany case held rum and wine; another, which had been given to Napoleon by Maria Teresa, held a hundred objects made of gold, including a breakfast service for tea, coffee and chocolate, with plates, candlesticks, knives, forks and spoons, a spirit lamp for making breakfast, a gold hand basin, and a whole range of perfume bottles. There was a tea-pot, a coffee-pot, a sugar-basin, a jug, a coffee-cup and saucer, and candlesticks, all made with gold and embossed with an Imperial and imperious N. At the bottom of the box, two thousand gold coins had been found, and the wood bore the scars made by the Prussian soldiers when they had forced it open. There was also a snuff box made of gold with a border of brilliants in the shape of bees, with Napoleon's initials picked out by a hundred and forty-four diamonds; and, in silver, a sandwich box, plates, knives and spoons, a pepper and salt-box, a mustard pot and a decanter. There were linen shirts, and handkerchiefs and stockings, which bore the Imperial crown. There was a writing desk which could be pulled out and used as the carriage moved, and beneath the coachman's seat a small leather case contained the polished steel poles of a make-up bed. In the front of the coach there were compartments for telescopes and maps, and in one of the doors, two pistol holders, which had held loaded guns, and, on the side of the coach, a large silver chronometer hanging on a silver chain. A spring-loaded mechanism triggered roller-blinds which had once hidden Napoleon from view, but which now could no longer prevent thousands of paying customers from gawping at the style in which the Emperor went to war.

Could Siborne's Model create as much of a stir as Napoleon's coach? While the museum-going public had relished its glimpse of part of the Emperor's life, Siborne had created a less obvious form of entertainment. But the Model was still an amazing sight. It lay within a protective glass case, upon which Siborne had insisted despite the extra cost, true to his written insistence a decade earlier that 'models should be provided with cases to protect them from dust, and should never be exposed to the sun.'

It is extraordinary today to see the Model in all its detail. It is so vast the mind can hardly take it in its perfect, miniature proportions. The rolling fields of Waterloo stretch as far as the eye can see. Through the centre of the landscape, disappearing into the distance, runs the Brussels to Charleroi road; to its side, at an angle, lies the Brussels to Nivelles road; both of them are crossed by a network of smaller roads, and tracks. The burnt-out château of Hougoumont, with its distinctive roof, is perfectly modelled, and so too the farmstead of La Haye Sainte and La Belle Alliance. Thousands of tiny soldiers, cast in a tin-lead alloy, are placed upon the landscape, one toy soldier representing every two on the actual battlefield. The detail is remarkable. Each weapon

The Great Model of Waterloo

or piece of equipment is attached separately to its owner; the wagon drivers have their own whips; individual soldiers, their arms raised or lowered in a variety of positions, were painted separately to show their uniforms, and even their helmet badges.

In the Crisis of the Battle, one attack by four battalions of the Imperial Guard has already been repulsed. Rallied by Napoleon, the survivors are regrouping on a rise of ground near the Charleroi road. The French artillery is bombarding the Allied positions. Sixteen battalions of French infantry, under d'Erlon, are moving past the farm of La Haye Sainte, now in French hands. The 27th Inniskilling regiment is standing in square in the exposed centre of the Anglo-Allied line, where British and Hanoverian infantry are standing firm, but the men are dying under the enemy barrage. To their right are Brunswick and Hanoverian infantry, with British and German cavalry in support. To the rear are the remains of the British heavy cavalry, the Union and Household brigades, which had suffered such terrible losses in their magnificent, flawed charge of the early afternoon. To their west are three large squares of Dutch-Belgian infantry, reinforced by British light cavalry led by Major-General Sir John Vandeleur.

The Great Model of Waterloo

But the main battle lies to the south. Six large battalions of the Imperial Guard, four from the Middle Guard and two from the Old, are advancing on two battalions of the 1st Foot Guards, while the British are pouring massed volleys of musket-fire into the enemy ranks. To their rear are columns of Dutch-Belgian infantry and cavalry. Men from Major-General Adam's Light Infantry Brigade, the 52nd, 71st Light Infantry and two battalions of the 95th Rifles, are wheeling as they advance, four deep, turning their right shoulders to pour fire into the enemy's flank. Between the angle of the two brigades stands the Duke of Wellington and his staff, placed at the point where the climax of the battle is being fought. Spread across the battlefield are the French troops at the time of the Guard's advance and of d'Erlon's final charge. Around La Belle Alliance are the 'greatly diminished' remains of the Imperial Guard, the chasseurs à cheval, the grenadiers à cheval, two squadrons of lancers, and two of Dragoons. It requires only a moment's imagination to see that the Imperial Guard will soon be broken, to be pursued by the British infantry past the partly-destroyed château of Hougoumont, and Wellington will order the general advance to win the battle.

Then, as now, the Model was deemed to be a marvellous sight. The *Morning Post* reported that the thousands of tiny figures had been created 'with so much accuracy that not only the nation, but the very branch of the service to which they belong, is perfectly obvious on the nearer points; while the more distant points are distinctly marked out by the various lines of fire, distinguished as they are by a representation of smoke, as ingenious as it is efficient . . . We strongly urge a visit to the Egyptian Hall.' Some of them, the dead and the dying, were scattered across the ground as if a giant hand had knocked them down, and all of them were so small that it was impossible to count them and come to an exact conclusion about how many had been placed on the battlefield. Siborne had supplied special magnifying glasses so that the spectators could admire the precision with which the models had been created, their tiny muskets and rifles, the artillery and horses, and in this way they could identify individual corps and companies, and even individual officers.

'The time chosen,' stated Siborne, as if to ensure that no one could doubt that this moment was the only one he could have selected, 'is that in which Napoleon made his last great struggle for victory; and which may be truly termed the crisis of the battle, for on the success or failure of this effort depended the fate of the Emperor of the French, and the destinies of Europe.' Nor was Siborne stinting in his praise of the Duke of Wellington, though he was careful to give due credit to the Prussians. 'The battle had already lasted eight hours and result still trembled in the balance. The steady, resolute, and unshaken front presented by the allied army under the Duke of Wellington, notwithstanding the most determined efforts, so frequently repeated, to force its line of battle, and the gradual development of the principal portion of the Prussian army under Prince Blücher Von Wahlstadt, by which so powerful a diversion was effected against the French right, rendered it imperative on Napoleon to resort to one of two alternatives – the commencement of a retreat, or to make another desperate attempt to break the Duke's line . . .'

A plan of the battle, showing the field at a quarter-past-seven, was printed in the guide to the Model which was sold at the exhibition, and there were more than a hundred footnotes to describe the positions of the soldiers on both sides. Despite his earlier promise not to produce anything which was at variance with one syllable of the Duke of Wellington's despatch, Siborne had positioned toy soldiers representing more than 40,000 Prussian forces on the Model. According to the guide, precisely 49,886 of their men and 123 guns were in action by 7 p.m. They were placed in three key areas: the leading column of Ziethen's men had joined up with the left of the Anglo-Allied line, and, separately, many of the Prussian toy soldiers were engaged in the heavy fighting with the Imperial Guard around Plancenoit and Smohain. The most controversial part of the Model lay between these two areas, for Siborne had positioned thousands more Prussian soldiers in the land which lay between the extreme left of the Anglo-Allied line and the fighting around Plancenoit itself. The implication was clear: that they had been present in force at the moment of victory and that, as the guide said, the Prussians had forced Napoleon to choose between retreating, or making 'another desperate attempt to break the Duke's line.' Siborne was showing that he believed that the bulk of the Prussian forces had precipitated the Crisis of the Battle, and that their presence, in front of Lobau's corps, had made a vital contribution to the overall victory. If he was right, then the Prussian army had brought unbearable pressure to bear on the right flank of the French army during the final moments of the battle.

By creating his Model in this way, Siborne was staying true to the evidence he had collated: the Prussians were fighting, and winning, the battle against the bulk of the French army at the moment of the defeat of the Imperial Guard. Siborne's questionnaire had been quite specific about the information he had wanted, asking surviving officers 'what was the particular formation at the moment when the French Imperial Guards, advancing to attack the right of the British Forces, reached the crest of our position? What was the formation of the Enemy's Forces?' If Siborne's Model was correct, however, then, by extension, Wellington could not claim the overwhelming credit for the triumph, and the Battle of Waterloo would have to be seen as the battle of three armies, and the victory of two.

Was Siborne right to make his Model in this way? His long-term supporter certainly thought so. 'I have no desire to take from the merits of the British,' Hussey Vivian assured him, 'but I cannot be blind to the advantage, the important advantage, the attack of the Prussian force was to us, and it's not fair not to give it its due weight and the Prussians due credit.' Not surprisingly, the Prussians thought so too. Captain Wagner, an historian in the Prussian army, wrote to Siborne to tell him that 'there exists neither in the German nor the French language a work that contains more details about the fighting in the village of Plancenoit than the description signed by you which I received.' His view seemed to be supported by a neutral observer at the battle, the Spanish general, Miguel Alava, who had told the *Madrid Gazette* that at the critical moment 'we perceived the fire of Marshal Blucher, attacking the enemy's right with his usual impetuosity; and the moment of decisive attack being come, the Duke put himself at the head of the English Foot Guards . . . (and) . . . they marched at the point of the bayonet, to come to close action with the Imperial Guard.'

Further backing had come from the Earl of Wiltshire, on a visit to Paris, who had tried to find out from the French what they made of the controversy. 'I am inclined to think,' he wrote to Siborne on 7 December 1835, 'that the last attack on *our right* was made by the *two columns* in question as a last serious effort in a moment of desperation on finding the Prussians arrived *under Blücher* and that it was made in haste without any support *whatever . . .*' But the military authorities in Britain inevitably disagreed, arguing that the Guard's defeat had occurred before the Prussian advance. Siborne faced an impossible task in proving his case to a sceptical high command. Wellington had insisted that he had repulsed the Imperial Guard before the Prussians' attack had begun to bite, and that was that. As Hussey Vivian put it: 'The Duke's despatch . . . speaks for itself and shows what were his feelings on the subject.'

In a sense, Siborne's crucial error was to ask the wrong question. He had carried out more research, more thoroughly, than any historian of his time. But through his Model he was reducing the battle to a single point in time. The staunch day-long defence of the ridge mounted by Wellington's troops could play no part in his vista. Nor could it concentrate on the heroic Anglo-Allied defence of Hougoumont, nor La Haye Sainte, nor the great cavalry charges which had disrupted the

French lines. Nor, for that matter, could the Model weigh up the importance of the Prussian march to Waterloo, the battles that Blücher's men had fought, and the day-long threat posed by the Prussian army that had forced Napoleon to weaken his battlefield army by sending troops to the east. None of this could be shown on Siborne's Model. Nor could the Model reflect on how Napoleon, rather than being irrevocably defeated at Waterloo, was finally brought down by political intrigue in Paris, forcing him into exile: indeed, it was only five days later, as he marched towards Paris, that the Duke of Wellington realised that the victory might be the climactic event it duly became. Ironically, by reducing the battle to a single moment, Siborne had stripped out each and every extraneous factor that had shaped the victory. For all its vastness, his Model was microscopic in its portrayal of time.

Despite the private criticisms he had faced from the military establishment, however, the public reception Siborne was accorded was nothing short of ecstatic. He had taken on the Leicester-Square Panorama, and its like, on his own terms – and won. The exhibition opened on 8 October, and ran for at least a year. On page eight of the *United Services Gazette*, below a brief report on a private who had been punished with a hundred lashes for mutiny, the newspaper reviewed the Model in glowing terms, in an article which spanned the length of one and quarter of its four columns. Its correspondent had seen the Model two days earlier, along with many distinguished officers who had fought at Waterloo. 'On Thursday last,' he wrote 'we had the gratification of attending the private view of this consummate exercise of skill and ingenuity; and have no hesitation in pronouncing it the most perfect model that has ever yet fallen under our notice.' There was a reference to its cost, and to the fact that Siborne himself had paid several thousand pounds over several years to complete it.

The *United Services Gazette* was overwhelmed by the impact of the Model, as if oblivious to the discontent it had provoked among Fitzroy Somerset and his colleagues. 'Nothing can be more perfect than the representation of the scene,' it declared. 'Not only is every undulation of the ground most faithfully represented, but the position of every regiment, and its muskets and artillery are most beautifully and ingeniously indicated. Moreover, the roads and enclosures, even to the various aspects of wood, corn, grass fields and potato plots, and ploughed land, are most elaborately marked.'

On a separate page, there was an even greater recommendation of the Model, which was described as 'not only the most perfect model of any battle that has ever yet been submitted to public inspection, but the only representation, in the slightest degree to be depended upon, of that glorious and final struggle.' There followed a long and sympathetic report on how Siborne had been deprived of the rightful funding of the project by the Whigs. 'Nothing daunted by this "heavy discouragement", Mr Siborne has proceeded (more slowly than he would probably have done under more auspicious circumstances) with his model; and, after a devotion of several years, and an expenditure of upwards of five thousand pounds, he has succeeded in producing a work, not only honourable in the highest degree to his own talents and perseverance, but worthy of being placed in some national depository.' For this to happen, the *Gazette* said, the public should launch a subscription to buy the Model, stating that it hoped every rank in the army would contribute. Siborne had clearly developed a new plan to recover his costs. Having completed the Model, he was now prepared to sell it to the nation if it could go on permanent display. 'In the meantime,' the *Gazette* concluded, 'every person, military or civil, who may desire to see a faithful representation of the greatest triumph achieved by modern arms will do well to visit Lieutenant Siborne's Exhibition.' After eight long years of hardship, with only his devotion to accuracy to sustain him, Siborne could finally bask in the glory of his project, and accept the plaudits of his peers and of the outside world.

A hundred thousand people came to see Siborne's Great Model of Waterloo, but the Duke of Wellington was not among them. He made clear his views in a letter which he sent to his friend Lady Wilton on 23 April 1840. Like many observers, he had noted the perfection of Siborne's topographical technique: 'I saw a preparatory sketch or drawing of the model of the Battle of Waterloo. But I have never seen the Model itself, I understand that it is beautiful; and the shape of the ground is accurately delineated making allowance for the Proportions.'

But there Wellington's praise ended. 'The Reason for which I have omitted to endeavour to see the model is that I understand from the inspection of the sketches or drawings that the Model would not give an accurate representation of the position of the troops of either or both armies at any particular period of the day, that is to say at the commencement or at the termination of the battle.'

Even if the Model had been as accurate in its positioning of the troops as it was in its depiction of the ground, Wellington would still not have approved. 'The position of every corps and individual at each of these moments might have been accurately ascertained, and marked on the model (but) ... no drawing or representation as a model can represent more than one moment of an action ... This model tends to represent the whole action; and every corps and individual of all the nations is represented in the position chosen by himself. The consequence is that the critical viewer of the model must believe that the whole of each army, without a reserve of any kind, was engaged at the moment supposed to be represented. This is not true of any one moment or event or operation of this battle.' So Wellington refused to give the Model the seal of his approval by visiting the Egyptian Hall. 'I was unwilling to give any sanction to the truth of such a representation in this model, which must have resulted from my visiting it, without protesting against such erroneous representation. This I could not bring myself to do on (any) account; and I thought it best to avail myself of my absence from London, and of indisposition, never to visit it at all.' Wellington, acutely aware of his image, both as a politician and as a military leader of legend, could not afford to suggest that he was endorsing the Model. For a man who wished to control the history of the battle, it would not do if people thought he was upholding what he considered to be a tendentious view of events.

None of this, initially, was allowed to detract from Siborne's triumph. In its own terms, the Model was a success, a stunning example of skill and dedication. Compared with the romanticised Panorama of the Battle, its dedication to accuracy was impeccable. But unlike the panorama, which claimed only as much adherence to the facts as it needed to in order to cover itself from charges of ignorance, Siborne would be judged by the highest historical standards because these were what he had demanded of himself. By contacting so many eyewitnesses, he had turned his Model from a nineteenth-century entertainment into a serious historical summary of the great battle, and this would not be forgotten, nor forgiven, by those who disagreed with the evidence he had so painstakingly gathered.

There was another problem, too, one which was both immediate and painful, and which had been spotted by the weekly magazine, *John Bull*: 'we earnestly hope that some portion, at least, of the heavy outlay incurred by the zealous and meticulous officer – its indefatigable constructor – may be returned to him in a shape which a little becoming and liberality on the part of the present Government ought to have saved him from having recourse to.'

Siborne might have won a battle but he was losing the war. The exhibition was failing to make enough money to repay his costs.

XIV

It has always appeared to me that the general opinion of the Prussians having been engaged at Waterloo early in the afternoon is wholly erroneous. Both the French and the Prussians are, naturally, anxious to fix as early an hour for this event as they can. The former to make out a case of having to contend with superior numbers; the latter to claim as great a share in the honours of the day as possible.

Ensign Robert Batty, letter to William Siborne, 5 February 1837

With his debts mounting, Siborne had only one course of action left to him. The Model was too big to go on permanent display, unless it could do so at no cost, and so he had it dismantled and shipped back, in its separate sections, to Ireland, where it was put in storage. All those years of struggle to bring his precious Model before the public, all those years of cold exchanges with the military authorities who had set out to baulk him, had come to this: his Model, the most perfect creation of its type, had been taken apart as if it was a jigsaw, to be boxed up and put away. If the authorities had so desired it, they could not have planned it better. Siborne's beautiful Model was hidden from public view.

It was curious that this should have happened. The 100,000 people who had passed through the splendid papryus columns of the Egyptian Hall had paid a shilling each for the privilege of seeing the Model, so the exhibition had taken £5000 of their money. In addition, Siborne had sold copies of his pamphlet, which was, for many, an essential

guide to the Model because without it many of its finer details would
have remained obscure. With money from the entrance fees he should
have recovered the cost of the Model's creation and recovered, too,
from the dreadful strain he had imposed upon himself for the greater
part of the decade. But his debts, of more than £3000, were not cleared.

There were, perhaps, several reasons for this. Siborne had to pay
for the cost of mounting the exhibition in the Egyptian Hall himself,
and by his own admission, he had miscalculated the expense of trans-
porting the Model across the Irish Sea, and of hiring and fitting out
suitable premises for the display of such a large work. The money he
made seems barely to have covered the cost of hiring the hall and the
accompanying expenses, and Siborne thought he might have been
cheated by the manager at the hall. But the model-maker, showing his
customary uncertainty with financial matters, could not say for certain
why he had failed to make enough money to cover his debts. 'I have
not succeeded in recovering more than a very slight portion of the
outlay,' he complained. 'Whether this has arisen from the expensive
establishment maintained, from mismanagement, or from the circumstance of my not having been able to devote my personal superintendence to the exhibition, I will not pretend to say, but such, most
unfortunately for me, is the result of my labour.' The public exhibition
of the Model, on which he had been relying to save him from bank-
ruptcy, had failed, even though, when it had ended, the Model went
on tour to big cities around the country, including an exhibition in
Glasgow.

On 3 September 1840, Lt. James Hope of the 92nd Regiment tried
to put his finger on the problem. 'It is a very general complaint,' he
wrote to Siborne, 'that, notwithstanding the explanatory remarks of
those in attendance, nine out of every ten take leave of the model,
without having added anything to their previous store of information
respecting that memorable event.' The Model was too detailed, too
complicated, for the British public, which wanted their entertainment
to be as straightforward, and as nationalistic, as the panorama. 'Last
November an officer of very considerable talent assured me that he
paid the model three very long visits before he could comprehend the
various details. This you may rest satisfied is the great cause of failure,

for the hundreds and thousands who have quitted the model under similar circumstances – having no doubt been the means of deterring thousands of their friends from visiting it – by assuring them that they would not gain any information from seeing the model.'

The Model was also beginning to attract criticism from servicemen for giving too much prominence to the Prussian advance. In June 1839, the *United Services Journal* reported that 'the Prussians are generally considered to bear too prominent a share in the battle, as represented in this model.' Lt. Hope shared this opinion, which he expressed somewhat witheringly, though he welcomed Siborne's suggestion that he might build a new model of the battle earlier in the day. 'I am very glad to hear that you are preparing a model to represent what you seem pleased to term "A Glorious Scene." Many were of the opinion that you ought to have selected this stage of the model for your battle in preference to the one you did, it proving the *latter was not truly a British scene*. Had there been fewer of father Blücher's children in the distance, the model would undoubtedly have had more (the look of) a British victory.'

Siborne was nothing if not resilient. He continued to send pleading letters to the government to ask if his debts might finally be written off. On 19 September 1839, Siborne sent a petition to the Lords of the Treasury, appealing to them to buy his Model for the nation. They declined. Two months later, the Model was advertised for sale by private contract as a 'profitable speculation' – ostensibly on the grounds that the proprietor could not spare the time to organise exhibitions across the country (and even in the United States) because of his professional duties. Clearly no one bought it, for the following months found Siborne making a number of attempts to try to sell his Model; first he asked Hussey Vivian to help him, and then, late in 1841, he approached the Royal Dublin Society, trying to persuade its members that the work was essentially one of Irish manufacture.

In September 1841, however, the political wheel came full circle, when the Tories, led by Peel, regained power. Siborne thought this was the opportunity for which he had been waiting, and as if to make his prospects brighter, the new Secretary at War, Sir Henry Hardinge, was the same man who had given financial backing to the Model back in 1830, when he had first held the office. Hardinge had also been the liaison officer who had witnessed the fierce debate between Blücher and Gneisenau, and he had been awarded the Prussian Order of Military Merit. If any politician would be sympathetic to his cause it would be Hardinge. Certainly, if the placement of the Prussian troops upon the Model was still a difficulty, then Hardinge, given his close relationship with the Prussians, might not be expected to raise it as a reason to block the release of government funds.

On 16 September 1841, Siborne sent Hardinge a long and detailed recitation of the events which had caused his financial problems. He made much of their past connection, recalling how, when he had first set out on his 'laborious task' matters had gone 'smoothly while you, Sir, continued in office.' He contrasted his treatment under Hardinge with that meted out by his successors. 'I need not trouble you with an enumeration of the difficulties I had to encounter, of the expenses I had to incur, or of the endless correspondence I had to maintain; neither will I advert at length to the constant anxiety, the immense labour, and the unremitting perseverance which the fulfilment of such a task entailed upon one.' Siborne, his lesson learnt, also reflected on the reasons why a public exhibition in the hands of a private individual could not be profitable, and appealed to Hardinge to buy it for the nation.

Siborne suggested that he was in more financial trouble than ever. It is possible, of course, that his plight was not as acute as he claimed, and that his motivation was more to do with his overall sense of injustice at the way in which the government had ended its funding of the Model. Certainly, he maintained that there was little hope that the Model would now bring him the money he so desperately needed. He had been compelled, he told Hardinge, to 'subject myself and my family to privations which I had never contemplated.' Now, he maintained, he was in danger of losing his life's work. 'To crown all, one of my creditors (who was my agent in London, and whom my friends strongly suspect of designing to get the Model into his own hands) will be empowered on the 1st of next December, should I not be prepared to pay him a sum of £500 by that date, and which I shall be utterly unable to do, to give me three months notice of his intention to proceed to a sale of the work, for the purpose of indemnifying himself to that amount.' Siborne said the Model might soon be taken from him, as a bailiff might seize a debtor's assets. 'I have no doubt that as a speculator he will turn it to good account, and thus deprive me of all possibility of retrieving myself, or of obtaining the slightest remuneration for the toil, the expense, the anxiety, as well as injury to my health which I have encountered in consequence of this unfortunate undertaking.'

Siborne appealed to Hardinge's sense of justice to end what he called 'my present embarrassment'. He begged him to remember that the Model had 'originated with the Government of which you were a member' and, somewhat disingenuously, suggested that he had been 'induced' to carry on with the project at his own expense by the succeeding government. 'I ask for no remuneration either for my seven years' labour, or for any ingenuity which the work may be considered to evince, and even should the cost of the construction be deemed too much for its purchase, I would make a great sacrifice rather than allow the Model to be seized by the individual to whom I have already referred.' Siborne, ostensibly optimistic, even suggested that there was not 'the slightest doubt' that the Model would increase in value over the years, should Hardinge agree to buy it for the nation. To aid his cause, he noted how the features of the battleground had been altered since 1815, with entire fields having been excavated by the Dutch government to create an enormous mound celebrating the Prince of Orange's role in the battle, and his survival, 'thus obliterating a most important portion of the Duke of Wellington's position.' Siborne also noted how several woods had disappeared, to become arable land, while new houses had been built, 'whereas the Model offers most minute, faithful, and mathematically correct representation of the celebrated Field, as it existed at the time, even in the most trivial details.' The British Museum, or the Tower of London, he suggested, would make a suitable home for the Model, which he said he had re-painted in brighter colours.

It was perhaps a measure of the predicament in which Siborne found himself that towards the end of his long letter to Hardinge, he made an astonishing offer, and one which directly contradicted the firm stand he had taken in support of the accuracy of his Model. For several years he had resisted the pressure exerted on him by Fitzroy Somerset and others to play down the role of the Prussian army at the moment of victory. In doing so he had refused to countenance the possibility that the evidence he had gathered could be contradicted. He had approached the deployment of his toy soldiers as he had approached the modelling of the fields, with an eye only on historical accuracy. His belief in the truth, as he portrayed it, was buttressed by the possibility that the exhibition of the Model would bring him his just financial rewards, as well as reflecting great credit on his skill and application. He had won public praise, to soften the blows of the private criticism which had been meted out to him; but now that his family's privations had not been lessened, he was prepared to do almost anything to recover his losses. So it was that, sadly, he made the following, desperate offer to Sir Henry Hardinge: 'There is another point to which I would wish to allude. I am well aware that in the opinion of some of our highest military authorities, the Prussian troops occupy too prominent a position upon the Model, an opinion to which I should be sorry to be so presumptuous as to oppose my own impressions, which may very possibly be erroneous, and the moment the work ceases to be my property, and I am no longer obligated to adhere to those impressions, I shall be most ready and willing to make any alteration that may be suggested in this or in any other respect.'

William Siborne had reached the end of a long and painful road. He wanted to sell his precious Model to the nation, and to try to do so, he was prepared to sell his soul. In his choice of words, he tried to find a way of salving his conscience, by trying to imply that by relinquishing ownership of the Model he was also relieved of his obligations to historical accuracy. Perhaps he even thought that the row he had unwittingly caused, by his adherence to the facts he had uncovered, was so great that the government might buy the Model simply to put an end to the affair. Once again he would be severely disappointed. Hardinge passed the buck, and Siborne received this reply from a clerk in the war office.

War Office
20 November 1841

Sir,

Your letter of the 16th September last, on the subject of your Model of the Battle of Waterloo, having been brought under the Secretary at War's consideration, I am directed to acquaint you that Sir Henry Hardinge very much regrets the failure you have experienced in the reimbursement of the expenses incurred in constructing a work of art so interesting to the public, and creditable to your ability, as that Model undoubtedly is.

Sir Henry Hardinge, however, cannot originate any proposal for the purchase of the work by the Government; any measure of that nature appearing to be one which should emanate from the General Commanding-in-Chief, or the Master General of the Ordnance, with a view to placing the Model where it may be made applicable to purposes of instruction, at the same time that it remains a record of the Battle.

I am Sir etc.

L Sulivan

Four days later came more depressing news, with a letter from the Master General of the Ordnance. Sir George Murray was generally sympathetic towards Siborne's predicament, but he could not see a way to buy the Model at public expense. 'It has not any direct connection with the peculiar branch of the service which belongs to this department; and could hardly be considered as being conducive to the instruction of officers of artillery or engineers.' Instead, Murray, like Hardinge, suggested that any decision to buy the Model was not his to take. 'If it is to be employed as a means of conveying instruction to military men, it must be in the branches of tactical and strategical operations, which are more connected with the department of the Quarter Master General than with the Ordnance.'

Siborne's letter was passed remarkably quickly between departments, with all the speed of a political problem looking for a home, until it reached the office of his old adversary, Fitzroy Somerset. In his reply, Somerset stated that the commander-in-chief, Lord Hill 'deeply' regretted that Siborne had lost money on a Model on which he had 'bestowed so much labour' and on which he had displayed 'so much ability.' He sympathised with the fact that the exhibition had not repaid Siborne's efforts by failing to produce 'as might fairly have been anticipated a considerable profit.' But Hill's sympathy did not extend to practical help. FitzRoy Somerset stated baldly: 'he does not feel at liberty to propose to Her Majesty's Ministers to buy it of you.'

Siborne had reached a dead end, though he did not at first recognize it, even though Sir Hussey Vivian spelled it out for him. On 28 November, Vivian listed the obstacles that Siborne was facing: first 'comes the Money, then comes the difficulty of disposing of the Model & lastly there comes the D of Wellington, for without him they will not one of them stir one inch.' Perhaps Siborne's blindness to political reality was, once again, a sign of his mounting desperation: he refused to take no for an answer. On 11 December, he again wrote to Fitzroy Somerset, stating that 'I think I may be permitted to give expression to the extreme regret which I feel on receiving this intimation of Lord Hill's decision.' Once again, he reflected upon the fact that he had started the work under Hill's leadership and said it was 'painful' to note that the praise for his many years' labour and ability should not have been enough to persuade Lord Hill to recommend that the government should buy it for the nation. Once again, too, Siborne made an offer to alter the placement of the Prussian soldiers on his model.

'I should feel greatly obliged by your informing me whether His Lordship's objections be founded upon any inaccuracy which I may have committed, because . . . I am most desirous of making any alterations which His Lordship, or any officers entrusted by him, might consider necessary, with a view to render the representation most faithful, and therefore deserving of His Lordship's patronage and support. I still venture to entertain a hope that Lord Hill may be induced, in consideration of the distressful circumstances in which I am placed, to recommend to government the purchase of the work, subject to the fulfilment, on my part, of the condition which I have above suggested, and then relieve me from the ruinous embarrassment in which I have become involved, by this unfortunate undertaking and which may yet compel me to ask His Lordship's permission to sell out of the service.'

In the draft of his letter, crossed out, was the following sentence: 'Such inaccuracy could only occur in the distribution of the figures (the model of the field itself being mathematically true).' Siborne was retreating into his professional heartland as a topographer, where his verities could not be challenged, and, under terrible financial pressure, he was prepared to fall into line with the establishment view of history. Unsurprisingly, however, in his reply on Christmas Eve, 1841, Fitzroy Somerset was not able to offer him any seasonal comfort.

> Sir,
>
> Having submitted to the General Commanding in Chief your letter of the 11th instant upon the subject of the purchase of your Model, and His Lordship having observed with regret that you still entertain a hope that he may be induced to recommend the purchase of it to government, I am directed to acquaint you, that his decision upon that point as communicated to you in my letter of the 7th instant must be considered final.
>
> I have the honor to be
> Sir,
> Your obedient
> humble Servant
> Fitzroy Somerset

Only now did Siborne realise that he had lost the fight. As Sir Hussey Vivian told him two days later: 'nothing now I fear remains to be done.' From now on Siborne's letters show that he did not raise money matters again. Either he had managed to pay off his bills, and had been disingenuous with the government by exaggerating his plight, or someone had helped him out by lending him the money. When, on 15 August 1842, Lord Hill, who had initiated his project, resigned as commander-in-chief through ill health, and Wellington assumed the role, even Siborne could see that the rules had changed. The model-maker turned his attention to writing history instead.

Perhaps the idea had come to him as suddenly, and belatedly, as the Prussians had to the Duke. Over the years, he had sent out around a thousand of his circular letters to survivors of Waterloo and the replies had provided him with a unique fund of general information about the battle. Siborne realised that no one had written the true history of the battle, because no one had gone to such extraordinary lengths to gather a wealth of firsthand information. So in 1835, when he had been turned down for promotion, he had decided to write his own book.

On 28 November 1836 he had written excitedly to one W.F. Wakeman for an introduction to Messrs Boone the publishers. He had acquired, he said, 'a store of valuable information' through issuing his circular letter, a copy of which he enclosed. They had gone mainly to British officers, but the 'liberality' of the Prussian and other foreign governments had helped him, too. He had, he said, 'the full conviction' that despite everything that had been published on the subject, 'there does not exist in England one good or true account of either Ligny, Quatre Bras, Waterloo or Wavre.' This, he said, had persuaded him to propose a history of the whole campaign 'in which the military operations, both strategical and tactical, and all the attendant circumstances, will be clearly set forth.' The selling-point was clear: Siborne insisted that he would write nothing that could not be confirmed by the independent testimonies he had gathered.

Siborne approached his history book as meticulously as he had approached his Model. He was particular, to the last degree, about how the book should look. The work, he insisted, 'must be accompanied by about half a dozen Plans, and these I should require to be engraved in a very superior manner.' Again, Siborne was determined not to cut any corners, but this time he would not bear the cost himself. Quite often in those days, the cost of a book was borne by the author, while the publisher acted as a salesman. Siborne could not afford for this to happen. He had, he said, spent between two and three thousand pounds on his Model (and it was perhaps a sign of his incompetence as a businessman that he could not say exactly how much he had spent), so he could 'spare nothing' for the engraving or publishing. At the same time, his determination to lay down the terms under which he would write the book was clearly shaped by his treatment by the government over the funding of his Model. He stipulated every cost that the publishers must bear, while he tried to ensure he retained editorial control of the finished product. It was almost as if he thought that the publishers needed the book more than he did. 'If Messrs Boone will consent to take upon themselves the expense of publishing my work including that of the engravings (which must be according to my own views and under my own superintendence), and allowing me 40 copies for presents, I am willing to come into the terms of half profits with them upon two Editions of 750 Copies each.'

The list of conditions did not end there. Siborne could see that the book might help to promote the Model, and that the Model might help to sell the book. He insisted that a pamphlet must be printed, which would contain an extract from the book describing the Crisis of the Battle as shown on the Model. This pamphlet had to be sold at the exhibition of the Model for sixpence, or perhaps a shilling, because he saw it as an 'excellent means' of promoting the book and inducing visitors to the exhibition to buy it. Finally, he declared, the book must be published in time for the exhibition of the Model which 'by dint of great exertions' he hoped to complete by the precise deadline of 18 June the following year. The publishers, perhaps reeling under the weight of Siborne's demands but doubtless attracted by the material he had gathered, agreed to his terms, with a solitary exception. They clearly thought the book could become, in its own way, a publishing success, and they increased the print run to a thousand copies.

While the book might ease Siborne's financial difficulties it was not, however, an immediate solution to his problems. The political rumblings over his Model continued, and there was clearly some criticism that Siborne's army work was suffering because of the time he was devoting to the Model. On 6 March 1838, a report in *The Times* suggested the Model had been made 'without at all interfering with his official duties, and we are all the more particular in mentioning the circumstance, having heard that a contrary opinion prevailed at headquarters.' And if the Model had been complicated to construct, then the book would be just as difficult to write. Unlike the Model, which had effectively frozen in time a single moment of the battle, with all the attendant controversy that it had provoked, the book could, in a more rounded way, give due weight to cause and consequence, and to the respective contributions of the two armies ranged against Napoleon. But at the same time, given Siborne's meticulous nature, it had to be thoroughly researched, and evidentially based, so that it would require many years of work before it could be produced. It would, in essence, be a lasting work of history, supported by reportage, the views and analysis of the participants themselves distilled into a unique record of the event that shaped the century. Once again, Siborne's ambition, his aim for a work of historical permanency, stood in direct opposition to his need for instant money.

Siborne had proved himself to be an inspired model-maker and a brilliant topographer. He was not, it is fair to say, a great writer. His history of the Waterloo campaign has the plodding style of a man who has many facts at his disposal, and wishes to use them all, rather than having the discernment to pick his way through them. Occasionally, however, Siborne is so struck by an event within the battle, such as the charge of the heavy cavalry, that he describes it with the abandon of a man who is relieved to be freed from the burden of his material, and this he does with all the imagery and nationalist fervour that tarnished the histories written by many of his contemporaries. 'I sincerely trust your venture will be a straightforward *British one*,' Lt. James Hope had warned him – and, essentially, it was. For all these faults, however, Siborne's *History* was unique. He alone had gathered together a vast repository of information from the survivors of the battle; he alone had collected hundreds of their accounts; he alone was prepared to mould them into an account of a conflict which shaped the century.

The task Siborne had set himself was vast. His book came to more than five hundred pages, starting with Napoleon's return from Elba, and ending with the Allied occupation of Paris. In his preface, he made a veiled reference to some of the difficulties he had encountered in the years which followed his survey of the battlefield in 1830. 'One of my Waterloo correspondents has humorously remarked,' he wrote, 'that if ever truth lies at the bottom of a well, she does so immediately after a great battle, and it takes an amazingly long time before she can be lugged out.' The battle over the Model had clearly taken its toll on Siborne, for he struck a far more emollient note than he had over the deployment of the toy soldiers on its battlefield, conceding that 'while I feel that I have brought to light much that was involved in obscurity, I cannot but be sensible that I may have fallen into errors.' Should that be the case, he offered, he would be 'most ready' to make any corrections 'that may appear requisite', though he insisted that any new information which was provided to him must be based on eyewitness accounts.

With his writing, Siborne managed to capture the financial support of the establishment in a way in which he had failed with his toy soldiers. As the book neared publication, he requested, and received, many statements of support from the very top of society. On 14 September 1842, he received a letter from Windsor, which informed him that the Queen would permit him to dedicate his history of the war to her and that she would subscribe to it along with Prince Albert. Two weeks later came a letter from the Duchess of Kent at Clarence House, saying that she too would subscribe; so too would the Marquess of Anglesey; and Queen Adelaide, the widow of William IV, who had died five years earlier, asked for two copies which, she hoped, 'Captain Siborne will have the goodness to forward for Her Majesty with a statement of the account.' Even Sir George Murray subscribed. In all, around five hundred people put their names forward, including European emperors, and the King of Prussia: but Wellington was not among them. On 28 September Fitzroy Somerset told Siborne that 'the Duke of Wellington has been pestered to subscribe to new publications to such an extent that I believe he resolved several years ago never to give his name again on such occasions.'

Siborne was keen to avoid the controversy which had bedevilled the building of the Model. If the book was to succeed, and to provide him with a financial lifeline, it could only harm his chances if he stirred up another row. Just as he had been prepared, belatedly, to change the position of the Prussians on the Model, so he was now prepared to confirm their changed role in his *History*. In order to do this, he wrote a long exculpatory footnote, which lay several hundred pages into the book. In writing this, he had somehow to justify his long-held belief about the veracity of his Model, and explain why he had changed his mind without appearing to be inconsistent, given that both the Model

and his *History* were based on eyewitness accounts. First, he acknowledged with some understatement, the difficulty this posed.

'The description given, in the present work, of the distribution of
the Prussian troops at the moment of the defeat of the attacking
columns of the French imperial guard by Maitland's and Adam's
British brigades, being at variance with the representation of those
troops upon the Model of the Battle of Waterloo when the latter was
first submitted to the public, some explanation of the grounds upon
which this deviation from my original arrangement is founded, appears
to be requisite.'

Then Siborne supplied his explanation for the change, an explanation which, in its own way, was a masterpiece. There was, he implied,
nothing wrong with the information he had gathered for his Model.
'Having applied to the Prussian government for the information I
required concerning the disposition of their troops at that particular
moment represented on the model, it was most readily and liberally
supplied to me by the officers of the headquarters staff in Berlin, at
the instance of the Prussian minister of war. This information, which
was given with minute detail, was rendered more complete by the
distribution of the troops having been laid down upon a plan, drawn
on a large scale.'

Siborne insisted that he had gone to great lengths to check that this
evidence had been correct, and that he had not just taken the Prussian
accounts at face-value. 'On comparing these data with the evidence I
had collected from officers of rank and intelligence, posted, some
throughout the greater part of the battle, and others, during the whole
day, on the left of the Anglo-allied line, whence the Prussian movements could be distinguished, I felt perfectly satisfied that there could
be no doubt as to their accuracy on certain points, whilst upon others,
this evidence was of too vague a nature, as regarded *time* and *situation*,
to enable me either to corroborate or to rectify the details with which
I had been furnished by the Prussian authorities. Thus, for instance,
the junction of the leading columns of Ziethen's corps with the left of
the Anglo-allied line, the forming up of the cavalry of that column
on the flank, and in the rear, of Best's Hanoverian brigade, the relief
of a Hanoverian battery by a Prussian battery upon the summit or

knoll on which the Anglo-allied left rested, as also the previous conflicts in and about both Plancenoit and Smohain, upon the extreme right of the French army, are facts satisfactorily confirmed by corroborative evidence.'

Then came his admission. The Model had, in some respects, he conceded, strayed into error. 'As regards the disposition of the Prussian troops between the extreme left of the Anglo-allied line and the immediate vicinity of Plancenoit, I feel equally satisfied, after a most careful and diligent investigation of the whole question of the Prussian co-operation, in all its bearings, that, according to the *original* arrange-ment of the figures upon the model, the Prussian troops distributed along that intervening space, immediately in front of Lobau's troops, were represented in too forward a position.'

In other words, Siborne was now in step with the official line. In effect, he was stating that the Duke alone had, at the crucial moment, won the Battle of Waterloo. Siborne did not offer an overt apology to the political and military authorities who had poured such scorn on his Model, though he took great care to praise the Duke of Wellington, and acknowledge tacitly that it was the Duke who had won the battle at its end. Instead he explained that he had received fresh evidence. 'It was only subsequently, when collecting that further information which has enabled me in the present work to describe with such minuteness of detail those brilliant dispositions of the Duke of Wellington, by which he not only defeated the French imperial guard upon his own position, but secured the victory, that I discovered the error into which the Prussian authorities had been unconsciously but naturally led, when laying down for me the distribution of their troops along that part of the field to which I have particularly adverted, and which distribution gave the appearance of a much greater pressure upon the French right flank than could have occurred at the *moment* represented on the model.

'The cause of this error,' said Siborne, optimistically, 'is very simple, and is easily explained.' The Prussian accounts of the battle, he stated, 'concur in representing the Duke of Wellington's defeat of the attack-ing columns of the imperial guard, and the advance of his whole line, as happening *at one and the same moment*; whereas, in reality, there was an interval of *at least* twelve minutes between these two incidents.' The Prussians, he said, had not previously known that when the British line advanced, Vivian's light cavalry was attacking and defeating Napoleon's last reserves of cavalry and infantry near La Belle Alliance, the centre of the enemy line; nor had they known that Adam's light infantry brigade was defeating the remains of the first wave of the Imperial Guard, which had rallied on the heights between La Belle Alliance and La Haye Sainte; nor that Vandeleur's light cavalry had moved forward to assist Vivian's attack. The reason Siborne gave for this was one which, as a skilled topographer, he could have realised before, if he had believed it to be true. The attacks 'could not, from the configuration of the ground, be observed by the Prussian army; to which circumstance may be attributed the origin of that miscalculation concerning the actual disposition of the Duke of Wellington's forces at the moment of the general advance of his line, which induced the Prussian authorities to confound that advance with the defeat of the attacking columns of the Imperial guard.'

Siborne now claimed that the Prussian breakthrough had only happened during the general advance ordered by Wellington. This advance, he said, 'was made by his Grace to follow up a victory he had *already* secured, and. in conjunction with the Prussian attack, to render the overthrow of the enemy complete in every respect.' The Prussians had finally been relegated to the role of a secondary player in the great drama which was the Battle of Waterloo. Theirs was no longer a central role; instead the defeat of the Imperial Guard by Wellington had, in itself, 'secured' the victory. It was a fine distinction but a crucial one.

Was Siborne telling the truth or had he simply reached breaking-point? There is no trace in his records of any correspondence from the Prussian general staff that would lead him to his new conclusion. Sadly, it appears he had taken his new line because of political pressure, and not because he had discovered any new facts to change his mind. Quite possibly, he was fed up with the whole business. William Leeke, the young ensign from the 52nd, recalled that 'some time after the completion of the model of Waterloo, and when it was about to be removed from London for exhibition in the large towns of England and Scotland, I went to see it for the first time, and met Captain Siborne there . . . I therefore introduced myself to him, and spoke in terms of admiration of his beautiful model; but I told him we of the 52nd were dissatisfied with the forward position he had given to Maitland's brigade of Guards, and to his representing a first French column as having been routed by them, and as flying in disorder towards and near to the Charleroi road, as we *know both these things to be incorrect.* He merely shrugged his shoulders as much to say he could not now help it, and that there was no use discussing the matter.' Siborne, the meticulous model-maker, had had enough of history.

William Siborne's capitulation was not, however, enough to stop the campaign against him from the Duke of Wellington's supporters. Wellington had drawn up his own private account of the battle, which he made known to his own circle, and it was used by his friends to mount a campaign of denigration against Siborne. One of Wellington's confidants at the time was the author, politician and philanthropist, Francis Egerton, the future Earl of Ellesmere, who had translated Clausewitz's history of the 1812 campaign, and who was himself an authority on military matters. Egerton, a Tory MP who had been Chief Secretary of Ireland, was particularly scathing about Siborne. On 23 September 1842 he wrote in condemnatory terms to Wellington's associate, Charles Arbuthnot: 'I see . . . that Siborne, the officer who made that curious model of the battle, is about to publish a detailed account . . . When I first saw Siborne's model I suspected he had been humbugged by the Prussians, & I remember mentioning my opinion to Fitzroy Somerset.'

Despite the private criticism that was circulating against him, the first edition of Siborne's history was published in March 1844, proudly declaring its dedication to 'her most Gracious Majesty, the Queen.' The *History of the War in France and Belgium* 'from the testimony of eye-witnesses and other sources, exclusive and authentic' was printed in two volumes, 'beautifully embellished with Medallion Portraits, engraved on Steel', of the Duke of Wellington, Blücher, Napoleon and eight of the other main actors in the drama, including Lord Hill. Wellington's profile, judiciously, faced the title page of the first volume, and Blücher's the title page of the second.

Malcolm Balen

Siborne had instructed two engineers to survey the field of Quatre Bras, and their maps appeared as 'Anaglyptographic Engravings on Steel, from Models' consisting of two plans of Quatre Bras 'shewing different Periods of the Action', and two of Ligny, Wavre and Waterloo. The anaglyptograph was a machine which produced engraved surfaces with raised objects, and it made Siborne's maps look as if they were three-dimensional, with highly intricate detail. Readers were instructed, at the top of each map to 'place this upper side nearest the light,' and when they did, the contours of the battlefield became extraordinarily clear. On top of the maps the position of all the different units of each army was printed, with red for the Allied army, green for the Prussian, and blue for the French. It was a triumph for 'Bate's Patent Anaglyptograph', and for the engraver, Freebairn, and for Siborne's insistence that the maps must be printed this way.

The book was an instant success. A second edition had to be printed five months later, in August, and this too sold out within days. The newspaper reviews were ecstatic. 'It is written in a free and impartial manner,' reported the *US Journal*, 'a standard history has been produced, remarkable . . . for its truth'; 'we hail this work,' applauded the *Naval and Military Gazette*; 'we heartily thank Captain Siborne,' stated the *United Service Gazette*; 'a Military Classic' asserted the *Dublin University Magazine*, 'and they will remain so while Waterloo is a word to stir the heart and nerve the arm of a British soldier'; 'it is this combination of accurate knowledge and unexaggerated description which has obtained for the work the character of one of the most complete and important histories of the eventful period it describes,' declared the *Morning Herald*. The only discordant note came from Colonel Basil Jackson, writing in *Colburn's United Service Magazine* of May and June, who suggested that Siborne's error over the Prussian position had originated 'in a design on the part of the Prussian officers to support, by their *minute detail, and plan drawn upon a large scale, containing a distribution of the troops*, the pretension made on the part of their gallant army, of having saved the Anglo-Allied force from impending defeat at Waterloo.'

A third edition followed, four years later, and Siborne, spotting an opportunity, had also brought out a separate atlas, containing the beautiful maps from his book. Wellington's circle was far from happy. Francis Egerton renewed hostilities in June 1845 in the *Quarterly Review*, an established Tory journal that was opposed to political reform. In a critique of three Waterloo historians, Egerton praised Siborne for the scientific approach he had adopted in making his models, for his zeal and honesty, and for the diligence of his search for the truth. He recognised that Siborne had pointed out, unlike some writers, that the French capture of La Haye Sainte had been a crucial event, and not a trivial one (as Egerton pointed out, FitzRoy Somerset had himself lost an arm in the attacks which followed). The anaglypto-graphic plates in the book were, thought Egerton, 'agreeable'. But he insisted that Siborne's book, if it was to be viewed as history and not a collection of anecdotes, was 'defective in one important particular. It seems to us, as far as the British operations are concerned, drawn from every source *except* from the commander-in-chief and the few officers attached at the time to head-quarters who really knew or could know anything of value about the great features of the business.'

This was Egerton at his most disingenuous, because he knew that Wellington had refused to help historians apart from Gurwood, the compiler of his Despatches. He was also implicitly criticising Siborne's history for being too democratic, relying as it did on hundreds of eyewitness accounts which, in Egerton's view, could not compare with the army leadership's knowledge of the battle. Egerton thought that 'this imperfection' was 'very observable' in one or two passages of the book, and he effectively set out to show that almost nothing that had happened before and during the battle had taken the Duke by surprise: 'no passage of the Duke's campaigns is more pregnant with evidence of the omnipresent, indefatigable, personal activity, and imperturbable coolness which distinguished him, than the period which has come under our notice.' Egerton also insisted that the Duke had always paid the 'highest testimony' to the cooperation the Prussians had afforded him, without stopping to consult 'whether by doing justice to the fame of his allies he might give a handle to his enemies to detract from his own.'

That this was the Duke's own view of the battle and of his sub-sequent conduct, there can be little doubt. Egerton based his account on details which Wellington had provided for him, details which were published after his death by Egerton's widow, Alice, Countess of Strafford, as a 'memorandum all in the Duke's hand' and which, it was said, still bore the pencil marks of his corrections. The *Memorandum on the Battle of Waterloo* clearly states that the despatches of military commanders should take historical precedence over eyewitness accounts, however numerous they might be. 'The duty of the Historian of a battle . . . is to seek with diligence for the most authentic details of the subject on which he writes, to peruse with care and attention all that has been published; to prefer that which has been officially recorded and published by public responsible authorities; next, to attend to that which proceeds from Official Authority . . . and to pay least attention to the statements of Private Individuals . . .' Wellington's comments stood as a perfect commentary on the years of agony Siborne had been forced to endure.

In attacking Siborne's *History*, the memorandum repeated, too, in trenchant terms, the Duke's criticism of Siborne's Model, damning it with faint praise for the accuracy of its topography. 'It is curious that the Historian of the Battle of Waterloo, Captain Siborne, having discovered that in his capacity of artist he had failed in producing an accurate, and even intelligible, representation of the Battle of Waterloo, on his beautiful and accurate model of the ground, by having listened to every hero of his own tale, and having introduced into the model the action represented by each individual to have been performed, without regard to time, order of time, or circumstances – the consequences of which have been to render ridiculous and useless that beautiful work, so that it is more like the picture of five (Acts) of a play, and its termination represented on canvas as one scene, than it is to anything else that can be imagined – should in his History of this great military event, have fallen into the same error, so far at least as to have listened to every individual who chose to tell his own tale.'

Some of the most important facts of the battle had been omitted, the memorandum declared, 'because the only authorities from whom information was never required were the Commander-in-Chief himself, and the Officers of the General Staff, and those acting under his immediate orders in the Field.' This was clearly nonsense: the documentary evidence showed that Siborne had made repeated attempts to engage Fitzroy Somerset, the Duke's military secretary, in the project and Wellington had been aware of the Model's progress, though dismissive of it. Far from Siborne not requiring information from the commander-in-chief and his officers, Wellington had not wanted to supply it. Indeed, the Duke himself, who was so staunchly of the opinion that only the army leadership could understand the course of the battle, had declared in his memorandum on the Model, written in 1836, that he could not himself judge 'the particular position of each body of troops under my command, much less of the Prussian army, at any particular hour.' And who was to say that the commanders had a better view of the battle than the men on the ground? Lt. Anthony Bacon, of the 10th Hussars, and a future general, wrote to Siborne to insist that he knew 'from experience how easy it is for a commander to be mistaken in the minutiae.'

Egerton, though supportive of the Duke, felt that Wellington's attacks on Siborne had gone too far and he wrote a letter to Charles Arbuthnot, on 18 May 1845 'in which I deprecated the Duke's severity towards Siborne.' Wellington wrote a reply down the side of Egerton's letter. In it, he stated that he had mentioned Siborne's Model 'only as an illustration of the manner in which he had made up his work. That is to say, he took down every man's story as true and certainly correct, as he had before he represented his act and supposed position in his model.' So much for all the years Siborne had spent checking all the evidence he had gathered.

To make matters worse, Siborne was soon to face publishing competition from within the Duke's inner circle. The Reverend George Gleig was a frequent guest of Wellington's at Walmer Castle, when the Duke was Warden of the Cinque Ports, and had been made chaplain at the Royal Military Asylum in Chelsea, with a reference provided by Fitzroy Somerset. In 1846, Gleig was commissioned to write *The True Story of the Battle of Waterloo*, a cheap and superficial account of the battle which sold for just six shillings, against the £2 2s Siborne's publishers were charging, a price which could only be afforded by the wealthy. Gleig's book relied, to an extent, on the Duke's private version of events. Siborne was incensed, both by the attempt to undercut him, and because he thought Gleig had pirated part of his work. In the preface to the third edition of his book, Siborne spent an inordinate time complaining about Gleig's plagiarism, comparing in parallel columns his account against Gleig's wording. Was he over-reacting, or was this a conspiracy against Siborne, so that the Duke's version of events would finally trump his own?

Despite his meticulous fact-checking, a second wave of attacks on Siborne came from within the ranks. Now that he had published their accounts, some soldiers were unhappy with the way he had tried to reconcile differing versions of events. Foremost among the discontented veterans of the battle was Edward Macready, the ensign of the 30th Foot at Waterloo, who was now a major. Major Macready sent Siborne a series of sharply pointed questions, and when he failed to elicit a response, went public with his unhappiness in the pages of the *United Services Journal*. At the heart of Macready's complaint was Siborne's refusal to acknowledge that the 30th and 73rd Regiments had helped to defeat the Imperial Guard, instead of which Siborne insisted that the Guard had attacked, and had been repulsed by, Maitland's brigade of guards exclusively. At stake for Macready was not just historical veracity, but the honour of the regiments, and he was adamant about what he had himself seen: 'I think the column of the Imperial Guard which we of the 30th saw directly in our front was one of 1000 men, or thereabouts, – that it advanced, so long as it did advance, directly on our front, and that, if it had moved in that direction till doomsday, it would never have struck the line of Maitland's brigade.' Macready, who also questioned Siborne's description of his regiment's actions at Quatre Bras, effectively repeated Wellington's attack on the validity of anonymous sources, and criticised Siborne for his 'rule never without permission to reveal the names of his informants.'

History, William Siborne had discovered, was an unforgiving mistress. The Duke of Wellington had made no secret that he had always doubted its merits when applied to warfare: 'some individuals may recollect all the little events, of which the great result is the battle lost or won; but no individual can recollect the order in which, or the exact moment at which they occurred, which makes all the difference as to their value and importance.' While Wellington thought history belonged exclusively to the army's commanders, ironically, he found support from one of the rank and file eyewitnesses of whose role in describing history he was so dismissive. The former ensign, William Leeke, was patronising about Siborne's methods. 'The history of a great battle, especially if the materials for it are collected by one who did not see the principal events which he attempts to describe, must necessarily abound in mistakes. Captain Siborne took immense pains in collecting information both when he determined to construct his beautiful model of the Field of Waterloo, and afterwards when he was about to write the history of the battle, nearly thirty years after it was fought. Of course after the lapse of so many years, the greater portion of those he consulted could not be expected to recollect much that they had witnessed with any great degree of accuracy . . .'

Perhaps the Duke had been right to be so scornful of Siborne after all.

In November 1844, Siborne finally moved from Dublin to become secretary and adjutant of the Royal Military Asylum, a home for army orphans, in which role he was appointed captain on half-pay. For the first time, he was living near to the political and military leaders he had tried so hard to court from Ireland. He still needed their favours for, despite the progress of his *History*, and perhaps emboldened by it, Siborne had continued with his beloved modelling. Undaunted by the hostility he had encountered over his depiction of the Crisis of the Battle, he proposed a series of models on a larger scale than his original Model in order to show the key turning-points of the battle. The irony, at which Siborne hinted, was that, for all the conflict it had caused, he agreed with the critics who had pointed out that it was hard to see precisely where the troops had been positioned. He declared that in order to present what he called 'a perfect illustration' of the battle, he needed to execute a further set of models which were limited to showing a specific scene, so that they only had to display a smaller area of ground, and could be built upon a larger scale, more appealing to the eye. The toy soldiers would be bigger, and the contest in which they were engaged would become much clearer for spectators.

How Siborne could afford to model his next subject, the charge by the British heavy cavalry, is a mystery, unless he had found a new backer, or unless his previous protestations of poverty had been exaggerated. Once again, he entered into a meticulous, diligent correspondence with the eyewitnesses to the cavalry charge he wished to portray: particularly with Major Evans, of the 5th West India Regiment, the extra aide-de-compte to Sir William Ponsonby, who had died such a dreadful death in the cavalry charge. This time, with the larger scale he had adopted, there was no mistaking the painstaking detail with which Siborne had modelled the toy soldiers. The countryside was created on the scale of fifteen feet to one inch, and the soldiers and buildings at six feet to an inch. Several thousand troops were positioned on the battlefield, representing, thought Siborne, exactly 13,200 French infantry, 1600 French cavalry, 2407 British cavalry, 3104 British infantry, 1139 from the King's German legion, and 805 Hanoverian infantry.

Once again, Siborne was aiming to be nothing less than precise in his depiction of the battle at the point when the Earl of Uxbridge had ordered the charge of the heavy cavalry brigade, to counter the advance of the French cavalry against La Haye Sainte, and the two sides had joined battle at full speed with a resounding clash of steel upon steel, horse upon horse, rider upon rider. The 1st Life Guards, and the 1st (King's) Dragoon Guards had charged forward to the west of the Charleroi road; from here, the 2nd Life Guards, from Lord Edward Somerset's 1st British Cavalry Brigade, had crossed over the road to the east.

The New Waterloo Model was built in ten sections and, with its case, measured 18 feet 7 inches by 7 feet 9 inches. Each of the soldiers was about an inch high, with movable arms, and a detachable backpack, which was held in place by tiny iron pins. The cavalry had movable heads and arms, and their breastplates were made of lead foil or brass, while the cannon were made of lead alloy, with wooden parts for their limbers. The soldiers cost Siborne the enormous sum of £600, but he was convinced that, with its larger scale, the New Model would be a spectacular success. On 28 December 1844, he placed a new advertisement in the *Illustrated London News*:

UNIQUE EXHIBITION – BATTLE OF WATERLOO

New Model, upon a very large Scale, representing the Splendid
Charge in the earlier Part of the Battle by the British heavy
Cavalry under the Marquis of Anglesey and by the British Infantry
under Sir Thomas Picton – **EGYPTIAN HALL PICCADILLY**

*Open from Ten till Five; and in the Evening,
brilliantly illuminated, from Seven till Ten.*

Admission, One Shilling.

While the action shown by the New Model was undoubtedly clearer
than that portrayed by the Great Model, the earlier work had been far
more impressive in its size and scope, and it had also been the first
time the paying public had seen Siborne's extraordinary creation. He
was now was facing stiff competition for their attention. In the same
newspaper a fortnight later, the Surrey zoological gardens was boasting
of its two new attractions, a 'living toucan', and a female elk, while at
Hyde Park Corner, there was a collection of portraits of sixty Chinese
figures 'as large as life . . . from the mandarin of the highest rank to
the wandering mendicant.' At the Glaciarium, for a shilling, there was
'Another Most Amusing Novelty' – a glacier, made from artificial ice,
'on which Skates and Sledges rapidly descend to the Frozen Lake,
forming with the Panorama of Lucerne and its snowy Alpine Scenery,
a delightful resort.' Meanwhile, Madame Tussaud's was advertising,
'The Shrine of Napoleon, or Golden Chamber'. Once again, Napoleon's carriage was on show, and also the camp-bed on which he had
died in exile (and for which Madame Tussaud and her sons had
apparently paid £550). There was also 'the cloak of Marengo', from the
Arab stallion which he had perhaps ridden on the long retreat from Mos-
cow, and various other relics, including the clothes he had worn in exile,
and a painting of Napoleon by Robert Lefevre, for which he had sat in
his coronation robes. Visitors to Madame Tussaud's could see all this,
'being altogether a matchless exhibition,' for the same price that
Siborne was charging for the New Model: 'Admittance, one large room,
1s; two rooms of Napoleon and Chamber of Horrors, 6d.'

The New Waterloo Model

Within six months, it was probably clear to Siborne that he had, again, miscalculated and that the public enthusiasm for his New Model was not going to pay his bills. Whether he could fulfil his stated ambition of creating a series of models was, he reflected, dependent upon how this first 'specimen' as he called it was greeted by the paying public. Nonetheless he did not wait for its approbation before starting work on the next models, including the 'Grand Charge on the British Squares', the French cavalry attack on the Allied position. His overall plan was not just to build the full series of models, however, but to ensure that they were collected together and exhibited in a public building 'so as to constitute a highly instructive, as well as a soul-stirring, national memento of the greatest and most important battle of modern times.' Wisely, perhaps, he also considered that this was a question which he should leave to the consideration of the government.

To that extent, he was perhaps testing the water when, in mid-1845, he announced that the Great Model and the New Model would be exhibited together. In the *Illustrated London News* of 14 June, among the advertisements expounding the merits of 'Cabburn's Oil, for the restoration of children and adults' and Human Magnetism, he declared

The New Waterloo Model

that both Models would be displayed at the Egyptian Hall, so that 'all admirers of British values may behold this very faithful representation of one of the most brilliant actions recorded in history.' But Siborne was also being realistic about his debts. The Models were not just for the public's education or entertainment, as his advertisement made clear: the Models were on sale: 'Captain Siborne, finding that a desire has been expressed that these Models should be placed in some public institution, takes this opportunity of stating that he is willing to dispose of them; and should it be desired, of those also (partly constructed) which are intended to illustrate the other prominent parts of the Battle.'

There was another revelation contained within the pages of the *Illustrated London News*. In the face of years of unremitting government and military pressure, Siborne had finally removed the Prussians from their forward position on the Model. The Model, he informed readers of the newspaper, has 'not only been repainted and otherwise renovated and improved, but has also been corrected, as regards the Prussian co-operation, so as to make it correspond to every particular with the description of the Battle given in Captain Siborne's "History of the

Waterloo Campaign."' Only a few thousand Prussians now occupied forward positions on the vast tableau. Thousands of their colleagues had been removed. Victory at Waterloo belonged exclusively to Wellington.

The two Models went on show together on Christmas Eve, 1845, but Siborne soon turned his attention away from the problem of trying to sell tickets. In the New Year, he agreed once more to a public subscription to secure the future of the Great Model. The 'Waterloo Model Committee' was formed, and from its offices at 29 New Bond Street, it undertook to raise enough money to buy it for the nation. The executive committee consisted of a colonel, three majors, Colonel Gawler himself, and Captain Kincaid of the 95th Rifles. They declared that the Model had received the 'fullest approbation from every class of the British public' and that a desire had been 'universally expressed' that the Model should be purchased for the country. Effectively, however, this was less a general subscription and more a money-raising exercise within the army, to remunerate Captain Siborne for 'his most praiseworthy and patriotic undertaking'. Thirty-eight army officers, including the Marquess of Anglesey, lent their names to the appeal, which aimed to raise enough money not just to pay Siborne's costs, but to find a permanent home for the Model. Subscribers were asked, when they paid their money, to vote for one of five places where they would like the Model to be shown: the British Museum, The United Services Institution, the Tower of London, Chelsea College, or the Woolwich Repository.

The Waterloo committee was unstinting in its praise of the Model. 'Every village, every house and farm-yard, every knot of trees, every undulation of surface, every field, nay every crop of wheat, or other produce which the field bore at the time, – in short, every detail is given with the closest accuracy, from a six months' personal observation, aided by the most authentic observation.' It mentioned the 'universally strong encomiums' of the press and of the 'most distinguished judges of military science'. But, above all, it singled out the Model's value to posterity, which, it said, 'becomes most apparent, when we remember how gradually the methods of war of every age undergo their inevitable mutations, and how utterly inadequate the best explanations of history have been found to convey distinct ideas of these changes to succeeding times. How great would be the interest we should now attach to models, executed with equal skill and accuracy of Cressy, Agincourt, or any of the celebrated battles of our ancestors!' The Model, said the committee, should become 'a national memorial and incentive, to our children's children,' though it was perhaps more in hope than expectation that it suggested that the general public would, for patriotic reasons, be as interested in subscribing to the Model as army officers. 'It is to the universal heart and feeling of the country – whether in or out of uniform – whether throbbing in the breasts of the stronger or of the gentler sex, that this appeal is made to combine in handing down to future generations of our countrymen this speaking monument of British Glory.'

Siborne sent out many of the early appeal letters himself. Queen Adelaide, who had paid for two copies of his book, clearly felt that she had done enough, and declined, citing the excuse that there were 'too many endless demands upon her purse towards objects peculiarly connected with the Religion and Education of the country.' But the Royal family was represented nonetheless. The first name on the list of subscribers was Field-Marshal His Royal Highness the Prince Albert, who, after receiving a letter from Siborne, volunteered to pay the astounding sum of one hundred pounds. This gave Siborne the establishment approval he needed, when he approached leading military and political figures for money. On 13 April 1846, he wrote to the Prime Minister, Sir Robert Peel, mentioning his 'pecuniary embarrassments' and his most recent attempt to persuade the government to buy the Models, but also the fact that Prince Albert had subscribed. His aim, he said, was to acquire a preliminary list of influential subscribers before the prospectus was sent out to the public. It was still not enough to convince Peel who gracefully declined, and the subscription raised barely £850 of the £4600 Siborne had wanted to recoup.

One reply stands out as an ironic testimony to the hopelessness of Siborne's financial position after so many years of hardship and controversy. It was written in the elegant, flowing hand of Christian Charles Josias de Bunsen, for Siborne had even approached the Prus-

sian Ambassador to England for help – offering him the chance to buy
the New Model.

Prussian Legation,
4, Carlton House Terrace
2 February 1847

Chevalier Bunsen presents his Compliments to Captain W Siborne
and begs to inform him in answer to his letter of the 16th of Sep-
tember last, respecting the purchase of the Model of the Battle of
Waterloo, which was exhibited in Berlin, by His Majesty the King of
Prussia, that he did not fail to recommend it to the Royal
Government.

Chevalier Bunsen is now directed to acquaint Captain Siborne that
the said Government although fully appreciating the praiseworthy
undertaking which is already removed from Berlin, has declined to
purchase it, not considering it of such an historical interest for His
Majesty, as if *that moment* of the battle were represented, when the
arrival of the Prussian army contributed to the Glory of that day.

Siborne, who had been so keen, both as a modeller and a historian, to
ensure that the Prussians were given proper recognition for their role
at Waterloo, had failed to sell them his second Model, because they
thought it was too British.

XV

So much has been said of what has been termed the crisis of Waterloo, that the only result, I think, truly established, is that no man can pronounce with certainty what the crisis was, except he who won the battle.

Lt.-Col. Henry Murray, memorandum to William Siborne, 27 December 1834

The dispute between Siborne's view of history and Wellington's was the equivalent of the French cavalry charge against the Anglo-Allied squares of infantry: it was glorious, seemingly without end, and ultimately doomed. In another respect, too, it bore comparison: like the cavalry charge itself, the need to win overcame all other considerations, so that the fight between the two men for the history of the battle became more and more an academic exercise, far removed from any reflection of the human cost of the conflict.

In this way, history began to distance itself, dispassionately, from the shock at the price that had been paid for the victory. It was true that there had been relief, too, and the celebrations had been long and heartfelt for a victory that marked the end of the Napoleonic wars. In Antwerp, Charlotte Waldie had seen how 'the highlanders, regardless of their wounds, their fatigues, their dangers, and their sufferings, kept throwing up their Highland bonnets into the air, and continually vociferating, – "Boney's beat! Boney's beat! Hurrah! Hurrah! Boney's beat!"' In Edinburgh, a lawyer, James Simpson, had been in court when the news came through: 'Further law proceedings were out of the question; adjournment was ruled; and judges, advocates, agents, and officers were speedily in the streets, already crowded by their excited and exulting townsmen. The schools were let loose. Business was suspended, and a holiday voted by acclamation ... as early as seven o'clock, the Castle flag rose, and nineteen twenty-four pounders sounded in the ears and filled the eyes – for the effect was overpowering – of the excited throng.'

But, at the same time, across Europe, the families of the soldiers in the Anglo-Allied army had been desperate for a different kind of news, not knowing for several days who had been killed, or injured, and who had survived. It was understandable that it had taken time to find out. Thousands of Allied soldiers were lying in five different hospitals, the Jesuits, Elizabeth, Annonciate, Orpheline, and Notre Dame, while the wounded French prisoners were moved to a former barracks in a lower part of the town, where there was held to be a greater danger of contracting a fever. Five more hospitals in Antwerp also housed the wounded, including the Corderie, a new building on the banks of the Scheldt, which was nearly a quarter of a mile long and contained more than a thousand French soldiers.

John Thomson, the professor of military surgery who recorded the state of the injured for the Army Medical Board, found there were so many casualties that he needed twelve days to make a full examination of them all. The medical staff was struggling to cope. 'To appreciate the value of such labours,' he wrote in his report, 'one must have been present at the horrors of the scene at which they were engaged, must have heard the groans, and seen the agonies of the dying; and, in what is still more painful to endure, must have listened to the cries, without having it in his power to relieve the sufferings, of the wounded.' Another surgeon, Charles Bell, who was later knighted for his discoveries on the nervous system, told of how he had worked incessantly, knife in hand, for days on end, neglecting 'all decencies' of performing surgical operations, until his muscles could barely move. 'While I amputated one man's thigh, there lay at one time thirteen, all beseeching to be taken next.' One officer had been attacked so violently by a cuirassier that a sword had pierced his thigh and pinned him to his horse, through the wood and leather of the saddle.

News of the casualties travelled slowly, by horse or ship, and when it came through, the victory celebrations were dampened by the sheer scale of the toll. Ensign William Leeke recalled how his family scanned a list of dead and wounded officers printed in a newspaper, and thought he was dead, before realising that it was in fact a namesake who had been killed. Lady Magdalene de Lancey went through even worse agonies. First she was told that her husband, Sir William, was safe because his name was not on the casualty list; then she was told he was dead; then she learned that he was in fact alive, but badly injured, his ribs separated from his spine by a spent cannonball which had knocked him from his horse. For six nights, she nursed him in a humble cottage at Mont St Jean until he died. They had been married for barely three months. 'These moments that I passed by his lifeless body were awful and instructive. Their impression will influence my whole life . . .' she wrote. 'Since that time I have suffered every shade of sorrow.'

Lady de Lancey, understandably, had a very different view of the battle from those who had experienced none of it firsthand. There were two classes in society – those who had seen, and recognised, its horrors, or who had lost members of their family, and those who knew nothing of it except its glorious outcome. 'I can hardly express what I felt on returning to England,' she noted, 'to see people surrounded with every luxury unhappy at the want of the smallest comfort. I can fancy no better cure for all imaginary evils than a week's residence at Waterloo.'

The men were not forgotten, however, even if the terrible price they had paid faded as the years went by: a special medal was struck, with Wellington's name on its reverse side, and it was given to all ranks 'in commemoration of the brilliant and decisive victory of Waterloo.' Pensions were awarded, although a private received only a shilling a day for the loss of a limb, and a sergeant only half as much again, which was barely a living wage. Each year Wellington would hold a Waterloo Banquet for his senior officers. Five towns and a railway station were given the name 'Waterloo'. Across the battlefield, plaques remember the victims: a nineteen-year-old lieutenant in the 15th Hussars; a twenty-year-old from the Royal Horse Artillery; an eighteen-year-old cornet in the 16th Light Dragoons; a sixteen-year-old ensign in the 1st (Royal Scots) Regiment of Foot. Lives had been ended, families destroyed, soldiers traumatised, the individual, personal, cost of a day of savagery. With time, however, the terrible cost of the battle helped to magnify its glory so that fifteen years afterwards, the clash between Siborne's relentless search for evidence and the official opposition to it became a vital, if clinical, historical debate. It was a fight for the control of history, and in its shadow, the suffering of the men and their families was quietly, if unintentionally, forgotten.

William Siborne did not prolong the battle of history for much longer. Worn out by his struggles, he died from a long-standing stomach complaint at the Royal Military Asylum on 13 January 1849, at the age of fifty-one. To the end he felt a sense of injustice at the government's withdrawal of his funding, and the lack of official recognition which he felt his craftmanship deserved. Perhaps, too, he was worn down by the continuing attacks on his accuracy from the Duke of Wellington's associates. Certainly, his friends thought so, using an obituary notice which they placed in *Colburn's United Services Magazine* to re-visit the issue: 'it is with pain we add, that this excellent officer and very amiable man succumbed to a lingering illness, which was originally produced by nine years of close application to his well known and splendid model of the Battle of Waterloo, and further exasperated by repeated disappointments as to its destination. This unequalled model was, in the first instance, undertaken at the behest of the Government, but became neglected and ultimately abandoned by them, to the bitter mortification and loss of the ingenious Captain; who also wrote an accurate and detailed history of the war in France and Belgium in 1815, to illustrate his laborious and elaborate work. The task was both onerous and expensive; and what ought to have been a sure means of preferment and profit, proved only the fruitful source of vexation and illness. Indeed, when we recollect how many officers have been placed on the Staff for having merely been able to copy a military plan, we think of Siborne, and grieve!'

The tragedy was that Siborne had almost realised his dream. Seventeen years after he had begun his project, and a year before his death, Siborne had contacted the United Services Institute, on 15 November

1847, suggesting the Great Model should go on display there. The charge for entry, he suggested, should be a penny. The Institute agreed in principle to his request and set up a subcommittee to take charge of the project. It decided, yet again, that there should be a general subscription, at five shillings a head, to buy the Model, and that it would build a special room in which to exhibit it. The Great Model would finally be the centrepiece of a new London museum, as Siborne's military superiors had originally envisaged. It was cruel, then, that he should die before his plan came to fruition. It was not until July 1851 that the Institute managed to sort out the legal difficulties of purchasing the Model. A month later it finally it went on show, and it remained there for more than a hundred years, through the First and Second World Wars, the battles which shaped the new century as much as Waterloo had shaped the old one.

Wellington outlived Siborne by three and a half years and only in death did he fail to control events. At half-past-seven on the morning of Thursday 18 November 1852, at the age of eighty-three, he was carried to his grave in St Paul's Cathedral in a vast, grotesque cata-falque, an object which the Duke might have rejected on grounds of its execrable taste, a great black and gold railway carriage of a vehicle, consisting of a flat surface which was topped by a golden dais, with halberds which held a black and gold cloth, and which was adorned with symbols of lions' heads, sabres and laurel wreaths. Not even the six wheels of the great carriage had escaped the artistic attention of the new superintendent of the Department of Practical Art, bearing as they did a pattern of truncated oaks and double dolphins, made of solid bronze, with a lion's head at the centre. Between each wheel was a figure of Victory, or Fame, a figure which was repeated on a larger scale at each corner of the truck. On the front of the whole device was Wellington's coat of arms, and at each edge, an elaborate pyramid of cuirasses, topped by a helmet, from which sprang swords and bayonets and other small arms. On each side of the pyramids there were the flags of infantry regiments, held in place by small drums. Wreaths of laurels and cypress hung from the sides of the car, with garlands of bay scattered on the coffin, and by its side there were date palms, from Kew Gardens, chosen because they were the same type that grew in

Jerusalem. On each side of the dais were five entablatures, each containing the names of three of the Duke's military victories. A dozen black horses, clothed from head to foot in black velvet, led the Duke on his final journey.

Tens of thousand of people lined the streets in silence to see the cortège pass by. The procession started from the Horse Guards, as the sun finally broke through a gloomy sky for the first time in weeks, and the mourners moved off as the band of the 2nd Battalion of the Rifle Brigade struck up 'Dead March' in *Saul*. There were six battalions of infantry, 3600 men in all, and eight squadrons of cavalry, seventeen guns from the artillery, and men from every regiment in the army. Such pomp and circumstance could not, however, prevent a mundane mishap. The Duke had only travelled as far as The Mall, when the road gave way under the great weight of his transport, and not even a dozen dray-horses could pull him free without the strenuous efforts of more than fifty constables.

At St Paul's Cathedral, the Lord Mayor led the procession, to the strains of the choir, followed by Prince Albert, in his Field-Marshal's uniform, and other members of the Royal family. Wellington's coffin, which rested on an eight-foot-high bier, now bore his Marshal's sword and hat, its plume lifting gently in a slight breeze. Veterans of his many battles, including Sir Peregrine Maitland, laid a hand upon his coffin; Sir John Colborne (now Lord Seaton) and Sir Henry Hardinge, faithful to the end, were among the nine pall-bearers. It took the Garter King of Arms several minutes simply to read out Wellington's extraordinary list of honours from across the world, some of which were well-known (Duke and Marquess of Wellington, Field-Marshal and Commander-in-Chief of Her Majesty's Forces, Prince of Waterloo of the Kingdom of the Netherlands) and some of which were more obscure (Knight of the Order of the Elephant of Denmark and Knight of the Most Illustrious Order of the Golden Fleece).

'What makes the difference between the obsequies of the Duke of Wellington and of any other great man?' asked *The Times*, the next day. 'It is this: that a long life, filled with the most distinguished services, made him so well known, so thoroughly appreciated, and so heartily admired by all classes of Englishmen that his death has affected everybody like a personal concern. When the independence of England and the World was assailed, Providence sent us a champion, and as the myriads of his countrymen yesterday watched with the deepest interest the transit of his body to the tomb, many a heartfelt prayer must have been uttered that, should days of darkness again come and this land of freedom be once more threatened, God may grant us another Wellesley to lead our armies and win our battles.'

William Siborne's funeral was more modest, befitting his station in life. He was buried alongside his mother in London's Brompton Cemetery, in a grave which bore no grand or obscure titles but a simple, factual inscription: 'Capt. William Siborne . . . who died on 13 January 1849 in the 51st year of age. The deceased was Secretary of the Royal Military Asylum Chelsea, Author of the History of the War in France & Belgium in 1815 and Constructor of the Waterloo Models'.

Siborne's death should have been the end of the matter, but he was not allowed to rest in peace. The ghost of Wellington haunted Siborne even in the grave. In July 1898, *Blackwood's Edinburgh Magazine* recounted the tale told by a judge's marshal, Stafford Northcote, in a letter which he had sent to his mother fifty years before. Northcote had visited Wellington, when the Duke, as Lord Lieutenant of Hampshire, was entertaining the judges of assize on the Western Circuit. In all, there was a party of thirty-five, including two MPs, and various magistrates from Hampshire and Berkshire. Northcote described how they ate their meal off some of the gifts which had been presented to the Duke in the course of his long and successful military career: there was silver plate, inscribed with the word 'Assaye', which had been presented to the victorious Sir Arthur Wellesley in 1803 after his triumphant campaign in India; silver epergnes, the gift of George IV, had been placed in the centre of the table; and there was a beautiful dessert service, each plate bearing a separate view of Egypt, which had been made for Napoleon and which a grateful Louis XVIII had presented to the Duke after Waterloo.

Wellington, who was by now feeble when he walked, was seated at the table, with a Waterloo medal hanging from his red collar, and a star upon his breast. Northcote recounted how, before the meal, the group spent some time talking about the Battle of Vittoria, of which there was a picture in one of the rooms. Then one of the judges, ill-advisedly, asked the Duke what he thought of Siborne's Model of the Battle of Waterloo. According to the magazine, Northcote described how the Duke responded fiercely: 'That is a question which I have often been asked, to which I don't want to give an answer because I don't want to injure the man. But if you want to know my opinion, it's all farce, fudge! They went to one gentleman and said "What did you do?" "I did so and so." To another, "What did you do?" "I did such and such a thing." One did it at ten and another at twelve, and they have mixed up the whole. The fact is, a battle is like a ball; they keep footing it all the day through.' And with that, as if to signal that the matter was closed, the Duke asked each guest whether they would have black tea or green.

The exchange, reported by *Blackwood*'s, caused a lawyer to write to Siborne's son, who had published a selection of his father's Waterloo correspondence, to say that he had, for years, taken delight in paying an occasional visit to the United Services Museum to inspect the Great Model. Now, he said, he had the mortification of reading what the Duke had said about it. 'I assume that he is correctly reported – can you in any way rebut it? Is the Duke's *ipse dixit* to be taken as gospel?' The questions were as pertinent half a century on as they had been when Siborne was first building the Model. In reply, Siborne's son, Major-General Herbert Siborne, pointed out that the Duke had never seen the Model. The barrister's relief, as well as his surprise, was palpable. 'I think I may assure you that your father's beautiful model, his wonderfully accurate history of the Campaign . . . would ensure a very favourable reception for any defence you chose to make. I think with regard to Waterloo all Englishmen are Sibornites now.'

Gradually, however, in the years after his death, Siborne slipped into obscurity. In November 1893, the *Sunday Times* noted that at a sale at Sotheby's, Siborne's 'magnificent collection' of letters from officers who had fought at the Battle of Waterloo had raised only twenty-five pounds, whereas a collection of manuscripts relating to the Borough of Ipswich had made forty pounds, an outcome which moved the newspaper to blame caprice for the valuation of old documents.

Siborne's skill as a model-maker, and his battle with the authorities, was forgotten, clouded by the passage of time, even as his *History* survived as the standard material with which scholars worked.

Like their creator, the models slipped in and out of public consciousness, with the New Model leading a more tangled life than its counterpart. We glimpse it here and there in the years after its creator's death. It went on display in Germany in the 1840s, after which it disappeared from public view, and was apparently stored at a Dublin ironworks. It emerged again to go on display at the Irish International Exhibition of 1907, but then, for more than two decades, the trail went cold, until, many years later, it was discovered again in the loft of a house in County Dublin. In the 1930s, the owner of the house, a Mrs Barrington Malone, presented the Model to the Camberley Staff College. The college placed the New Model in a small room, but, unaware of its true historical value, and needing the space, decided to destroy it. Fortunately, the Model came under the nominal authority of the curator of The Armouries at the Tower of London, Charles ffoulkes, and he intervened to insist that it should be sent to him at the Tower. ffoulkes suspected immediately that the Model was of historical value. 'When I saw this model it was relegated to a storeroom and was in a most dilapidated condition, ' he recalled in his memoirs. 'But I could visualise that with careful repair it could be brought back to its original condition.' He noted that the figure of Wellington had been lost, and decided to have another made, and he quickly established that the quality of Siborne's model toy soldiers was superior to anything the toymakers of his day could provide. To find out more about the Model's history, in April 1935 he sent the following letter to the *Daily Telegraph*: 'Sir – I shall be greatly obliged if you will give me the hospitality of your columns in an endeavour to trace the surviving relatives of Capt. William Siborne or Siborn (1797–1849), author of the "War in France and Belgium" and "Waterloo Letters." I am anxious to obtain information respecting the remarkable models of the battle of Waterloo made under his direction.'

Charles ffoulkes received an unexpected and immediate response from one of Siborne's few remaining relatives, the husband of his granddaughter. He said that the family still possessed a number of prints showing military uniforms and their colouring, which had been collected by Siborne and which had been annotated and corrected by him in pencil. Many had been borrowed from Sir Hussey Vivian and they were probably drawn for the makers of the model figures to work from. But, during the correspondence with ffoulkes, it became clear that not even Siborne's own family knew that he had built his second Model.

22 April 1935

Dear Sir,

My wife and I read your letter with the greatest interest. It is news to us that there was this other completed model of a section besides the large one in Whitehall of the whole battle. All we knew on this point was that my wife remembers her father, Maj.General HT Siborne (1826–1902) saying work on the model had been started on a scale which proved too large and had to be abandoned for a smaller. In her childhood she remembers numbers of the bigger leaden figures knocking about as toys for her brother and herself; and the one survivor of these, which is the mounted figure of Napoleon, we still possess. Like you we have always been struck by the workmanship.

Needless to say, we are delighted not only to hear of this model, but to know that it has fallen into such good hands as yours after so many vicissitudes.

Kenneth Henderson

Charles ffoulkes asked a sculptor who had created models for the War Museum and the Imperial Institute to restore the New Waterloo Model and two months later he placed it in the small-arms room of the White Tower, with an ingenious arrangement of moveable magnifying glasses so that every detail could be seen. Separately, he exhibited a dozen toy soldiers from the British and French armies with typewritten labels below so that visitors could identify the uniforms of the troops on the tableau, among them the Scots Greys, the Dragoon Guards, and the Rifle Brigade.

By his intervention, ffoulkes had succeeded in rekindling interest in Siborne's craftsmanship. When the New Model went on show, the author Philip Guedalla wrote a letter to *The Times*, congratulating the

Tower on the 'striking addition' to its exhibits. He called the toy soldiers 'little miracles of accuracy', pointing out their moveable arms and knapsacks, and the tiny brass breastplates of the French cuirassiers. 'Nothing could exceed the vividness of the charging cavalry,' Guedalla wrote. In its news pages, *The Times* marvelled at the New Model, much as the *United Services Journal* had once praised the Great Model. 'A wonderful model of the battlefield of Waterloo is being placed on public exhibition in the Tower of London today,' *The Times* declared. 'The figures, each about one inch high, are modelled with consummate skill which no craftsman of today could surpass. Uniforms are painted with meticulous accuracy. The troops are set in every conceivable attitude of attack and guard. Tiny hats of generals, knapsacks of the infantry, and brass breastplates of the French cuirassiers are all removable. Cavalry officers are distinguished from troopers by microscopic sabre taches. Wellington, on his brown charger, surrounded by his staff, is picked out in a quiet area of the field. An officer saluting has just approached; another rides away with orders. A single square of British red-coats is shown, the men tightly wedged shoulder to shoulder, the officers within the formation. Few parts of the field are quiet. At La Haye Sainte, the King's German Legion – according to legend, out of action by reason of faulty ammunition – are being attacked by French infantry, who have barricaded the Charleroi road with trees and overturned vehicles. On the lip of the sandpit the Rifle Brigade (95th) enfilade the French advance. Batteries are in action with their attendant limbers in the rear. All over the field are stragglers, walking wounded, prisoners and dismounted officers searching for their units, and, of course, many dead men and horses.'

A few days later, the secretary of the Royal United Services Museum was moved to publicise the model his institution had held for more than eighty years, declaring that the public had the opportunity to compare the Great Model with a 'remarkably interesting representation of the mechanised Army of today in action – set in a 40ft diorama complete with all its modern details.' Once again, the Great Model, it seemed, was competing with a rival attraction, akin to the panorama which had proved to be such a success at Leicester Square for Henry Aston Barker.

As the years went by, however, both models fell into disrepair again. After thirty years in the Tower of London, the New Waterloo Model was loaned to Dover Castle, but by this time it was discovered that the repairs overseen by ffoulkes had only delayed, not prevented, its deterioration. Many of the soldiers and their cannons had corroded, and the Model was sent to the Ancient Monuments laboratory in Ruislip, near London, whose scientists were more accustomed to building models of new roads and historic buildings than repairing them. The worst affected figures were the cavalry, with their tin breastplates, and the chief conservator at the laboratory concluded initially that the source of the decay could be traced to some hardboard which had been inserted during a previous restoration attempt. He thought that vapours from the oak had eaten into the lead soldiers. In the end, it was thought that fumes from the glue used by Siborne had caused the problem.

In 1962, the Great Model, so long on display at the United Services Institute, found itself homeless, and it was put into army storage at Aldershot. It remained there for thirteen years, until, in November 1975, two eminent military historians, Dr David Chandler and Antony Brett-James, the head of war studies at Sandhurst, opened a few of the crates which held the separate sections of the model and carefully examined the contents. They found to their surprise that they were in a surprisingly good condition. The joints between the different sections of the model had been weakened by its dismantling, but there was no sign of rot or dampness, and Siborne's meticulously modelled pastures were still in a reasonable state of repair, despite some cracking in the plaster of Paris.

The surface of the model, which Siborne had lovingly repainted was, however, very dirty, and some of its colours had almost entirely faded. In some places, the toy soldiers which had been made to represent the dead and the dying were virtually indistinguishable from the ground area on which they lay. Some of the infantry, cavalry and artillery figures simply needed touching up; but others required re-painting completely. This, the historians considered, was a difficult task, given how closely together the ranks were packed and the minute scale on which they had been modelled, and they concluded that it might only be possible to paint the outside figures. The buildings, Hougoumont, La Haye Sainte and La Belle Alliance, had survived the years reasonably well, but they too needed repair.

But the main problem was the one which had bedevilled Siborne. The Great Model was so large that there was nowhere obvious to display it. The historians unconsciously echoed its maker when, in their report, they concluded that 'to be properly appreciated in its vast detail, it would need to be raised at least 3 feet from the ground, carefully lit, properly cased in glass, with a full explanatory key.' But, like Siborne, they insisted the Great Model should be made available to the general public.

Chandler and Brett-James ran through the options that faced the army, much as Siborne had done more than a century before. There was no room at Sandhurst for a model of such a great size, and the public would not be able to gain access easily because of security fears. The National Army Museum in Chelsea might be prevailed upon to take it, even though its staff was dubious about its ability to carry out the reconstruction work. Another option, but one which was only regarded as a 'better than nothing' solution was to display part of the Model, perhaps the section between La Belle Alliance and the Mont St Jean crossroads, including La Haye Sainte and Hougoumont. Once again, they echoed Siborne by suggesting that 'it might be possible to charge a fee for admission to the model – and thus recoup the financial outlay inseparable from the model's restoration and re-siting.' With great insight, they concluded that, whatever the solution, the Model was a unique masterpiece and had to be preserved. Only one solution would not have occurred to Siborne himself, because he would have quickly realised the impossibility of the dream. The historians suggested that they could approach the Duke of Wellington to display the Model at his estate at Stratfield Saye.

Today the two Models are both on show: the Great Model, restored by experts, is to be found at the National Army Museum in Chelsea, a cannonshot or so from William Siborne's grave, the vast, sprawling contours of its landscape contained safely within a glass case, as he himself had always demanded. The Model is the centrepiece of a Waterloo gallery which was opened by the Duke of Wellington, which would have surprised William Siborne, but doubtless pleased him too. With time, history learns how to forgive.

The New Waterloo Model is housed, unsung, in a corner of the Royal Armouries Museum, by the riverside in Leeds, near a portrait of Napoleon on his charger, and cruel cabinets of weaponry. On the green rolling battlefield around La Haye Sainte, cut through by the Brussels highway, straight as a Roman road, its soldiers and horses look as if they were modelled yesterday. But the crowds prefer their history more direct, just as they did in the day of Henry Aston Barker and his famous panoramas. The Model vies for attention with interactive rivals: 'a Norman warrior recalls his part in one of the most decisive battles to be fought on British soil;' 'Trafalgar, 1805 – a British gunner's mate describes his part in one of the largest battles in naval history.' Against such voices, William Siborne is still struggling to be heard.

He deserves an audience, however, for, unlike Wellington, he realised that history is not the preserve of any one individual, and certainly not the gift of officialdom, to be dispensed as and when it feels appropriate. His great triumph was to gather and record hundreds of accounts of the battle of Waterloo, so that he has bequeathed to us an unparalleled record of the extraordinary, bloody day when the future of Europe was decided. That he did so in the face of the establishment's obstructionism made his achievement all the more remarkable, not least as his sympathies instinctively lay with the political and military leaders he had been brought up to obey.

But, in making his Model, William Siborne was attempting the impossible, in trying to reduce nine hours of bloodshed to a single frozen moment. The truth, which neither Siborne nor the Duke would publicly acknowledge, was that the Battle of Waterloo could not have been won without the two armies cooperating as they did. Whatever the time of the Prussian arrival on the battlefield, the day-long threat of their presence sapped the strength of Napoleon's army, diverting thousands of his men from where they were most needed. Whether the Prussians broke through the French lines before, during or after Wellington's repulse of the Imperial Guard was, to that extent, irrelevant: except that, through his Model, Siborne had dared to ask the question.

In doing so, he failed to realise that great victories require unambiguous heroes, whose glory will grow ever stronger with the passage of time, not least if their valiant deeds are followed by politically difficult periods of peace. Unwittingly, through his Model, Siborne showed that heroes rarely bring about victory single-handedly, but need a supporting cast, in this case actors from another nation. In doing so, before his country was ready to accept the fact, he made the Battle of Waterloo a far more complex and subtle affair than his nationalistic audience required: a man before his time.

If William Siborne had been a wiser, or a less honest, historian he would have heeded the advice of Lt.-Col. Henry Murray of the 18th Hussars, who warned him that 'too critical an inquiry as to who has the greatest claim to praise engenders a jealousy which never should exist between companions in arms.' But he failed to listen, and for that we should be grateful. What was he to do with the Prussians? To look at the battleground he created is to marvel at a man who tried to turn the history of a war into a model of the truth.

A Note on Military Terms

Cavalry was divided into Heavy Cavalry (Cuirassiers who were armoured and Dragoons who weren't) and Light Cavalry (Lancers, Hussars and Light Dragoons). Cavalry battalions were made up of ten troops, each of about 90 men, which joined together to form five squadrons.

The British Infantry was divided into two groups: the Foot Guards and the line regiments. The Foot Guards were the elite. Infantry regiments were made up of between two and four battalions. The battalion was the main tactical unit, and was commanded by a lieutenant-colonel or a major. There were about ten companies of around a hundred men in each battalion. The best two companies were chosen to protect the battalion's vulnerable flanks: the right flank company was called the Grenadier Company (as it had originally carried grenades); the left flank company was called the Light Company and had the best marksmen. The centre company was called the Battalion Company.

A **brigade** was made up of two or more battalions, usually from different regiments. Wellington created **divisions** by mixing together several brigades, of varying levels of experience, and adding artillery. He had eight of them.

Further reading

The Battle of Waterloo is fought over by as many authors as soldiers, but several historians should be mentioned in despatches. Dr David G. Chandler's writing has that rare quality of being both academic and accessible to the general reader. He also gave generously of his time to answer my queries. Sadly, he died in 2004, but I would like to thank him and his wife, Gill.

Jac Weller's *Wellington at Waterloo* is still, I think, a classic. For a more detailed study, *The Hundred Days* by Antony Brett-James consists of hundreds of eyewitness accounts, which read as if it were yesterday. Peter Hofschröer has done exhaustive work in many archives, reflected in his books on the Waterloo campaign. He was very generous with his advice about William Siborne. Mark Adkin has compiled an extraordinary book called The *Waterloo Companion* which is a cornucopia of information and an invaluable source of reference. Finally, William Siborne's correspondence with the veterans is to be found in the British Library. After his death, many of his Waterloo letters were edited and published by his son. Late into this project, Gareth Glover published the remaining material – a remarkable feat, as those of us who have tried to decipher the veterans' handwriting can testify, and one which has confirmed the scrupulous adherence to historical accuracy of both father and son.

General reading

Mark Adkin: *The Waterloo Companion*, Aurum, 2001

A.F. Becke: *Napoleon & Waterloo*, reprint Greenhill, 1995

ed. Lord Chalfont: *Waterloo, Battle of Three Armies*, Sidgwick & Jackson, 1979

David G. Chandler: *Waterloo – The Hundred Days*, Penguin, 2002

David G. Chandler: *Campaigns of Napoleon*, Weidenfeld & Nicolson, 1966

W.B. Craan: *An Historical Account of the Battle of Waterloo*, Samuel Leigh, 1817

Col. Charles Chesney: *Waterloo Lectures* (1868), reprint Greenhill, 1997

Charlotte Eaton: *Narrative of a residence in Belgium*, John Murray, 1817

Ian Fletcher: *A Desperate Business*, Spellmount, 2001

J.W. Fortescue: *History of the British Army*, vol. X, Macmillan & Co., 1899–1930

Sir William Fraser: *Words on Wellington: the Duke, Waterloo, the Ball*, John C. Nimmo, 1902

George Gleig: *Battle of Waterloo*, John Murray, 1849

George Gleig: *The Life of Arthur, Duke of Wellington*, Green & Co., 1891

Philip Guedella: *The Duke*, Wordsworth, 1997

ed. Alan Guy: *The Road to Waterloo*, National Army Museum, 1990

David Hamilton-Williams: *Waterloo, New Perspectives*, Arms & Armour, 1999

Philip J. Haythornthwaite: *Waterloo Men: The Experience of Battle*, Crowood Press, 1999

Peter Hofschröer: *1815, The Waterloo Campaign*, 2 vols, Greenhill, 1998/9

Peter Hofschröer: *Wellington's Smallest Victory*, Faber, 2004

Henri Houssaye: *1815 – Waterloo*, A&C Black, 1900

David Howarth: *Waterloo, A Near Run Thing*, Phoenix, 2003

George Jones: *The Battle of Waterloo, described by eye-witnesses*, London, 1852

John Keegan: *The Face of Battle*, Cape, 1976

Christopher Kelly: *A Full and Circumstantial Account of the Battle of Waterloo*, London, 1828

Sir James Shaw Kennedy: *Notes on the Battle of Waterloo*, John Murray, 1865

Magdalene De Lancey: *A Week at Waterloo*, John Murray, 1906

Elizabeth Longford: *Wellington: The Years of the Sword*, Weidenfeld & Nicolson, 1969

Elizabeth Longford: *Wellington – A new biography*, Sutton, 2001

Colin McNab: *From Waterloo to the Great Exhibition*, Oliver & Boyd, 1982

Albert Nofi: *The Waterloo Campaign*, Greenhill Books, 1993

Charles Oman: *Wellington's Army*, reprint Greenhill, 1986

John Sutherland: *Men of Waterloo*, Frederick Muller, 1967

Roger Parkinson: *The Hussar General – The Life of Blücher*, Wordsworth, 2001

Capt. William Siborne: *History of the Waterloo Campaign*, reprint Greenhill, 1995

Julian Paget & Derek Saunders: *Hougoumont, The Key to Victory*, Pen & Sword, 2001

Jac Weller: *Wellington at Waterloo*, reprint Greenhill, 1998

Andrew Uffindell & Michael Corum: *On the Fields of Glory*, Greenhill, 1996

Mark Urban: *Rifles*, Faber, 2003

The Soldiers' stories

An account of the Battle of Waterloo by a British officer on the staff, Gosling Press, 1993 (Facsimile reprint of the edition published in London: J. Ridgway, 1815)

The Hundred Days: Napoleon's Last Campaign from eye-witnesses, compiled, edited and translated by Antony Brett-James, Macmillan, 1964

Matthew Clay: *A narrative of the battles of Quatre Bras and Waterloo*, Thompson (no date)

Edward Cotton: *A Voice from Waterloo*, Mont St. Jean, 1862

ed. W. H. Fitchett: *Wellington's Men. Some Soldier Autobiographies*, Elder & Co., 1900

George Gawler: *The Crisis and Close of the Action at Waterloo*, Dublin, 1833

Rees Gronow: *Reminiscences and Recollections*, London, 1899

James Hope: *Letters from Portugal, Spain and France*, Edinburgh, 1819

Basil Jackson: *Notes and Reminiscences of a Staff Officer*, London, 1903

John Kincaid: *Adventures in the Rifle Brigade*, London, 1830

John Kincaid: *Random Shots from a Rifleman*, London 1835, reprint Spellmount, 1998

William Leeke: *The history of Lord Seaton's Regiment at the Battle of Waterloo*, Norwich, 1866

Cavalié Mercer: *Journal of the Waterloo Campaign*, reprint Greenhill, 1985

Thomas Morris: *Recollections of Military Service*, London, 1846

William Tomkinson: *The diary of a cavalry officer 1809–15*, reprint Spellmount, 1999

Edmund Wheatley: *The Wheatley diary*, ed. Christopher Hibbert, Windrush, 1997

The Duke's story

George Gleig: *Personal Reminiscences of the First Duke of Wellington*, ed. Mary Gleig, Blackwood, 1904

The despatches of Field Marshal the Duke of Wellington, vols 1–13, compiled by Lt.-Col. John Gurwood, John Murray, 1837–9

Supplementary despatches and memoranda of Field Marshal Arthur Duke of Wellington, India 1797–1805, ed. by the 2nd Duke of Wellington, 15 vols, John Murray, 1858–72

Wellington and his Friends; Letters of the first Duke of Wellington, selected and edited by the 7th Duke of Wellington, Macmillan, 1965

Ellesmere, 1st Earl of: *Personal Reminiscences of the Duke of Wellington*, ed. Alice, Countess of Strafford, John Murray, 1903

Ellesmere, 1st Earl of: *Essays on History, Biography, Geography, Engineering, etc. Contributed to the* 'Quarterly Review', London, 1858

Philip Stanhope, 5th Earl of: *Notes of Conversations with the Duke of Wellington 1831–1851*, John Murray, 1889

Controversies, pamphlets and periodicals

David Hamilton-Williams: *Siborne – The Unpublished Letters*, Military Historical Society, Aug. 1987

Malcolm Henderson: *A Short History of the Siborne Family*, National Army Museum, 7510–93

Peter Hofschröer: 'Waterloo – New Perspectives', *First Empire* magazine, Oct. 1995

Peter Hofschröer: 'Were the Sibornes Frauds?', *First Empire* magazine, June 1995

Peter Hofschröer: 'The Model of the Battle and the Battle of the Model', *Journal of the Society for Army Historical Research*, 79, 2001

Lt.-Col. George Gawler: 'The Crisis at Waterloo', *United Service Magazine*, part 2, 1836

John Hussey: 'Conversations with the Duke of Willington', *First Empire* magazine, November 2003

John Hussey: 'Further Intelligence Reports, 14–15 June 1815', *First Empire* magazine, March 2005

Maj. Edward Macready: 'Correspondence on Waterloo', *United Service Magazine*, vol. 1, 1845

Maj. Edward Macready: 'Comments on Capt. Siborne's History of the Waterloo Campaign', *United Service Magazine*, vol. 1, 1844; vol. 2, 1845, vol. 3, 1852

Derek Mill: 'Waterloo – New Perspectives', *First Empire* magazine, December 1995

C.M. Woolgar: *Wellington's Dispatches and their Editor, Colonel Gurwood*, Southampton University archive

Blackwood's Edinburgh Magazine, vol. 164

Britain Triumphant on the Plains of Waterloo, John Tregortha, 1817

'Summoned to Waterloo', Alf Cooke

The Models and their rivals

A collection of descriptions of views exhibited at the Panorama, Leicester Square, and painted by H. A. Barker, Robert Burford, John Burford and H. C. Selous, London, 1798–1856

Bernard Comment: *The Panorama*, [transl.by Anne-Marie Glasheen], Reaktion, 1999

Description of Messrs. Marshall's grand historical peristrephic painting of the ever-memorable Battles of Ligny, and Waterloo, etc., W.H. Jyrell, 1816

Ralph Hyde: *Panoramania!*, Trefoil, 1988

Henry I. Kurtz: *The art of the toy soldier*, New Cavendish, 1987

Description of the Model of the Battle of Waterloo, Whitehall, 1896

Guide to the Model of the Battle of Waterloo now exhibited at the Egyptian Hall, Piccadilly, London, P. Dixon Hardy, 1838

Guide to Captain Siborne's New Waterloo Model Representing the Splendid Charge between One and Two o'Clock by the British Heavy Cavalry under The Marquess of Anglesey and by the British Infantry under Sir Thomas Picton, London, 1844, Military Tracts XVIII, MOD Library

Description of the Model Constructed by Capt. William Siborne (late of the 9th and 47th regiments) of the Battle of Waterloo now in the Museum of the Royal United Service Institution, with explanatory notes and short account of the campaign, Whitehall, 1896

Friends of National Army Museum Newsletter, vol. II, no. 2, 1991

Soldier magazine, vol. 39, no. 18, 5–18 September, 1983

A description of the costly and curious military carriage of the late Emperor of France, London Museum, 1816

Letter to Maj.-Gen. R.C. Ford, Commandant, RMAS, from A. Brett-James: 'The Future of the Siborne Model', (kindly supplied by Dr D.G. Chandler)

Detailed reading

George Caldwell & Robert Cooper: *Rifles at Waterloo*, Bugle Horn, 1995

Charles Dalton: *Waterloo Roll Call (1890)*, reprint Naval & Military, 2004 (army lists)

Gareth Glover: *Letters from the Battle of Waterloo – Unpublished Correspondence by Allied Officers from the Siborne Papers*, Greenhill, 2004

Philip Haythornthwaite: *Uniforms of Waterloo in Colour*, Blandford Press, 1974

Yolande Hodson: *An illustrated history of 250 years of military survey*, Military Survey Defence Agency, 1997

Alan Lagden: *The 2/73rd at Waterloo*, privately published, 1998

ed. Maj.-Gen. H.T. Siborne: *Waterloo Letters*, (1891), reprint Greenhill, 1993

William Siborne: *Instructions for Civil and Military Surveyors in Topographical Plan-Drawing*, G&WB Whittaker, 1822

William Siborne: *A Practical Treatise on Topographical Surveying and Drawing*, C&J Rivington, 1827

William Siborne correspondence, British Library Add. MSS. 34703–34708

John Thomson: *Report of Observations made in the British Military Hospitals in Belgium after the Battle of Waterloo; with some remarks upon amputation*, Blackwood, 1816

Acknowledgements

I would like to thank Peter Robinson at Curtis Brown and Mitzi Angel at Fourth Estate for their help and constant encouragement. Thanks, too, to Clive Priddle who was there for me at the start, and among others, to the staff at the National Army Museum in London, the British Library, the Newspaper Library at Colindale, and to staff at the Ministry of Defence archive.

Karen Meager, Mischa and Katya, again gave me their love and support.

Finally, this book is for my father, Henry Balen (1919–2004), who always did the same.

Index